Bluestocking Feminism and British-German
Cultural Transfer, 1750–1837

Bluestocking Feminism and British-German Cultural Transfer, 1750–1837

ALESSA JOHNS

The University of Michigan Press
Ann Arbor

Published in the United States of America by
The University of Michigan Press
Printed and bound by CPI Group (UK) Ltd, Croydon, CR0 4YY

2017   2016   2015   2014   4   3   2   1

A CIP catalog record for this book is available from the British Library.

Library of Congress Cataloging-in-Publication Data

Johns, Alessa.
    Bluestocking feminism and British-German cultural transfer, 1750–1837 / Alessa Johns.
        pages cm
    Includes bibliographical references and index.
    ISBN 978-0-472-11938-7 (hardcover : alk. paper) — ISBN 978-0-472-03594-6 (pbk. : alk. paper) — ISBN 978-0-472-12047-5 (e-book)
        1. Feminism—Europe—History—18th century.   2. Social change—Europe—History—18th century.   3. Culture diffusion—Europe—History—18th century.   4. European literature—18th century.   5. Great Britain—Civilization—18th century.   6. Germany—Civilization—18th century.   7. Great Britain—Relations—Germany.   8. Germany—Relations—Great Britain.   I. Title.
    HQ1587.J64   2014
    305.4094090'33—dc23

                                                        2014004812

For my parents
Jorun and Donald Johns

Acknowledgments

I would like to thank Professors Barbara Schaff and Frank Kelleter for sponsoring my fellowship at the Lichtenberg Kolleg, the Institute for Advanced Study at the University of Göttingen, which provided the ideal environment for completing this book. I am grateful to Director Dagmar Coester-Waltjen, Deputy Directors Doris Lemmermöhle and Gerhard Lauer, Coordinators Dominik Hünniger, Johanna Schott, and Turan Lackschewitz, as well as the many lively staff members who saw to every convenience from handling computer glitches, library access, and visa acquisition, to housing, bicycles, meals, and attendance at local cultural events. I thank my fellow Fellows and Associates for intellectual stimulation, engaging conversations, and friendship: in particular Shaheen Ali, Regina Bendix, Elke Brendel, Don Brenneis, Ingrid Hehmeyer, Christine Langenfeld, Joep Leerssen, Jason Mittell, Dorry Noyes, Per Øhrgaard, Roland Pfau, Ann Rigney, Heinrich Schäfer, Norbert Schappacher, Lalit Vachani, and Christiane von Stutterheim. My work was also generously supported by a fellowship from the Herzog-August Bibliothek, Wolfenbüttel; a University of California President's Research Fellowship in the Humanities; and ongoing assistance from the Committee on Research of the University of California, Davis.

I gratefully acknowledge advice on individual chapters from John Brewer, George Starr, Chris Reynolds, Jennie Batchelor, Cora Kaplan, Gerhard Lauer, and Thorsten Unger. And I thank the anonymous reviewers of my complete manuscript; their judicious comments and criticisms were very helpful to me as I revised. It has been a pleasure to work with the University of Michigan Press, and particularly Tom Dwyer. For collegial advice and support I thank Paula Backscheider, Sean Burgess, Adriana Craciun, Gesa Dane, Fran Dolan, Margaret France, April London, Colin Milburn, Liz Miller, Ruth Perry, Nicole Pohl, Betty Schellenberg, Julia Simon, and Birgit Tautz. I could not have completed my study without the copious resources of the State and University Library at the University of Göttingen; I am especially grateful to former director Elmar Mittler and librarian Reimer Eck. I benefited also from conducting research at the Herzog August Bibliothek, Wolfenbüttel; the Goethe and Schiller Archive and Anna Amalia Library, Weimar; the publishing firm Vandenhoeck & Ruprecht, Göttingen; the British Library, London; the Bancroft and Doe Libraries, UC Berkeley; and the Shields Library, UC Davis. I thank publishers for permission to reprint earlier work in revised form: a prior version of chapter 1 appeared in Jennie Batchelor and Cora Kaplan, eds., *Women and Material Culture* (2007), published by Palgrave Macmillan, reproduced with permission of Palgrave Macmillan. The full published version of this publication is available from: http://us.macmillan.com/ QuickSearchResultsV3.aspx?search=women+and+material+culture&ctl 00%24ctl00%24cphContent%24ucAdvSearch%24imgGo.x=0&ctl00%2 4ctl00%24cphContent%24ucAdvSearch%24imgGo.y=0. Parts of chapter 3 were published in *Das Erdbeben von Lissabon und der Katastrophendiskurs im 18. Jahrhundert*, edited by Gerhard Lauer and Thorsten Unger, Das achtzehnte Jahrhundert—Supplementa (Hg. von der Deutschen Gesellschaft für die Erforschung des achtzehnten Jahrhunderts), Bd. 15, Wallstein Verlag, Göttingen 2008, 351–63.

I am indebted to Sabine and Andreas von Tiedemann, Luise, Hans, and Felix, for their generous, kind, and frequent hospitality to me and my family as I researched in Göttingen; to Rima Holland for happy stays in Heidelberg before and after Frankfurt flights; to Elke Schauer for tips about life in Göttingen and Lower Saxony; to Salvatore Ciniglio for delightful meals and conversation; and to Tom and Chris Crozier, Anna Maria and Karol Berger, Ana Peluffo, Pablo Ortiz, Emily Albu, and Alan Taylor for friendship and unstinting moral support.

I am grateful for the steadfast and loving encouragement of my family. My parents, Jorun and Donald Johns, and my brothers Karl and Andreas have consistently cheered on my academic pursuits. I thank my mother for her patience in looking over my many translations from the German and Andreas for checking my French; Karl could be counted on for art-historical information. My husband, Chris Reynolds, and our son Gabriel have daily supplied love, distraction, joy, and companionship; I have appreciated their readiness to travel back and forth between California and Germany, and indeed in the course of this project Göttingen has become a second home. My talented in-laws Joel, Ellen, Anne Marie, Susan, and Martha Reynolds and their far-flung families have been an unfailing source of support and vacation fun. I dedicate this book with admiration and gratitude to my parents, who, by going to the trouble and expense of raising me and my brothers biculturally and bilingually, enabled me to take on this project in the first place.

Contents

Illustrations

Introduction

Cultural Transfer and the Terrains Vastes

This book elucidates processes of cultural transfer between Britain and Germany during the period of the Personal Union—the time from 1714 to 1837 when the kings of England were simultaneously Electors of Hanover—by focusing on how certain exchanges, especially those undertaken by bluestocking feminists, furthered social reform. Britain and Germany, by contrast with America and France, sidestepped revolution but nonetheless generated discourses of individual and social liberty. Often in reaction to French continental cultural hegemony and imperial designs, some English and German actors undertook programs of social change inspired from beyond their own borders. They engaged in a process of *cultural transfer,* which involved the reciprocal movement of knowledge, methods, people, and goods between regions that were not impenetrably bounded but dynamically interrelated, regions better viewed as porous and internally differentiated cultural zones.

Cultural transfer, drawing on notions from postcolonial theory, emphasizes complex processes and hybridity and modifies the idea of simple influence or reception: that is, the pat, unidirectional impact of one nation, perceived as impermeably bounded and inhabited by a monolithic population imbued with a homogeneous national identity, on another entity equally uniform. As Stefanie Stockhorst has pointed out, "The paradigm of European national cultures and their independent origins appears no longer sustainable in the light of the manifold interrelations in politics, economics, science, philosophy, religion, and literature which constitute the ensemble of European history: what is alleged to be a genuine part of the 'own' culture, on closer inspection often turns out to be imported, and *vice versa.*" The notion of cultural transfer thus becomes necessary "in order to integrate the cultural dynamics of both the original and the target cultures and of the very transmission process into one theoretical concept."[1]

The idea of cultural transfer is to be distinguished from, even as it is related to, other recent exchange terms such as *transculturation, acculturation,* or *cultural appropriation,* terms more frequently heard in the American academy. "Transculturation," for example, emerged from postcolonial studies of Latin America and described the efforts of colonized peoples selectively to employ the culture of the colonizer, which was imposed upon them, to their own ends.[2] "Acculturation" has been used to describe transculturation on a large scale, generally with attempts by minority groups to come to terms with a dominant culture, and "cultural appropriation" has been applied loosely to the absorption of elements of a dominant culture. These designations share a concern for intercultural impacts in asymmetrical exchanges, with colonized peoples, immigrants, or minorities coming up against a more powerful, dominant group.[3]

The term *cultural transfer,* by contrast, has more often been used in the European context and derives from the work of Michel Espagne, Hans-Jürgen Lüsebrink, and others engaged initially in analyzing French-German exchange; it has spread to describe mostly intra-European and transatlantic reciprocities.[4] It denotes a broader type of interaction that can but need not involve cultural impositions and disparities of power between the participants. Though it may expose exploitation and critique ideology, it need not necessarily do so. Cultural transfer is therefore an expansive term and the more useful for this study, which portrays processes of interaction as varied, often reciprocal, and occurring in a complex power setting that frequently involves not just two asymmetrical parties (as in the other terms) but trilateral or even multilateral ones that may engage in assimilation, discrimination, repulsion, or a combination of these. Transculturation and the other terms could thus be seen as categories of cultural transfer; they are certainly not opposed or unrelated types of intercultural links, even though they have not been used in tandem with the language of transfer.

My study of cultural transfer reveals how new discourses were gathered and disseminated in a dynamic British-German field that was not bounded by, but that affected and was affected by, revolutionary, Napoleonic, commercial, and colonial activity. I trace the process by viewing chronologically, in separate chapters, four pivotal moments of transfer: (1) the expansion of the book trade from roughly 1750 to 1789; (2) the rage for translation, with a focus on the 1790s; (3) the effect of revolution on intra-European travel and travel writing up to the 1820s; and (4) the impact of transatlantic journeying on visions of reform, with a focus on the 1830s. The period of the Personal Union saw new avenues of cultural contact between Britain and the German principalities just when commercial and colonial enterprises were accelerating and revolutionary activities preoccupied America and France; for German and English women and reformists, such circumstances expanded the possibilities for articulating fresh views of what personal freedom, national character, and international interaction might be. Some feminists I discuss, for example, utilized the opportunities to promote expanded educational opportunities; the chance to work and control money; the right to self-expression and publication; the possibility for physical self-determination in the form of independent travel and sexual freedom; the increased access to divorce; and the end to war and the promotion of international peace. These goals are remarkably consistent throughout the period, even if they are unevenly emphasized or expressed in varied ways by different writers. Consequently, though my subjects' perspectives may not have dominated in their time, their writings and activities nonetheless had a cumulative impact and eventually were brought to bear on public discourses, social mores, and national legislation. Occurring even before first-wave feminism, these interventions, in addition to speaking to women's lives, offer an important corrective to more general cultural and historical interpretations: they help us, for instance, to modify ongoing debates about definitions of nationalism and cosmopolitanism, about English insularity, about Romantic masculinism and individualism, about myths attempting to justify European imperialism, and about the national stereotypes that still characterize Germany and Britain.

While studying reformist interventions from nonrevolutionary countries, I attend to other theoretical issues and historical problems. First, even though Britain and Hanover shared a sovereign from 1714 to 1837, scholars have largely ignored the Personal Union; their histories have treated the German electorate and the British monarchy as separate political and cultural entities. And yet the very legislation governing the Hanoverian succession in Britain concerned itself above all with the extent of the monarch's ties to his native land. The 1701 Act of Settlement placed serious restrictions on the German-born king: he was obliged to take communion in the Anglican Church; he could not leave

Britain without parliamentary consent; parliament moreover would review any assistance in foreign military actions; and foreign-born men could not hold public office. These measures are said to have assured the mutual independence of Britain and Hanover, but at the same time they could not fully Anglicize the German-born king, and they assured a degree of British parliamentary reach into the monarchs' extended visits and actions on the continent. Germans were no less concerned with this issue. The term "Personal Union" itself was coined by a political scientist at the University of Göttingen, Johann Stephan Pütter, to mark distance from Britain after the French invaded the electorate in 1757 in response to British agitation in North America. The loose term sought to underscore how "each state remains independent from the other" in the face of an incursion that in fact threatened to announce the opposite.[5]

Despite the thought-provoking mutual anxiety occasioned by the Personal Union, it is only recently that English-language scholars have produced volumes addressing Anglo-German ties in any depth: Jeremy Black's *The Continental Commitment: Britain, Hanover and Interventionism, 1714–1793* (Routledge, 2005); Andrew Thompson's *Britain, Hanover and the Protestant Interest, 1688–1756* (Boydell, 2006), Nick Harding's *Hanover and the British Empire 1700–1837* (Boydell, 2007), the edited volume of Brendan Simms and Torsten Riotte on *The Hanoverian Dimension in British History, 1714–1837* (Cambridge, 2007), and the anthology *Migration and Transfer from Germany to Britain 1660–1914*, edited by Stefan Manz, Margrit Schulte Beerbühl, and John R. Davis (Saur, 2007).[6] On the German-language side are Michael Maurer's pathbreaking *Aufklärung und Anglophilie in Deutschland* (Vandenhoeck und Ruprecht, 1987), Heide N. Rohloff's anthology *Grossbritannien und Hannover: Die Zeit der Personalunion 1714–1837* (Frankfurt, 1989), the collection *Aneignung und Abwehr: Interkultureller Transfer zwischen Deutschland und Großbritannien im 19. Jahrhundert*, edited by Rudolf Muhs, Johannes Paulmann, and Willibald Steinmetz (admittedly with a predominant focus on the pre-WWI decades, Philo, 1998), and the informative Göttingen exhibition catalog edited by Elmar Mittler, *"Eine Welt allein ist nicht genug": Großbritannien, Hannover und Göttingen 1714 bis 1837* (Göttingen, 2005). The books available in English generally emphasize high political and diplomatic history; I focus instead on the sociocultural ramifications of the significant political ties between the two lands, something that the German-language books have been more likely to explore. My study therefore contributes to a process of historical revision that these scholars and others have called for, a process that is, thankfully, gradually gaining momentum.

Second, recent discussions of international transfer and cosmopolitanism have overwhelmingly concerned globalization of the twentieth and twenty-first centuries; discussions of earlier ideas, if they occur, are generally represented by Immanuel Kant, who appears not as one voice among many but as a convenient figure against whom a more modern politics can be measured.[7] My study draws on the recent work of Pauline Kleingeld and Adriana Craciun to address historically, and in the plural, cosmopolitanism*s* (as well as emerging nationalism*s*); a more nuanced account of intertwining nationalist and internationalist ideas in the period is necessary.[8] Third, recent swings in scholarly approaches toward the Enlightenment—from postmodern skepticism, with its tendency to caricature Enlightenment humanism, to neoliberalist triumphalism— suggest that finding a middle way, something advocated by scholars such as Seyla Benhabib, Keith Baker, Peter Hanns Reill, and Daniel Gordon, is a goal that must constantly be kept in view.[9]

Though female actors loom large on my historical stage, this book is not strictly women's history, though it is feminist and gender history. Male figures participated in crucial ways to facilitate the circulation of (proto-) feminist discourses. However, while the historiography of cultural transfer has so far been populated mostly by men, women played crucial parts at every juncture. Johannes Paulmann, for example, has pointed out that women's reformist involvement appears to a greater degree in the study of British-German ties in the mid- to late-nineteenth century than it does in German-French ties for the same period; I extend that consideration to an earlier period with case studies beginning from around 1750.[10] Highlighting women's participation in cultural transfer is central to the accurate telling of the story of British-German interaction, with the effect that female experience is integrated into "mainstream" historiography.[11] The existing literature on Anglo-German relations, in focusing on high politics and diplomacy, has largely left women out, whereas the multifarious cultural activities I consider—publishing, book collecting, translation, and travel—are all ones in which women participated fully, constantly, and ubiquitously. The rigorous appraisal of cultural transfer demands attention to women alongside men and to the workings of gender overall; it underscores the centrality of gender to the period's discourses and suggests that in many cases women's activities can be seen as representative.

1. Moments of Cultural Transfer

My study begins by examining the book market. Precisely because France dominated continental literary culture in the eighteenth century, there is much to learn from examining the increasing intensity of British-German links. Benedict Anderson has described this moment as a nationalist one, in which local languages took over the discourses previously carried on in the lingua franca by a learned, cosmopolitan elite.[12] I argue, however—drawing on the notable work of Bernhard Fabian— that *both* nationalism and internationalism characterize the moment, and I foreground gender by suggesting that women, exactly because of their ill-defined political identities, were well positioned to promote what Kwame Anthony Appiah has called patriotic cosmopolitanism.[13] My case studies are Anna Vandenhoeck, a British woman who settled in Göttingen and, at the death of her husband, directed one of the most significant German publishing houses in the eighteenth century; and Duchess Philippine Charlotte of Brunswick-Wolfenbüttel, sister of Frederick the Great, niece of George II, and mother of Anna Amalia of Weimar. She was an avid collector of books who continued a tradition of female intellectuals begun by her great-grandmother Sophie of Hanover. Using materials from the archives of the Herzog August Bibliothek in Wolfenbüttel and the firm Vandenhoeck und Ruprecht (manuscript catalogs of book collections, rare publication records and translations, letters and personal documents) I show how these women, despite their lack of a legal and political identity, shaped politics by cultural means. Reinforcing substantial British-German royal ties, these enterprising women— whose different class affiliations and national origins did not keep them from sharing profound gender identification—fostered a protofeminist, rooted cosmopolitanism by publishing, collecting books, forming reading groups or leading salon-style discussions, contributing to libraries, and bequeathing substantial wealth.

Chapter 2 considers translation. In this period, as James Raven, Mary Helen McMurran, and Mirella Agorni among others have shown, up to 36 percent of the titles published per year in Britain were translations, and in Germany English works were translated with amazing rapidity: in 1776, for instance, 76 percent of the novels published in England were translated into German.[14] We must revise our notion of what constitutes "British" and "German" literature in the period; scholarship has followed the anachronistic aims of "English Studies," "German Studies," school curricula, and university departments that developed in the nineteenth century. I probe theories of translation beginning with Johann David Michaelis, a famous Göttingen biblical scholar who traveled and resided for a time in England, maintained frequent and lifelong correspondences with British scholars, advocated women's education, and completed a translation of Samuel Richardson's *Clarissa* for Vandenhoeck (1748–53), which took Germany by storm. He also raised an independent-spirited daughter, Caroline (best known today by her married names Schlegel-Schelling). She was only one of a group of accomplished Göttingen professors' daughters. Dorothea Schlözer, for instance, whose father August undertook an educational experiment on his firstborn child, became a prodigy and Göttingen's first female PhD at age seventeen. For her part Caroline Michaelis, along with Therese Heyne, daughter of a philology professor and director of the library, and Margarethe Wedekind, daughter of a philosophy professor, pursued a program of translating books— mostly in the 1790s, in the Mainzer revolutionary circle guided by Georg Forster—as a textual means of liberation from poverty, obscurity, sexual restriction, and political powerlessness. Translation in this period has been interpreted as a feminine pursuit, a means especially significant for women of earning a living respectably and participating in the republic of letters.[15] The Mainzer revolutionary sympathizers favored translating the radical texts published in England by Joseph Johnson, and like Johann David Michaelis they felt that a literal rendition of the books would facilitate absorption of British ideas of liberty in the German context. By contrast I consider the English feminist Mary Wollstonecraft. She herself wrote for Joseph Johnson, shared an interest in the radical pedagogies of German educationalists, and undertook a translation of Christian Gotthilf Salzmann's *Elements of Morality* (1790). Yet the theory of translation implied in her work is one of "naturalization"; it affords a certain resistance to the absorption of foreign cultural practice and unlike the original circumscribes notions of gender and national difference. A look at other translations from the German, published by Joseph Johnson, reinforces the sense that some "naturalization" appealed to the British market around 1800, even as it emphasizes the need for seeing English translations in their full western European and American context, a point driven home by consideration of Johann Christoph Friedrich GutsMuths's *Gymnastics for Youth*. A study of translators and translations thus opens a window on the effects of the French Revolution among radicals in Britain and Germany and highlights the complications posed by gender and emerging ideas of nation and Romantic aesthetics.

In chapter 3 I expand my purview to study intra-European travel and the impact of travel literature and artistic likenesses on English and German discourses of reform. In particular, I consider representations of Vesuvius, which was not only the culmination of the Grand Tour but also a potent revolutionary symbol, something capitalized upon more recently by Susan Sontag, whose popular novel *The Volcano Lover* (1992) uses the mountain to weave together images of eighteenth-century political, scientific, affective, and aesthetic eruptions. Sontag follows in the footsteps of Germaine de Staël, who famously located scenes of her novel *Corinne* (1807) on the slopes of the fiery mountain. Staël, however, is only the most illustrious writer or artist who employed the volcano as a means of furthering or critiquing social roles and norms; others include Friederike Brun, Elisa von der Recke, August Tiedge, Johann Wolfgang von Goethe, Duchess Anna Amalia, Johann Gottfried Seume, Angelika Kauffmann, Michael Wutky, Philipp Hackert, Joseph Wright of Derby, Anne Miller, John Moore, Hester Lynch Piozzi, Mary Shelley, Percy Shelley, and Felicia Hemans. There are also artistic caricatures and cartoons, one of which, from the 1830s, depicts Vesuvius with the word "Liberty" erupting out of the revolution-volcano. While considering all of these, I will ultimately focus on the writings of Anna Jameson, whose works emphasize how an aesthetic category facilitates the volcano's literary and ideological deployment. Jameson's semifictional autobiography *Diary of an Ennuyée* (1826) challenges the newfangled sentimental-sublime style of representing the volcano—promoted enthusiastically by Georg Forster in Germany—through a reversion to the picturesque, suggesting that consideration of aesthetics under the pressure of disaster, especially of this storied burning mountain, can expose the naturalization as well as the critique of sexual politics in the revolutionary and postrevolutionary period. It also demonstrates the broad extent of cultural transfer, since British-German relations are not consistently determined by people who are citizens of those nations, or limited to geographies that fall within those nations' bounds—bounds that were in any case shifting in this period.

Chapter 4 opens out my study yet further to explore the impact of transatlantic travel on the discourses of social reform in pre-1848 Britain and Germany. I return to Anna Jameson, who in addition to visiting Vesuvius journeyed to Upper Canada. In all of Jameson's writings she focused on women's roles and needs, whether the subject were life in Canada, German art, Shakespearean characters, female sovereigns, forms of charity, or labor. Jameson first traveled to Germany in 1833 and 1834–36 and resided in Weimar (the cultural center created by Anna Amalia, the daughter of Philippine Charlotte, patron of Goethe, and traveler to Vesuvius—chapters 1 and 3). Jameson became close to Ottilie von Goethe, daughter-in-law of the renowned poet, with whom she shared a long correspondence; moreover she proved an energetic cultural translator between Britain and Germany. She wrote extensively on German literature, art, and architecture to introduce it to a British audience, and her works on Shakespeare as well as on Canada were translated into German. In considering the impact of her books, their translations, her correspondence, as well as her overall reception, I explore the extent to which Jameson's transatlantic experience was brought to bear on the dialogue she established between London and Weimar in the 1830s and '40s. The image of America became, for many German as well as British writers, a utopian alternative to the disappointments in the wake of the French Revolution. I trace the part transatlanticism, and especially understandings of Native American or First Nations practices, played in Jameson's feminism and in the discourses of liberty she promoted in the European context, ultimately leading to legislation concerning the expansion of education, women's property rights, and divorce.

Bluestocking Feminism and British-German Cultural Transfer, 1750–1837 is therefore a study in bluestocking transnationalism spawning discourses of liberty and attempts at sociocultural reform. While the French Revolution loomed large, it did not fully determine the content of the alternative enlightenments within and beyond the geography of the Personal Union. Such links had their own history and were carried on by hitherto understudied German and English actors. My periodization foregrounds the central significance of gender and sexual politics to my study, as the year 1837 marks the end of the Personal Union: Salic Law prevented a woman, Victoria, from reigning over Hanover. My book moves chronologically toward 1837 and is roughly divided into two parts; part 1 centers on the cultural significance of Göttingen, with its university (founded by George II and attended by hundreds of Britons), publishing ventures, educationalists, and translators, and its enterprising daughters; part 2 shifts to people associated with Weimar, where a convergence of thinkers and ideas generated cascading intellectual and cultural impacts felt to this day.

This bipartite structure, however, cannot obscure the dense interweaving that connects and reconnects my chapters. Instead, there emerges a thick description of British-German networks, whose protagonists appear and reappear at various moments and places to initiate actions and ideas with lasting reverberations. The ideas, goods, and people that make up the study of transfer, as Johannes Paulmann has suggested, are not to be viewed in isolation, but within, as part of, the elaborate context of their social and political environments.[16] Such a project endorses the call of such thinkers as Bruno Latour, Michel Callon, and John Law for an encompassing account of the manifold factors—human as well as non-human, material, geographical, cultural—that serve to contrive, establish, and then reassemble dynamic interactive networks.[17] Anna Vandenhoeck, for example, as university publisher and Göttingen bookseller after her husband's death, not only released Richardson's *Clarissa* in Germany but her work is shown in different chapters to affect the course of English-language learning in Germany and the collecting habits of Brunswick aristocrats. One of these nobles, Duchess Philippine Charlotte, *salonnière* and book collector, and Johann David Michaelis, translator of *Clarissa*, are not only involved in furthering German-British ties but also raise daughters crucial to late-eighteenth and early nineteenth-century cultural transfer. Philippine Charlotte's daughter Anna Amalia, for example, the "muse of Weimar," helps to bring Goethe and other literary lights to that small principality (including, later, Germaine de Staël and Anna Jameson), and Caroline Schlegel-Schelling becomes hostess of the nearby Jena Romantic salon, an equally attractive destination for British intellectuals. Georg Forster, German-born and English-bred participant in James Cook's second voyage, husband of Therese Heyne, a Göttingen professor's daughter, not only sets up a translation factory that employs the radical Göttingen "Universitätsmamsellen"; he also gives South Sea artifacts to Prince Leopold Friedrich Franz of Anhalt-Dessau. This enlightened prince displays these items—along with a functioning replica of Vesuvius, a copy of the Coalbrookdale Bridge, Wedgwood vases, and other examples of modern invention and thought—to further the enlightenment program of his garden at Wörlitz, which was inspired by the English gardens he had seen on his travels. This same prince, prompted also by the Dissenting academies he saw in England, employs the progressive educator Johann Bernard Basedow to found his famous Philanthropist school in order to educate the youths of Dessau. The ideas generated within that movement make their way back to Mary Wollstonecraft and Joseph Johnson, who publish translations of German Philanthropist work in order to further new pedagogies in Britain.

Such intricate concatenations of figures, ideas, and material goods in this dynamic and fertile historical period not only suggest the kind of actor-network proposed by Latour, Callon, and Law, but also provide this study with the possibility for what Clifford Geertz has called thick description of British-German transfer. According to Geertz the task is "to uncover the conceptual structures that inform our subjects' acts . . . and to construct a system of analysis in whose terms what is generic to those structures, what belongs to them because they are what they are, will stand out against the other determinates of human behavior."[18] The four moments of cultural transfer I analyze supply the ground upon which feminist conceptual structures and their significant meanings can be construed. They reveal the significance of Germany to histories that have often shuttled only between Britain and France, make a place for the sustained consideration of gender and early feminism in international exchange, and complicate the sometimes oversimplified views of movement from Enlightenment to Romantic thought by tracing ideological continuities and preoccupations, here with a view to reform and social renewal, moving from the mid-eighteenth century into the early Victorian period. Ideas for sociocultural change did not emerge only from revolutionary agents, and they sometimes take on an apparently, but not statically, conservative cast.

Thick description also allows an adjustment of the metaphors we use to characterize our historiography. Just as members of the Annales school argued the profit of viewing the past in the long term, the *longue durée*, I would suggest that seeing the eighteenth and early nineteenth century as broadly as possible, over *terrains vastes*, allows for a stronger understanding of British-German links. These ties, after all, often worked through French and Dutch and American or other geographies, personages, and networks, and these others left their mark on the exchanges, even if they did not determine their trajectory. Viewing the *terrains vastes* thus traces identities and conflicts through movements within their surroundings, shifts foci between local and general, and acknowledges an ongoing and dynamic prerevolutionary and revolutionary European and global context. The results may perhaps appear untidy, but they capture a larger piece of the fabric of events so that patterns can be discerned; they account for the mobility and intermittent connectedness of individuals and social groups; and they acknowledge the contingencies of the period to a greater degree than the conclusions of studies that are contained through a focus on single influences, solitary figures, or unique historical phenomena. Importantly, attention to cultural transfer allows scholars to contemplate historical roads not taken—what might have been but did not gain ground or precedence—by surveying the lay of the land: that is, by viewing the spread of options or range of choices that existed for historical actors, especially neglected female ones, the reader can come to conclusions about the extent to which a wider set of human or social factors could be said to have played a part in shaping the lived reality of cultures during the period under consideration. Historiography stands a chance, then, of shedding tendencies toward determined trajectories, simplistic etiologies, or Whig-style interpretations of progress.

To that extent transfer study absorbs the goals of counterfactual history, which, by considering points of divergence—moments where different decisions might have been made—draws attention to individuals' choices and to the alternate histories that might have emanated from those different decisions. While counterfactuals are employed (if not acknowledged) in most historical thinking as a way of mentally filling in blanks or setting factual trajectories in relief, pondering alternate histories is particularly useful for determining the value of subalterns' or reformist positions. The outlooks of those who were disadvantaged, powerless, or marginalized may or may not have influenced people in charge or determined the flow of events, but deciding what those outlooks were or might have been is helpful. As Lubomír Doležel has written, the historian is forced to "place himself in the position of the contemporaries to whom the various possible alternatives were still available, for whom the selection was not closed by the actualization of one of them."[19] To evaluate the meaning of actual events, historians must determine whether an alternate and perhaps preferable sequence might have followed had other voices been heard and other decisions taken. This helps the effort to establish the significance of progressive discourses by women, subalterns, and reformists.

2. *Bluestockings, Actor-Networks, and the* Terrains Vastes

Integrating feminist contributions into historiography has been a long-term project for feminist historians; I focus here on the eighteenth- and early-nineteenth century "bluestockings," a term developed in the mid-eighteenth-century to denote, initially, a social circle interested in intellectual improvement and the exchange of ideas through salon-style conversation and correspondence.[20] I will use the term in its broadest possible sense, applying both its original reference to both sexes and to interest in intellectual and philanthropic pursuits, as well as including later members of feminist intellectual circles in Britain and on the Continent. It is a way of marking the ideological transfer that took place through time and space to link these individuals. Scholars have successfully rescued the term *bluestocking* from the scorn of its early-nineteenth-century detractors; moreover, they have discussed the bluestockings in generational terms and have called for ever broader considerations of their activities. Recently, for example, Elizabeth Eger, Karen O'Brien, Harriet Guest, Nicole Pohl, Ruth Dawson, Ina Schabert, Ulrike Gleixner, Marion W. Gray, and others have favored a view of women's lives in relationship with communities and collectives and have considered their work and its influence through time as well as in modes beyond the literary.[21] Although such considerations can obscure differences among individuals, they have the advantage of allowing broad and long-term evaluation.

For one thing, they let scholars begin to explicate how these bluestockings came to perceive themselves as a transnational interest group with a particular ethos and epistemology that developed over the late-eighteenth and early nineteenth centuries and came to fruition in first-wave feminist programs. This is a project to which this study aims to contribute. As Elizabeth Eger has argued, the early British bluestockings "stand as inspiring pioneers . . . in the history of feminism"; however, it is perhaps not so much their "contribution to the formulation of a national canon of literature"[22] that measures their significance as it is the influence they exerted on intellectuals and reformers removed in space and time—the common cause they delineated among European feminists overall. Female innovators such as Anna Vandenhoeck and Duchess Philippine Charlotte of Brunswick-Wolfenbüttel were of course limited by the range of their commercial and social power, but that range was significant and, like Elizabeth Montagu or the French *salonnières*, their decisions represented a self-conscious effort to promote women and their interests in an international context. They had been reached by a (proto-) feminist impulse from British bluestockings that was self-consciously promulgated in the third quarter of the eighteenth century; it was epitomized in Sarah Scott's utopian novel *Millenium Hall*, a book available in translation at Anna Vandenhoeck's Göttingen shop. It was conveyed also in Vandenhoeck's edition of *Clarissa*, lending impetus to the more radical sociopolitical visions of the Göttinger daughters and Mary Wollstonecraft in the 1790s. These in turn enabled the kinds of critiques articulated in the second quarter of the nineteenth century by female travelers who took stock of their circumstances via comparison with practices and peoples in the lands they visited and analyzed. Although, before Wollstonecraft, we have no systematic feminist manifesto, we view what Gary Kelly has termed the "Bluestocking programme"[23] and discern self-conscious efforts to pursue persistent feminist goals articulated by earlier writers of different political and religious persuasions and nationalities: education, personal mobility, control over resources and time, intellectual independence, the right to self-expression, the chance for meaningful and, increasingly over time, remunerative work.

Feminist scholars devising a new literary history of female authorship have suggested recently that women's writing itself emerged through transnational links. According to Anke Gilleir and Alicia C. Montoya, "It was through international contacts, by creating new female networks, that early women authors also created something we would call today 'women's writing'—by definition not bound by any national or geographic limitation. . . . A sense of gender identity acquired its meaning not from a sense of national sameness, but transnational difference."[24] Along these lines I am arguing that not only women's writing and gender identity but feminism itself was promoted through cultural transfer. Accounting fully for bluestocking activities around 1800 requires consideration of the *terrains vastes*. The bluestocking program, mutually reinforced through a process of European cultural transfer, offered a template through which feminist knowledge and a feminist critique was formulated and eventually moved from mostly fictional to nonfictional discourses to become a ground for activism and sociopolitical reform.

The *terrains vastes* also provide space for a model of expanding networks. Feminist critics have expressed interest in the actor-network theory of Bruno Latour, Michel Callon, and John Law because, among other things, it includes and accounts for previously ignored "actants" as parts of the association. Actor-network theory focused initially on technology and science and the laboratory environment, taking account not only of human experimenters but also the lab itself, the scientific equipment, the rats, the microbes, the printer and copier, the custodial staff, the supply chain, and the recipients of the results. Thus the theory came to offer a more heterogeneous and inclusive model of connections and activity, giving a fuller and more detailed picture of what constitutes work and what goes into creating and sustaining a scientific "fact." Such a model speaks to other feminist issues addressed here: first, the interest in moving beyond borders to approach particular concerns transcending the nation-state, especially about gender; second, the focus on translation to facilitate this movement, with a fascination about the changes, additions, and corruptions that can occur in the transmission from one context into another; and third, the conviction about creating connections, with a focus on travel and alliance-building, based on a recognition that ends are not achievable through isolated individual efforts but require the actions of collaborators over time.[25] According to Latour the task is to "follow the actors . . . to learn from them what the collective existence has become in their hands, which methods they have elaborated to make it fit together, which accounts could best define the new associations that they have been forced to establish."[26]

Influenced by actor-network theory, Donna Haraway has argued, "Non-human nature (including most white women, people of color, the sick, and others with reduced powers of self-direction compared to the One True Copy of the Prime Mover) has been especially patient," but scholars must now recognize with Latour "that the agencies and actors are *never* preformed, prediscursive, just out there, substantial, concrete, neatly bounded before anything happens, only waiting for a veil to be lifted and 'land ho!' to be pronounced. Human and nonhuman, *all* entities take shape in encounters, in practices; and the actors and partners in encounters are not all human, to say the least."[27] My geographic metaphor, the *terrains vastes*, is a call, not only to make space for new classes of actors and to see beyond the borders of the nation-state, but also to meet mountains of data without fear or an inclination to ignore piles simply because the way past a stack seems simpler and more direct. Such a turning away seems to me more likely than not to leave out precisely those "non-human" figures identified by Haraway, the "white women, people of color, the sick, and others with reduced powers of self-direction" who have inhabited the regions farther off the main track.

Scholars of historical cultural transfer, in addition to feminists, have sought ways to employ the idea of networks. Ann Thomson, Simon Burrows, and Edmond Dziembowski have discussed the eighteenth century and have pointed out that it is difficult at this scholarly juncture to move away from considerations of the individual: "We are still mainly at the stage of studying individual 'egocentric' networks, generally centred on particular figures." As a result, scholars must work to identify and define these associations: "Does a network consist merely in the relationship between several individuals and is it a question of the number of people involved or the intensity and nature of the links between them? . . . Can one approach in the same way a formally constituted and self-conscious network such as that of the correspondents of a learned society and a network reconstituted by the historian from an individual's web of correspondents or from overlapping interests? . . . Further research is needed in order to obtain a more comprehensive understanding of the functioning of networks in this period and the degree to which local, national and international systems intersected."[28] Without disregarding individuals, it seems to me that seeing them within the *terrains vastes*, as actors within the intersections of international systems, is furthered by employing an expanded notion of associations in the manner of Latour, with the inclusion of material elements and a recognition of ongoing realignments.

The expanding feminist networks that constitute the *terrains vastes* thus help to shape the current historiographical "spatial turn," evaluated recently by David Blackbourn: "In their different ways, environmental history, oceanic and transoceanic history, transnational history, the history of cultural transfer and connections (*Beziehungsgeschichte, l'histoire croisée*) have all been a part of [the] spatial turn. . . . Zooming in allows you to see things previously invisible; stepping back, widening the lens, has the same effect, although the things you see are different."[29] My concern in this study is clearly to widen the lens, to allow for the aerial view that offers a glimpse of significant actors and networks that have been missed and unaccounted for. At the same time, there is a zooming in too: one has to begin somewhere, and so the movement of my argument necessarily shifts from individuals and from individual case studies outward and back again as I attempt to account for associations and consider their broader effects. Blackbourn has contemplated this task and suggested that "we must be able to hold two ideas in our heads simultaneously": both the results of taking a close look and the place of the details in the big picture.[30] My study of British-German cultural transfer thus sees bluestockings individually promoting the transnational project but also collectively constituting it, influencing the forms and norms governing life in these distinct but linked lands as they publish, collect, translate, travel, correspond, form alliances, take part in debates, engage and shape the culture of their time.

CHAPTER 1

The Book as Cosmopolitan Object

Anna Vandenhoeck, Publisher, and Philippine
Charlotte of Brunswick-Wolfenbüttel, Collector[1]

Ihr Toren, die ihr im Koffer sucht!
Hier werdet ihr nichts entdecken!
Die Konterbande, die mit mir reist,
Die hab ich im Kopfe stecken. . . .

Und viele Bücher trag ich im Kopf!
Ich darf es euch versichern,
Mein Kopf ist ein zwitscherndes Vogelnest
Von konfiszierlichen Büchern.

[You fools, who search in the suitcase!
You'll discover nothing here!
The contraband that travels with me,
Is tucked away in my head. . . .

And I carry many books in my head!
I can assure you of it,
My head is a twittering birds' nest
Of books to be confiscated.]
　　　　　—Heinrich Heine, from *Deutschland. Ein Wintermärchen*

Heinrich Heine's speaker of the 1840s ridicules the border guards who inspect his luggage for smuggled texts and thereby critiques the censorship, repression, and exile suffered by liberals in the Vormärz period.[2]

Though Heine's poem did not save his political allies from persecution, his image defiantly conveys the free and cosmopolitan status of the book, an object that will elude reactionary authorities and, bird-like, fly into minds and chirp unrestrainedly in subversive dialogue with other texts. Heine's depiction of books thus figures unhindered cultural transfer, a smooth movement of oppositional ideas across mental and political borders and an efficacious occupancy and activity in new territories. For all the satirical bitterness of his poem, the upshot of the image is idealistic and hopeful.

It may be surprising to find Heine introducing my chapter featuring two establishment late-eighteenth-century women who would perhaps have winced at his strident political stance, could they have seen into the future. However, I wish to suggest that Heine's capacity to imagine the efficacy of books as cosmopolitan objects, challenging a parochial and nationalistic politics in the 1840s, follows upon decades of intense interest, exemplified by my protagonists, in unimpeded literary transfer for the purpose of promoting enlightenment, internationalization, and the expansion of sociocultural authority. Heine will reappear in chapter 4; here, I will focus on how Anna Vandenhoeck, a British woman who became bookseller to the University of Göttingen, and Duchess Philippine Charlotte, a princess of Prussia who married the Duke of Brunswick-Wolfenbüttel, contributed significantly to the enlightenment transfer project in a milieu of increasing multilateral cross-Channel exchange.

Literary historians have delineated the major roles played by women in the eighteenth-century book market and the shape they gave to the republic of letters.[3] Given women's centrality to each national culture, what part can they be said to have played in intra-European cultural transfer overall? It is a complex undertaking to contemplate simultaneously trade, gender, and nation, but doing so reveals facets of international exchange that have been inadequately studied and that alter the common story. I will consider books as material objects of transfer in eighteenth-century Europe, and I will ask how these texts, moving throughout the region in spite of wars and political tensions, shed light on feminist questions, particularly as they relate to cosmopolitanism and the rise of nationalism. Such questions are especially interesting with reference to Germany, not yet a country in the eighteenth century but a region with a confusing array of principalities and political alliances. Since Germany was not a unified nation, we can learn much from examining how the absorption of books from another culture, in this instance the British, paradoxically aided in national self-definition and at the same time furthered international connection.

Moreover, precisely because France dominated continental literary culture in the eighteenth century, there is much to learn from studying English-German links. Delving into relationships between Britain and the German principalities after the Hanoverian succession and before the French Revolution brings to light aspects of cultural exchange that scholars, both from the English and the German side, have largely ignored. Books as objects of exchange can tell us about the history of two nations generally viewed separately, but which were tied politically and in complex sociocultural ways.

For one thing, such a study aids our understanding of European literary history and highlights the political role of women as producers, consumers, and cultural promoters. Duchess Philippine Charlotte's role as a book collector is augmented by her goals as a hostess; her activities ultimately draw attention to the gradual displacement of French products from dominance in Germany. This meant both an opening for English books as well as German, and what has been viewed as incipient nationalism based on a bourgeois demand for an indigenous, German literature is shown simultaneously to have carried an international element. In addition, a look at the book trade allows us to revise how we think about class distinctions. The standard story is that of a court culture dominated by the products of French culture, and, again, a rising bourgeoisie demanding and producing German goods. The two are said to have come together only in the 1780s, especially in the court of Anna Amalia of Weimar.[4] But a view of book publishing and collecting, particularly among women, suggests that a merging of aristocratic and bourgeois interests occurred earlier. Finally, the eighteenth-century European book market reveals what might at first appear to be a paradox: gendered cosmopolitanism. Rather than engaging in nonnational detachment based on notions of *liberté* and *fraternité*, as would the supporters of the French Revolution, bluestocking women display a patriotic cosmopolitanism characterized by cultural attachment. Tracing the movement of books between Britain and (what came to be) Germany thus offers fascinating insights into general European cultural links in the eighteenth century and suggests that women, despite their lack of a legal and political identity, were shaping politics by cultural means. In so doing they were beginning to create a class of their own, characterized by cultural and intellectual pursuits and a distinctive bluestocking ethos.

1. Göttingen: Academic Interests and Publishing

Some cultural ties between Britain and Germany clearly had political origins. After the establishment of the Personal Union, which made the Elector of Hanover, Georg Ludwig, King George I of England in 1714, the most prominent cultural link was represented in the founding of the University of Göttingen by George II in 1734. This institution was the brainchild of Gerlach Adolf von Münchhausen, a privy councillor of Hanover who became curator of the university and who energetically encouraged British-German transfer. The University of Göttingen was to be a modern institution, engaging in practical subjects to create a well-educated class of public servants and citizens. It would emphasize not only law, medicine, and theology but also political science and history. It would develop a botanical garden and an observatory. It would promote religious tolerance in order to appeal to students from beyond the borders of the electorate; and, indeed, it drew students from all over Europe. Among international students British were the most numerous. Matriculation records suggest that in a representative decade, 1770–80, up to 5 percent of students were British.[5] George III sent his three youngest sons to study there, and many aristocratic and gentry families followed his example.

Professors had strong ties to Britain. Münchhausen encouraged Göttingen scholars to spend time there and to update their knowledge, especially in fields where British thinkers were at the forefront.[6] Albrecht von Haller, for example, undertook educational travels in England, wrote a travel account, and remained influenced by things English his entire career, even publishing in late life a novel on Alfred the Great (1773) that touted the British political system and lionized George III.[7] Extracts of his writings on physiology and blood circulation were translated and published in the *Monthly Review* and the *Scots Magazine* in the 1750s, his novel *Usong* was translated within a year of its German publication, and his *Letters to his Daughter on the Truths of the Christian Religion* appeared in three separate British editions between 1780 and 1807.[8] He became first president of the Göttingen Academy of Sciences and the first editor of its internationally respected critical journal, the *Göttingische Anzeigen von gelehrten Sachen*. He promoted the German translation of Samuel Richardson's novel *Clarissa* and wrote influential early reviews; these were translated into French and English, were published in the *Gentleman's Magazine*, and persuaded Richardson to revise the novel by adding footnotes to clarify Lovelace's character.[9]

Other professors with strong ties to Britain included Gottfried Achenwall, a prominent political theorist who traveled to England and wrote extensively on what he viewed as the sources of English freedom;[10] Johann David Michaelis, a renowned Biblical scholar who also traveled and corresponded with colleagues in England, was invited to join the Academies of Sciences in Paris and London, had works excerpted in the *Monthly Review* before they were fully issued in several British editions, and translated *Clarissa* into German (1748–53), which I will discuss in the next chapter.

Georg Christoph Lichtenberg (1742–99), however, is the best known of the Göttinger professors to travel to England. He first came to accompany Göttingen students William Irby and Thomas Swanton home in April-May 1770. His connection with these high-ranking families (the young men were sons of a lord and an admiral) made possible introductions into elevated social circles, and he was even invited by King George III to visit the observatory in Richmond. The king then financed Lichtenberg's second trip to England, September 1774 to December 1775. Lichtenberg was a royal guest at Kew for the winter. He followed the political fortunes of John Wilkes and reported on the crisis with the American colonies; he observed English ways closely, commenting vividly on English street life, theater, manufactures, science, philosophy, and literature. Clarissa Campbell Orr has recently delineated his connections to Queen Charlotte. Surely with the queen's blessing he eventually became tutor to the three English princes who came to study in Göttingen.[11] He was elected a member of the London Royal Society in 1793. Although he was a professor of physics, with interests in mathematics and astronomy, he is best known today for his trenchant aphorisms. His literary flair led him to coedit, with Georg Forster, the *Göttingische Magazin der Wissenschaften und Literatur* (1780–85), and in his last years he introduced Germans to the work of William Hogarth with his *Ausführliche Erklärung der Hogarthischen Kupferstiche* (1794–99).[12] Among his prized possessions were a copy of Newton's death mask and a picture of the English king and queen that hung over the sofa in his garden house.[13]

Other Göttingen institutions furthered the anglicization of the region. Münchhausen paid particular attention to the university library. He hired energetic and ambitious librarians, Joachim Matthias Gesner and later Christian Gottlob Heyne, who were themselves professors and developed a first-rate collection. From the start the Göttingen library vigorously bought English books; Bernhard Fabian calls it the "greatest repository of English books in eighteenth-century Germany."[14] New books were quickly reviewed in the *Göttingische Anzeigen von gelehrten Sachen*, and they were incorporated into the first full bibliography of eighteenth-century English authors compiled, surprisingly, not by an Englishman in England but by the Göttinger assistant librarian Jeremias David Reuss: *Alphabetical Register of all the Authors Actually Living in Great-Britain, Ireland, and in the United Provinces of North-America, with a Catalogue of their Publications* (1791). Reuss wrote that since he possessed "most of the literary resources upon which an English author could draw . . . it may perhaps not be too daring if he attempts to supply a work [i.e., this bibliography] which the English have not yet produced." From 1799 one could also consult the Göttinger Johann Gottfried Eichhorn's *Litterärgeschichte*, which, according to Fabian, represented "one of the most incisive accounts of literature and learning in England that were written in eighteenth-century Germany."[15] Scholars in the area participated in an early form of interlibrary loan: Georg Forster in Kassel and Johann Gottfried Herder in Weimar requested that Heyne send them English volumes from Göttingen since the books could not be obtained any other way.[16]

The founding of the university naturally had an impact on Göttingen's commercial life. Most notable was the creation of the influential publishing firm Vandenhoeck. Abraham Vandenhoeck, a Dutch bookseller born in The Hague around 1700 and active in London, was called to be bookseller and printer to the university in 1735. Münchhausen's international ties and his ambitions for the university clearly led him to choose Vandenhoeck for the job. Vandenhoeck died soon, however, in 1750. As a result his English wife, Anna, took over the firm. Born Anna Parry in 1709, she married Vandenhoeck in the 1720s. His London shop was to be found "at Virgil's Head over against the New Church in the Strand," and a broad variety of publications were sold there, including medical and theological and political titles in Latin and French as well as in English, alongside fictional, historical, and travel texts from all over Europe.[17] Vandenhoeck expanded the business to Hamburg in 1732, and they moved to that city for a short period before being recruited to Göttingen in 1735.[18] It took time and effort to import their equipment and set up shop; even procuring type and paper could prove difficult. But their position must have improved substantially by 1749, when we learn that Anna was able to afford a pleasure trip to Kassel via post coach, accompanied by English friends.[19]

When Abraham Vandenhoeck died, Göttingen professors lamented his loss but expressed confidence in the capability of his wife to take over the work. In a letter to Johann Matthias Gesner, Albrecht von Haller wrote: "Nuper obiit Van den Hoeckius (magna mea cum iactura), sed vidua inceptos libros ad finem perducet" ("Vandenhoeck died recently, a great loss for me, but the widow will bring the initiated books to completion"), and Münchhausen too announced to the university his readiness to leave the business in Anna Vandenhoeck's hands under the current terms ("man [ist] nicht abgeneigt, der Wittwe das Capital auf den bisherigen Fuß in der Handlung zu lassen").[20] Vandenhoeck was not alone; she ran the operation with the help of her business manager Carl Friedrich Ruprecht, to whom she ultimately willed the establishment when she died in 1787. (The company, still going strong, is now called Vandenhoeck und Ruprecht and was run by the Ruprecht family for seven generations.) Vandenhoeck published landmark works of celebrated professors—Haller, Michaelis, Johann Stephan Pütter, August Ludwig Schlözer among them—alongside printing the necessary catalogs, notices, and incidental items for the university. By 1751, however, she found it expedient to divest herself of the printing side of the business in order to concentrate entirely on book publishing and selling.

For over thirty years Vandenhoeck was pivotal in making her company into one of the most respected publishers in Germany, and the shop in Göttingen was a destination for intellectual exchange. The law professor Johann Stephan Pütter explained how, especially during the Seven Years' War when French troops occupied Göttingen and citizens' movement was restricted within the town gates, Vandenhoeck's shop was the place for scholars to meet and enjoy conversation.[21] She set special emphasis on foreign books, and English volumes in particular were available: the firm published the German translation of Samuel Richardson's *Clarissa* as early as 1748–53, and it created a reading circle so that foreign-language journals and newspapers would be available to customers. But Vandenhoeck's was not alone in promoting an English connection. Another later, prominent Göttinger bookseller, Johann Christian Dieterich, planned an entire series of English works to be edited by Georg Christoph Lichtenberg, and the Weidmannsche Buchhandlung began translating English books with amazing rapidity. This firm was based in Leipzig, not Göttingen, but perhaps encouraged by the practice of booksellers exchanging volumes among themselves at the book fairs (gradually displaced in this period by payment in hard currency), it meant that Anna Vandenhoeck always had hundreds of English books, in the original and in translation, on offer at her shop.[22] Friedrich Wilhelm Unger would later write, "It was Vandenhoeck's widow and Diet-

FIG. 1. Anna Vandenhoeck. Courtesy of Vandenhoeck & Ruprecht, Göttingen, Germany.

erich from Gotha who first brought life to the local book trade. . . . There was hardly another place in the position of Göttingen to offer foreign and especially English books."[23] Given the interest in international publications, a plan was developed around 1751 for a "world book company" to be established by selling stocks to 250 parties in order to raise the considerable capital of one hundred thousand taler, with the aim of facilitating the import and export of books to and from other European countries. A formal proposal was drawn up, an advertisement generated, and another Dutch bookseller, Elias Luzak, contracted to become the commercial organizer of this project, which was much favored by the Hanover regime. However, the scheme was never realized, though Luzak settled in Göttingen anyway and became a competitor for Vandenhoeck.[24]

Göttingen was therefore a node of expanding internationalization and especially anglicization, a characteristic it shared with Hamburg, which had long had close commercial ties with Britain. In Hamburg there was an Anglican church; British diplomats resided there; social organizations with international ties, such as the Patriotische Gesellschaft and the Freemasons, were very active. An English bookshop and English journals emerged, and many of the people spreading Anglophilia during the eighteenth century had some Hamburg or Göttingen connection.[25] Anna Vandenhoeck's commercial activities thus formed part of a larger tendency in the culture toward increasing interest in England and demonstrate how the market was opening up to non-French literature and language. German buyers of English books were of course people with means, mostly aristocrats and rich bourgeois. I will therefore consider aristocrats and their ties to the bourgeois expansion of trade, considering the aristocratic approach to book-buying and focusing on Braunschweig (Brunswick), which was allied both with England and Prussia.

2. Braunschweig: Cosmopolitanism and Court Culture

Göttingen, in the Electorate of Braunschweig-Lüneburg (which was generally called Hanover), was closely tied not only to England through the Personal Union but also to other Brunswick duchies as well as to Prussia, since they were territorially contiguous and linked through intermarried ruling families (see figure 2). Especially noteworthy was a family dynasty of female intellectuals, beginning with Sophie of Hanover. These women—with the exception of one crucial male figure, Frederick the

Great, and a lesser one, Karl I—were central in fostering the intellectual and cultural growth of northern Germany in the period and promoting the type of cosmopolitanism I will be describing. There is a significant salon tradition to be witnessed in provincial courts that culminated in Anna Amalia's late eighteenth and early nineteenth-century Weimar. And while the bluestocking aristocrats who were central in this process are familiar to Germanists and royal historians, they remain virtually unknown to other scholars. I will therefore offer brief introductions to these dynamic noblewomen before turning to the example of Philippine Charlotte, Duchess of Braunschweig-Wolfenbüttel.

(1) *Sophie von Hannover* was Electress of Hanover and slated to become queen of England, but she died only months before Queen Anne. She traveled extensively, collected books and paintings, corresponded with significant figures, and possessed enormous energy. She was the patron of Gottfried Wilhelm Leibniz and took an active part in shaping his career, for example setting up and mediating his productive theological correspondence with the Huguenot Paul Pellisson.[26] On the day that she died, in her eighties, she was taking a vigorous walk in her beloved garden in Herrenhausen.

(2) *Sophie Charlotte von Preussen* was the only daughter of Sophie von Hannover. She also supported Leibniz, whose *Essais de Théodicee* derived from conversations with her; he is said to have been "in despair for weeks" when she died.[27] Lietzenburg castle was the location of her renowned salon, and her husband renamed it Charlottenburg in her honor.[28]

(3) *Caroline of Ansbach* learned much at Sophie Charlotte's gatherings. She was orphaned and came under Sophie Charlotte's guardianship. In this context Leibniz became her instructor; he suggested books to her and they corresponded for years. Caroline was courted by and encouraged to marry Archduke Karl, the future Holy Roman emperor. This would have meant converting to Catholicism. Caroline, however, was devout and independent-minded and debated the formidable Jesuit Father Ferdinand Orban for hours in front of an open Bible before she turned down the marriage proposal. She finally married Sophie Charlotte's nephew, Georg August, who became George II of England and who felt so confident of her powers that he appointed her regent during his long trips to Hanover. As Sophie von Hannover and Sophie Charlotte had done, Caroline mediated and moderated the correspondence of Leibniz, this time with Samuel Clarke.[29]

(4) *Sophie Dorothea*, sister of George II, married Sophie Charlotte's son Friedrich Wilhelm, the irascible and miserly "Soldier King" of

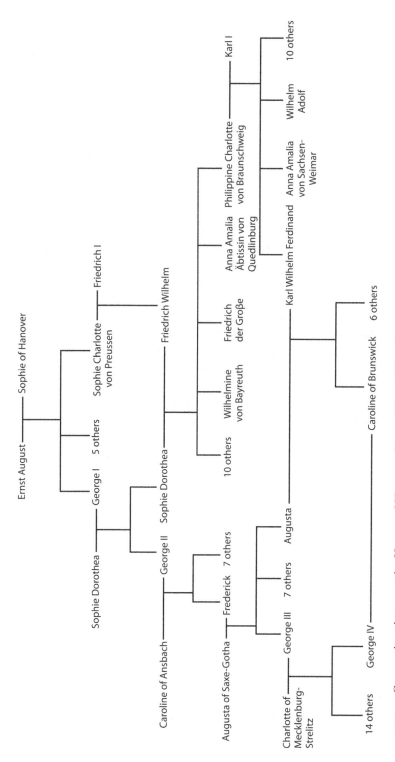

FIG. 2. Connections between the Houses of Hanover, Brunswick, and Prussia

Prussia. She instilled in her children a love of music and the arts. She worked indefatigably to arrange twin marriages between her daughter Wilhelmine and the Prince of Wales and her son Frederick and Princess Amalia, but her plans were thwarted by her husband, who greatly disliked his cousin George and wanted to create stronger German and imperial connections while frustrating British continental ambitions.

(5) *Wilhelmine von Bayreuth* was the favorite sister of Frederick the Great, with whom she corresponded for over thirty years. She built a famous rococo opera house, where the latest compositions, including many of her own, were performed; she was close to Voltaire; she helped to found the University of Erlangen; she introduced innovations in the gardens of the court at Bayreuth; and she amassed a book collection of five thousand volumes.

(6) *Philippine Charlotte* was a younger sister of Frederick the Great, and also kept up a lifelong correspondence with him. She was lively and apparently appealed to everyone, even her moody father. She married Karl I, the Duke of Braunschweig-Wolfenbüttel, and in what appears to have been an unusually peaceful partnership they created a court atmosphere in the tradition of Sophie Charlotte and Sophie Dorothea. I will expand on her role below.

(7) *Anna Amalia of Sachsen-Weimar-Eisenach* was a daughter of Philippine Charlotte and is perhaps the best known of these learned noblewomen. The patron of Goethe and Friedrich von Schiller and "muse of Weimar," she transformed that small town into a cultural center where the brightest talents of the era congregated. It has been said that her parents' court epitomized the baroque, while Anna Amalia brought court culture into the classical era. Though her contributions are better known than those of her predecessors, she was clearly drawing on a family history of promoting arts and letters, a family history that moved mostly through the women. Only recently has her education in Wolfenbüttel and Braunschweig received closer attention; thanks to Joachim Berger we now have a thoroughgoing biography of this significant figure in German political-cultural history.[30]

3. Book Collecting and Borrowing in Braunschweig

In addition to promoting salon discourses, the Prussian-Braunschweig women participated in the book market. They created substantial collections and some of these were then donated to public libraries; the

Herzog August Bibliothek, central to this story, possesses manuscript cat-alogs of the aristocratic book collections that were willed to this remark-able library. Not only do these catalogs offer fascinating evidence of con-tinental European reading habits but they also reveal how the collections were gendered (the duchesses kept libraries separate from the dukes), and what the nature of influence from one generation to another might have been (we have catalogs from parents as well as sons and daughters). Jacqueline Pearson, in her book on *Women's Reading in Britain, 1750–1835*, has lamented the dearth of evidence concerning *English* women's libraries: "Following the fortunes of women's libraries is . . . problem-atic since few women had independent libraries . . . though they might have access to those of fathers, husbands, or sons."[31] In contrast, there is ample German evidence of independent women's collections, as for example that of Duchess Philippine Charlotte. She is not well known—incredibly, we have no full biography—but her social centrality makes her a good representative.

Philippine Charlotte was a formidable woman, proud of her birth and rank, which she enjoyed displaying (figure 3). Visitors commented on her diamonds and lavish table, to which she frequently invited her preferred guests, professors from the Collegium Carolinum and the Uni-versity of Helmstedt. Because she left her library to the Herzog August Bibliothek, we know that she had about four thousand volumes, a very impressive number for a private library in this period—about the same size as the other most notable libraries of female aristocrats of the time, including those of her sister Wilhelmine of Bayreuth, her daughter Anna Amalia, Luise-Dorothea of Sachsen-Gotha, and Caroline of Hessen-Darmstadt.[32] She had a catalog compiled of this impressive collection and even spent an afternoon reading the catalog to a visitor. Despite Philippine Charlotte's penchant for show, she clearly intended the cata-log and the library for personal edification. In the sermon preached at her funeral J. W. G. Wolff, the cathedral clergyman, said that Philippine Charlotte saw the collection more as a useful means to enlightenment and inner development than for outward display. Indeed a letter to her librarian confirms this; she wrote that he should remove 140 volumes and exchange them for thirty-three others, since the 140 she had identi-fied "aren't helpful and are more for show than use."[33]

Philippine Charlotte demonstrated a remarkable cosmopolitanism in her collecting habits and in this she appears representative of the other aristocratic women I have mentioned. Hers were the choices of a liberal, enlightened, and well-informed intellectual, even if there are

FIG. 3. Johann Heinrich Tischbein the Elder, *Philippine Charlotte and Karl I of Brunswick-Wolfenbüttel and their Family*. Courtesy of Museumslandschaft Hessen Kassel, Gemäldegalerie Alte Meister, photograph by Ute Brunzel.

no works in Latin and Greek. In fact most works are in French, the language in which she always wrote and often spoke. Subject headings in the systematic catalogue include Theology and Church History, Morals, Politics, History, Natural History, Law, Medicine, Math, the Arts, Games, Logic, Literature, Comedies, and Novels. The library is dominated by male authors, including, among the English, Joseph Addison and Richard Steele, Gilbert Burnet, Daniel Defoe, David Hume, Samuel Johnson, John Law, John Locke, John Milton, Alexander Pope, the Earl of Shaftesbury, William Shakespeare, Laurence Sterne, and Jonathan Swift. There does not appear to be much self-censorship; the authors often reflect controversial and reformist points of view. Among the French and Italian authors are Jean Barbeyrac, Cesare Beccaria, Niccolò Machiavelli, François Rabelais, Jean-Jacques Rousseau, Bernardin de Saint Pierre, Voltaire, and the Comte de Volney. She collected politically provocative works, edifying moral tracts and philosophical treatises, as well as gossipy secret histories and novels about love.

Despite the preponderance of male authors, Philippine Charlotte was particularly interested in works by and about women, something typical of engaged aristocratic women in this period.[34] Philippine Charlotte collected women's translations, letter collections, biographies, autobiographies, poetry, novels, scientific works, courtesy books, and secret histories.[35] Wide-ranging, cosmopolitan, women-oriented collecting habits are true also of Philippine Charlotte's sisters Wilhelmine and Anna Amalia. (This Anna Amalia is not to be confused with her daughter; her sister was the abbess of Quedlinburg and an accomplished musician.) Marc Serge Rivière and Annett Volmer have helpfully compared Anna Amalia's library with that of her brother, Frederick the Great, and concluded: "Amalia was far better read and more cosmopolitan than her celebrated brother; she grew into a more universal and a more rounded individual who, admittedly, had much more time to use her library than the warring king . . . He read mostly in French translation; she was very proficient in French, English and German, though not in Latin and Greek," and she "was true to her sex" in collecting works by women writers and about female figures.[36] Philippine Charlotte's library, nearly twice the size of Amalia's, reveals the same differences from Frederick's and the same preoccupations. If Frederick encouraged the reading of his sisters, they were inspired to move beyond his particular predilections.

In addition to feeling solidarity with women of different nationalities, Philippine Charlotte maintained a cosmopolitan outlook that was prompted by her ambitions for her family. There were marriages to be arranged, and Philippine Charlotte had her sights on England. That she and her brother had strongly differing views on this is evident in her half of an exchange of letters.[37] She wrote to Frederick how she enjoyed a visit from the English king George II, who was polite and gracious and reminded her of their mother (George II's sister): the same face, eyes, manner, and way of speaking. She was forced abruptly to change her tune, however, in a response to what must have been an angry letter from Frederick. She wrote: "You are quite right that there's no comparison to be made between him and our worthy mother"; he is ignorant, vain, conceited, and believes no one to be more powerful than he is. "I expect nothing from his breed."[38] But she then went on to ask why Frederick was angry with her husband, so that one gets the distinct impression that her backtracking on George II was intended to appease her impetuous sibling.

This conclusion is supported by her undiminished pursuit of family links with England: she worked to arrange a marriage between a daughter and George's grandson, the future George III. Having borrowed a

copy of a *History of England* from the Herzog August Bibliothek to pre-
pare for her trip to Hanover, she traveled with her daughters Caroline
and Anna Amalia to meet George II, who offered "every distinction
imaginable." He was most impressed with Caroline and gave Philippine
Charlotte hope that "l'affaire en question sera bientôt decidée." That
match was not to be, but Philippine Charlotte eventually married her
son to George III's sister and her granddaughter Caroline to George
IV. Philippine Charlotte respected her brother, but felt no compunction
about resisting his will when it served her own family.[39]

The same independent spirit manifested itself in her ideas about
reading. Frederick made suggestions, but Philippine Charlotte came to
her own conclusions. When Frederick sent her a volume of Cicero, for
example, she challenged the ancient author's notions about the virtue
of denying pain and defended what she felt constituted a natural human
response: "On voit bien que Cicéron n'est jamais accouché." In her next
letter she expressed delight that Frederick agreed with her, and went
on to mention that she was reading Epictetus, Bernard Le Bovier de
Fontenelle, "la mort de Socrate," and Johann Gustav Reinbeck on the
immortality of the soul.[40]

Most of all, however, Philippine Charlotte's international interest
was fostered by the Collegium Carolinum professors. To be mentioned
in this regard are especially Johann Friederich Jerusalem (1709–89),
Johann Arnold Ebert (1723–95), and Johann Joachim Eschenburg
(1743–1820). The latter two were prominent German translators from
the English. Ebert is best known for his translation of Young's "Night
Thoughts"; he also taught the crown prince. Eschenburg is best known
for translating Shakespeare as well as aesthetic works, for instance of
John Brown, Daniel Webb, Richard Hurd, and Charles Burney.[41] He was
trained in Göttingen, where he studied with Michaelis. Most notable of
all was Jerusalem, whom Karl and Philippine Charlotte hired in 1742 to
be tutor to their sons and preacher to the court. Jerusalem had traveled
in Holland as well as in England, where he resided for three years. There
he made the acquaintance of important intellectuals and clergy (Arch-
bishop Potter, Bishop Sherlock, Daniel Waterland, William Whiston,
James Foster) and was swayed by latitudinarianism. He almost decided
to stay in England but returned to Germany. He was the most prominent
intellectual in the court; he must have been one of Philippine Charlotte's
favorite dinner guests and exercised some influence on the choices of
books for her collection. He became head of the Collegium Carolinum,
a new-style institution that emphasized modern languages, the sciences,

engineering, and practical subjects rather than a classical curriculum. It fostered religious tolerance, emphasized the development of judgment and taste, and sought to minimize class distinctions. According to Jerusalem the performance of students alone, not their rank, would determine how they were judged.[42] The sons of the duke and duchess attended alongside members of the bourgeoisie. Like the University of Göttingen it was influenced by English ideas and it too attracted British students.[43]

Certainly the book collection of Philippine Charlotte's son, Wilhelm Adolf, reflects his education at Jerusalem's hands: when he died in battle at age twenty-five in 1770 his collection came to the Herzog August Bibliothek, where it remains to this day. The manuscript catalog compiled at that time lists dozens of English authors, most of whose books are in the original: represented are works by Addison, Francis Bacon, Henry St John Bolingbroke, Burnet, Defoe, John Dryden, Henry Fielding, Sarah Fielding, Adam Fitzadam, Thomas Hobbes, Hume, Locke, Delarivier Manley, Sherlock, Steele, John Tillotson, William Warburton, Isaac Watts, Francis Wollaston, Edward Young. He also owned a two-volume edition of *English Miscellanies* edited by John Tompson, which must have served him as a language-acquisition text. Tompson was the first English professor at the University of Göttingen, and his anthology, first published in the 1730s, went through four editions published by Vandenhoeck. The full title reads: *English Miscellanies consisting of various pieces of divinity, morals, politicks, philosophy and history; as likewise some choice poems; all collected out of the most approved authors in the English Tongue Viz. Tillotson Nichols Lock Milton Cowley Waller Denham Dryden Buckingham Prior Addison Pope etc. And chiefly intended for the Advantage of such, as are willing to apply themselves to the Learning of this usefull Language.* Wilhelm Adolf acquired the third edition, published in Göttingen "for the widow of Abram Vandenhoeck, 1755."[44] We therefore see the direct connection between Göttingen and the provincial courts, between Anna Vandenhoeck and Philippine Charlotte, between the anglicized milieu of the Hanoverian university town and the Braunschweig duchy that was on so many levels—geographically, politically, ideologically, maritally—located directly between England and Prussia.

Unlike her brother Frederick, Philippine Charlotte collected not only English books but also German ones, and in a number of ways the welcome given to British texts occurred simultaneously for German ones—both were reactions against French hegemony. Though the emphasis on German language authors in this period is generally associated with bourgeois writers and thinkers, there were crucial aristocratic supporters of the new intellectual developments. For her part, Philippine Charlotte is credited alongside her husband with hiring Gotthold Ephraim Lessing to be librarian at the Herzog August Bibliothek, and her book collection contained many of his works in German. He was a leader among bourgeois eighteenth-century German writers who first produced his celebrated tragedy, *Emilia Galotti*, in Wolfenbüttel to honor Philippine Charlotte on her birthday. If that play critiques aristocratic ways, Philippine Charlotte herself was ready to take up progressive points of view. She, together with her sister Amalia over dinner on a visit to their brother, argued the value of German literature and thereby provoked Frederick's famous and disparaging essay, "De la littérature allemande, des défauts qu'on peut lui reprocher, quelles en sont les causes, et par quelles moyens on peut les corriger" (1780).[45]

Philippine Charlotte also inspired, in rebuttal, Jerusalem's letter-essay, "Ueber die Teutsche Sprache und Litteratur. An Ihro Koenigliche Hoheit die verwittwete Frau Herzogin von Braunschweig und Lueneburg" (1781).[46] Addressing his arguments to his patron Philippine Charlotte, Jerusalem defended German authors from Frederick's criticisms. He insisted that recent indigenous writers had come far and achieved a national literature worthy of international recognition. He wrote that far from being provincial, the productions of Friedrich Gottlieb Klopstock, Solomon Gessner, Christoph Martin Wieland, Christian Fürchtegott Gellert, and Lessing "are classic for all of Germany."[47] Jerusalem's focus on national literature had as its goal not only the development of a German identity but also participation in international exchange. He argued, for example, that because it is only the difficulty of the German language and the illegible script that keeps other nations from benefiting from German productions, German orthography should be changed. Jerusalem's argument challenged French domination and made space for indigenous German writing as well as English contributions. The essay was considered important enough to be summarized and evaluated in the British critical journal, the *Monthly Review*, in the same year, 1781;[48] clearly Britain's intellectual elite was intensely interested in the literary developments of the Germans, who, alongside increases in commercial, diplomatic, and intellectual exchanges between the countries, had done so much to support British interests in the Seven Years' War.

Indeed, in the last four decades of the eighteenth century British magazines published a good deal of German material that appealed to an ever-expanding audience. First, for example, the poetry and oratory of Frederick the Great offered British readers a picture of the intellectual and artistic warring king; religious texts by the Count von Zinzendorf, resident in England in the early 1750s, allowed an understanding of the Herrenhuters and Moravian practices; and medical work of Albrecht von Haller gave insight into state-of-the-art experiments undertaken at the University of Göttingen. The purview then broadened in the 1760s and 1770s to more general works catering to a bourgeois and feminine audience, for example the periodicals offered translations of Gessner and Gellert, travel literature, poetry of Anna Karsch, Sophie von LaRoche's novel *Sophia Sternheim*, Goethe's sensational *Sorrows of Young Werther*, and eventually the popular plays of August von Kotzebue. Journals then backtracked as well to translate earlier works, for example of Lessing, Klopstock, and Wieland.[49]

Increasing two-way transfer, buttressed by arguments of accommodation such as those of Jerusalem's, encouraged rather than discouraged cosmopolitanism. This therefore calls into question overly simplified interpretations reinforced by such recent theorists as Benedict Anderson: that is, that a tradition of humanist, universalist cosmopolitanism deriving from an early modern tradition and depending on Latin communication was overtaken in the eighteenth century by nationalist tendencies promoting indigenous writers and a national literature. When one considers the evidence of the literary-cultural activities of a provincial German court, its energetic duchess, and the thinkers she sought out to surround her, we see that the arguments in favor of German literature went hand in hand with enlightened internationalist ideas. At the same time, the enthusiasm of the British magazines and their lay English readership for translations from the German attests to a corresponding interest in European productions beyond the French.[50]

This more complex view is corroborated by larger economic trends. Bernhard Fabian has pointed out that, in the early decades of the eighteenth century, journals in Germany, like those in England, moved from addressing an elite educated audience to reviewing, in German, literature for a regional readership. This did not mean a retreat to parochialism, since editors consistently "drew attention to significant foreign publications," thereby "opening new perspectives on the intellectual life abroad." That is, long-standing humanist paradigms were giving way to an era of general cosmopolitanism. Already before the French Revolution, cultural movement was away from the intellectual elite to the mainstream, and away from being female-exclusive to female-inclusive. In the reviews, Fabian notes, foreign works were evaluated "not in the older tradition as contributions to an international body of scholarly literature, but in a more modern fashion as the products of a foreign literature."⁵¹ Despite being written in foreign languages and therefore seemingly nation-bound, works of literature were actually becoming more available, crossing borders, more likely to be translated, and reaching more diverse readers rather than being limited to a small scholarly circle. The content of British magazines reflects this moment as does Philippine Charlotte's library and Vandenhoeck's translation of *Clarissa*.

Moreover, such increased availability of foreign works is resoundingly reinforced by the astonishing catalog of books available in Vandenhoeck's shop in 1785, a fascinating and rare document from which, for the sake of space, I will mention only titles by British women authors available in German translation (along with the year of that edition): Aphra Behn, *Oroonoko* (1770); Frances Brooke, *History of Emily Montague* (1769); Hester Chapone, *Letters* (1774); Sarah Fielding, *Countess of Dellwyn* (1761); Sarah Fielding, *David Simple* (1746); Sarah Fielding, *Familiar Letters* (1759); Sarah Fielding [?], *Life of Octavia* (1761); Sarah Fielding, *Ophelia* (1763); Mary Hamilton, *Duchess de Crui* (1776–77); Eliza Haywood [?], *History of Miss Jenny* (1770); Charlotte Lennox, *Henriette* (1761); Delarivier Manley, *New Atalantis* (1740); Mary Wortley Montagu, *Letters* (1763); Sarah Scott, *History of Cornelia* (1762); Sarah Scott, *Millenium Hall* (1768); Frances Sheridan, *Miss Sidney Bidulph* (1770); Elizabeth Singer Rowe, *Friendship in Death* (1777); and Elizabeth Singer Rowe, *Poetical Works* (1772).⁵² Since this list represents only the books on her shelves in the early 1780s, one can imagine the wealth of volumes that moved through her shop over the course of three decades.

The democratization implied by this development concerned class as well as gender. The Herzog August Bibliothek in Wolfenbüttel—remarkably, a public library from the 1660s—offers a special opportunity to examine this revolutionary shift. For it possesses not only the manuscript catalogs of the aristocrats such as Philippine Charlotte and her son Wilhelm Adolf but also the *Ausleihbücher* (withdrawal books) that show what the lower classes read. Mechthild Raabe has published and analyzed the astonishing withdrawal books of the library, which show that readers of all classes and both sexes checked out volumes: carpenters, servants, soldiers, students, clergy. Their participation reached a peak in the period 1760–80; they brought about an enormous increase in the withdrawal of belles-lettres. Many foreigners visited the library and consulted volumes; Philippine Charlotte herself checked out books she could not consult in her own collection, for example the Koran and a book concerning Indian philosophy. After the French Revolution many

French émigrés settled in Wolfenbüttel and Braunschweig, and judging from the number of their withdrawals, they were clearly delighted to have a library so well stocked for their use.[53]

A study of the eighteenth-century European book trade, its relation to the political ties between England and Germany, and the interesting picture of bookselling and book-buying that we can glean from transnational case studies transpiring in Lower Saxony offer us occasion for revising our views of eighteenth-century international understanding. Pauline Kleingeld has documented how cosmopolitanism in the eighteenth century was advocated by German thinkers on various levels—moral, political, intellectual, cultural, economic, and spiritual—and she traces how it gave way to growing nationalism after the French Revolution and the Napoleonic wars.[54] Yet the women's version evident in the court of Philippine Charlotte and the shop of Anna Vandenhoeck, situated within the broader cultural movements I have traced, suggests that their orientation and type of cosmopolitanism was of a more pragmatic, embedded nature.

Studies of the rise of nationalism in the eighteenth century have tended to concentrate on individual nations and their imperial strivings, privileging analysis of colonial competition between European lands while downplaying intra-European ties. Consequently the place of gender in the international political European context has hardly been broached. I have therefore chosen to emphasize case studies from the same geographic region, Lower Saxony, that involve women of different national origins and classes in an attempt to show how politically marginal figures such as Anna Vandenhoeck and Philippine Charlotte nonetheless contributed to the larger picture. The expansion of the book trade, as Benedict Anderson has pointed out, was crucial for national self-definition in this period, but I am suggesting that it simultaneously enabled internationalism on the ground. These women's cosmopolitan inclinations shared certain sources, being closely related to their social positions and family fortunes within a context of growing British-German transfer. Vandenhoeck in Göttingen supported the translation of significant British publications, encouraged British journals through a reading circle, and offered great numbers of British volumes, in the original and in translation, for sale at her shop. She willed substantial money—and she was one of the richest citizens of Göttingen—to two telling groups: the Reformed Church, a congregation at this time involved with Huguenot immigrants and perhaps even conducting services in French, and the fund for professors' widows.[55] Philippine Charlotte likewise remembered the widows of the Helmstedt professors in her will. She also left an income to the émigré French princess of Montmorency to be sure this aristocratic, exiled Frenchwoman would not be left without resources in another land. These monied women sought to the end to mitigate the adverse effects of a restrictive sociopolitics of gender and nation; their wills demonstrate acute sensitivity to the plight of vulnerable ladies in donations that saw beyond national boundaries.[56]

The evidence we have from female participants in the eighteenth-century book market thus reinforces a sense of the depth of gender identification and the importance of family connections. Women's lack of political identity and clout contributed to their interest in promoting a quotidian rather than transcendent cosmopolitanism that can be contrasted with the type derived from theories of liberty and fraternity that inspired revolutionary activity. Cosmopolitanism has been seen to derive from a sense of detachment, where universal notions of human behavior and the well-lived life outweigh a person's loyalty to hearth and home. But I argue that a look at women's activities and intellectual preoccupations demonstrates that gender position can trump rigid national and social identities, that there is a type of cosmopolitanism deriving from some women's experience that allows for both patriotism and international identification. Anna Vandenhoeck and Duchess Philippine Charlotte thus demonstrate what Kwame Anthony Appiah has called "patriotic cosmopolitanism" in the process of furthering their political inclinations by cultural means.[57] In their literary activities they foreshadow the impatience of Heine's *Deutschland* narrator, shirking suspicion of foreign products, defying artificial borders, and delighting in the capacity for intellectual transfer in spite of customs threatening to thwart them.

CHAPTER 2

Translation Following *Clarissa*

Georg Forster and Meta Forkel,
Mary Wollstonecraft and Joseph Johnson

Johann David Michaelis, translator of Vandenhoeck's edition of *Clarissa*, was a professor of Near Eastern languages and literatures at the University of Göttingen. He was internationally known for his biblical translation and exegesis; a member of the Academies of Sciences in Paris and London, he was also named a Knight of the North Star by Swedish king Gustavus III. He gained prestige as advisor to the royal Danish expedition to Yemen, carried out by Carsten Niebuhr and others from 1761 to 1768, an undertaking Michaelis hoped would demonstrate how studies of contemporary Near Eastern culture could shed light on practices of biblical antiquity. Much respected in Britain, he enjoyed the favor of the British king and queen and corresponded frequently with notable scholars such as Sir John Pringle, Benjamin Kennicott, Robert Lowth, Jacob Bryant, Robert Wood, and Charles Godfrey Woide. Possessed of tremendous self-assurance, he was a lively speaker said to arrive at the lecture hall in riding gear, with his sword at his side and a Bible under his arm. He came to enjoy the highest salary of any Göttingen professor, owned the biggest house in town, and entertained renowned guests such as Benjamin Franklin, Lessing, Goethe, and Alexander von Humboldt.[1]

In 1745 he was new to the Göttingen campus; he had traveled in England from the spring of 1741 to the autumn of 1742, learned the language, met important personages, and had read Samuel Richardson's groundbreaking epistolary novel *Pamela*. He was therefore apprised of the innovation and celebrity of Richardson, and when in 1747 Albrecht von Haller, the illustrious professor of medicine, Anglophile founder of the Göttingen Academy of Sciences, and editor of the prestigious *Göttingische Anzeigen von gelehrten Sachen*, suggested that he translate Richardson's new novel, Michaelis agreed to undertake the task.[2]

The translation of *Clarissa*, which was published in segments between 1748 and 1753, was pivotal and marks a significant moment in the literary and cultural relationship between Germany and Britain. The novel was an international sensation and no less significant in the German principalities than it was to Denis Diderot and the French; it spawned literary imitations, popularized sensibility, and inspired new understandings of feminine expression and female agency.[3] The story is made up of epistolary exchanges between Clarissa, her friends, family, and her deceiving suitor and pursuer Lovelace; it engendered lively debates about the wisdom of arranged marriages, the extent of female autonomy, and the social efficacy of bourgeois virtues. It contributed at midcentury to a new sense of women's subjectivity, offering a compelling model both of a writing female subject and a self-willed being. Göttingen daughters, influenced by such representations as well as by the upbringing in their unusual academic environment, felt empowered to assert a new approach to personal, literary, as well as political freedom. Michaelis's version of *Clarissa* demonstrates how translation involved far more than the movement across national boundaries of literary ideas; it implied the transfer of cultural registers and epistemologies with very real implications for transnational social understanding and gender politics in particular. I therefore invoke a broad Latourian definition of translation, one closer attuned to its Latin root meaning "carrying across" than simply probe the rendering of a text into another language, although I consider this as well. Hence we view a transformative moment in British-German cultural transfer, a dynamic and mutual interchange moving beyond simple ideas of reception or influence and challenging essential notions of national identity.[4]

I consider Michaelis's translation of *Clarissa* not only as a way of assessing eighteenth-century theories of translation, then, but also as a means by which protofeminist debate was carried over into Germany with impacts on the next generation. For the Göttingen daughters, who themselves formed a tightly knit social and intellectual community enmeshed and alongside that of their fathers, ended up furthering the process of the cultural transfer of British ideas, among other things by translating literature themselves. Like Johann David Michaelis's approach, their theory of translation suggested that a generally faithful rendition of the books translated would facilitate the absorption of British ideas of liberty in the German context. An interesting contrast emerges when we probe translation in the other direction: the theory governing Mary Wollstonecraft's translation of German educational writing is one of "naturalization" and of cultural influence viewed with circumspection.[5] Such different attitudes toward literary cultural transfer exist despite their chronological simultaneity and the surprisingly similar situations of the translators: Caroline Michaelis, Therese Heyne, and Meta Wedekind lived conflict-ridden personal lives, grappled with poverty, and addressed issues of gender and politics in ways remarkably similar to Mary Wollstonecraft, Catharine Macaulay, and Charlotte Smith in Britain. At the same time, the French Revolution and the Napoleonic wars, as well as the discourses surrounding them, altered the avenues and aims of cultural transfer within the Personal Union. Following a discussion of Michaelis's *Clarissa*, the issues raised for translation theory and the intellectual and cultural context, I will consider three case studies: first I will compare translations of Meta Wedekind Forkel and Mary Wollstonecraft. These translations measure the changing cultural relationships between Germany and Britain at the end of the eighteenth century and suggest how a look at the Personal Union highlights women's role in furthering reformist discourses—discourses substantially inflected by the ongoing transnational exchange of ideas of gender and nation within the context of the French Revolution. This point will then be expanded upon with a conclusion discussing British publisher Joseph Johnson's larger project of German translations, focusing on his edition of GutsMuths's *Gymnastics for Youth* of 1800: the history of this book returns us to the question of western European networks and the need for viewing translation through the *terrains vastes*, as Johnson, like Georg Forster in the case of Meta Forkel's work, used translations both to influence national politics and deepen transnational links, now under the pressure of Napoleon's increasing sway.

1. Johann David Michaelis: Translation and Gender in Göttingen

Johann David Michaelis, translator of the Bible and an expositor of ancient literary texts, was also interested in questions of women's education and was influenced by British gender ideas on his travels to England. Soon after arriving at Göttingen in 1745 he published a letter to Frederick the Great proposing a university for women: "Allerunterthänigste Bittschrift an Seine Königliche Majestät in Preussen, um Anlegung einer Universität für das schöne Geschlecht" (A Most Humble Appeal to His Royal Highness in Prussia concerning the Establishment of a University for the Fair Sex). It takes up the cause of Mary Astell and Daniel Defoe on the need for women's academies. As did Astell and Defoe, he declines imagining equality between the sexes; he shares Defoe's view that women's intellectual and moral powers were clearly to be employed in support of men. Women, he wrote, take the role of "Lehrerinnen / Von munterm Geist, von aufgeklärten Sinnen / Die . . . uns von ihrem Fleiss den süssen Honig gönnen" (teachers / of a lively spirit, of enlightened minds / who . . . do not begrudge us the sweet honey of their hard work).[6] In appended verses addressed to poets in this text, he imagines a new Athens guarded by women empowered through knowledge and virtue: "Athen nimmt statt der Legionen, / Ein Heer von tapfern Amazonen / Zum Schutz in seine Mauren ein, / Dass niemand unsern Fleiss verstöre, / Und beydes unsre Ruh und Ehre / In unsern Zimmern sicher seyn" (Instead of legions Athens takes / An army of courageous Amazons / Into its walls for defense / So that no one can disrupt our industry / And both our peace and honor / Are secure in our offices). The development of taste in a nation depends upon women, as Michaelis suggests elsewhere: "Je freyer unter einem Volke das Frauenzimmer erzogen wird, und je mehr es in Gesellschaften koemmt, desto zaertlicher wird hierinn auch unter Europäern der Geschmack" (The more women are raised at liberty among a people, and the more they come into society, the more taste will become refined even among Europeans).[7] Such ideas about the social efficacy of the feminine would have been familiar to British readers of the *Spectator* and other popular periodical literature; Michaelis is clearly inspired by such ideas in his own formulations.

Michaelis thus appreciated the shifting gender roles he perceived in British culture and furthered the idea of an enhanced social role for German women; his protofeminism is not only visible in his views on women's education but also is apparent in his translation of *Clarissa* (first published in England in three sections between December 1747 and December 1748; translation published 1748–53), where he foregrounds the abilities of writing women. He does feel compelled to justify the translation of a sentimental novel: in the preface to *Clarissa* he first explains the bookseller's compelling reason for publishing this book (because Haller, the most famous critic in Germany, had suggested it) and why he himself was chosen to undertake the work (because he had lived in England sufficiently to have superb command of the language and an ability to render the story in a manner appealing to Germans). Going beyond Vandenhoeck's reasons for publishing a work of belles lettres—such a popular book was by no means a typical title for the university bookseller Vandenhoeck, though the firm did occasionally publish fiction—Michaelis says that he feels translating this text will be a real benefit to the world. He hopes a reasonable reader will not think him vain: he aims for no glory, since he plans to establish his reputation with other works, and he is so overburdened with his own writings and university lectures that he would never give up the chance to spend time with good friends if this project were not of such significance.[8]

Michaelis balances his urge for justification and his extravagant stance of humility with a forceful gender argument: "Some have felt that Clarissa writes better than a woman could," he says, but in fact, he argues, there are women of understanding and learning who can write better than men, such as Madame de Sevigné. He goes on to prove this point expressly by refusing to translate one passage, the famous "Ode to Wisdom." This Ode was inserted by Richardson into the text of *Clarissa* as verses "by a Lady," and the unacknowledged female contributor, whose identity was only revealed later, turned out to be none other than the learned Elizabeth Carter.[9] To show how well a woman can write, Michaelis says, he "did not venture . . . to translate the Ode, because according to the British author it is written by a Lady, and it redounds to the honor of the Sex" (vii–viii). Richardson commissioned music for a number of the verses and had the song engraved on a separate fold-out sheet that was then pasted into the volume. This drew attention to Carter's "Ode to Wisdom" and displayed it in type large enough to be deciphered and performed by readers at their instruments. Consumers of the novel could thereby deepen their identification with the protagonist on another level as they sang and played themselves into what the story suggested was the moral, lyrical, and musical imagination of the talented Clarissa. Michaelis the protofeminist let Carter's words stand on their own in order to show German readers what an Englishwoman had accomplished and what respect her verse commanded from a famous, best-selling British author.[10]

Translation theory today questions openness to foreign literary influences; issues of gender and nation are seen to complicate rather than enable transfer, so that an approach like Michaelis's is anachronistically interpreted as naive and weak on the one hand or minimizing difference on the other. Sherry Simon discusses the "historical continuity of gendered theorizing of translation," with the original seen as masculine and active and the translation as passive and feminine.[11] Drawing on Jacques Derrida she argues that the rigid binary must be deconstructed; "the hierarchy of writing roles, like gender identities, is increasingly to be recognized as mobile and performative."[12] From such a perspective Michaelis's goal to offer Germans a new view of women's potentialities via the English text is rendered problematical, since the target culture with its prejudices is as involved in constructing the translation as in absorbing it. Lawrence Venuti has questioned the process of "domesticating" translation. If the translator is "invisible" and the work is incorporated seamlessly into the target culture, the translator has obscured his imperial goals of cultural appropriation. In this view the very success of Michaelis's translation is held against him while the value he ascribes to the English work and author is called into question.

Venuti draws on the theory of Friedrich Schleiermacher to argue that translators should instead "foreignize" texts, estranging the original to make the cultural difference of the text readily apparent.[13] One could argue that Michaelis, in leaving the "Ode to Wisdom" untranslated, has in effect done just this. Yet one might also suggest that there is a danger involved in highlighting the foreign and what is different. Nationalist theorists during the Napoleonic wars insisted that the foreignness of a work be flagged so that Germans might not absorb alien influences unawares. "Foreignizing" can therefore further nationalistic ends as much as it can promote anti-imperialistic ones. Stuart Gillespie and Robin Sowerby have argued against Venuti's conclusion in the Enlightenment British context by suggesting that a survey of translations in that period shows they generally worked to expand the canon and encourage literary innovation; "the translator's objective was . . . the reproduction of the original's qualities by any means possible."[14] In the German context, a look at translations and translation theory suggests that, while thinkers in the early nineteenth century may have raised issues spurred by baldly nationalist views, earlier mid-eighteenth-century German innovators like Michaelis espoused a less vehement, more confident viewpoint. The worthy literary products of another culture, recognized as different but rendered understandable to Germans, could, they felt, be incorporated harmoniously, enhancing German literary and cultural life.

Michaelis's translation should therefore be viewed within its historical context; it should be evaluated internally and externally as an agent of reciprocal cultural transfer rather than as a narrowly national political document. As Márta Minier has concluded, many voices, not just one or two, "make themselves heard in the translation process," not only on the part of authors and translators but of readers as well. As a result, "cultural differences inevitably shape the result of the translation process,"[15] both in production and reception. Consequently to situate Michaelis in the mid-eighteenth century both in terms of the debates about theory and the historical context, I would suggest that his *Clarissa* offered a pre-Napoleonic demonstration of the possibility of not "either-or" but "both-and" translation in a liberal Göttingen environment not yet jolted by revolutionary upheaval and militarization.

This middle-of-the-road approach, seen from the production side, recalls John Dryden's notion of "paraphrase" (as opposed to the word-for-word "metaphrase" on the one hand and the much freer "imitation" on the other). Such a sense of translation sought to offer the target audience access to the best fruits of a foreign culture, thereby implying a wish for the absorption of these ideas, and at the same time demonstrated a recognition of that culture's difference. Michaelis's translation of *Clarissa* was in the first place a faithful one, aiming to stay as close as possible to the original text while making it understandable to his German target audience.[16] At the same time, by leaving the Ode untranslated, Michaelis allowed the English writer, and the English woman's voice, to come through unaffected. The Ode could offer uncompromised access to the original culture's estimation of women's creative powers and thereby teach German readers about female potential, which was then further reinforced in the unfolding plot about Clarissa's trials rendered into German. Such a move suggests that Michaelis was fully aware of the alteration forced by any translation, and at the same time it shows that he did not embrace "invisibility," "weakness," or, on the other hand, a coercive, domesticating, cultural-imperial agenda. Translation in general, whether literal or free, faithful or spirited, domesticating or foreignizing, can instruct about or exploit another culture or both, and to determine the actual political valence of the translation we have to look more closely at the particular work and its consequences; the type of translation itself cannot convey this information. Michaelis's approach to and the subsequent history of the *Clarissa* translation show that his work set in motion significant cultural shifts in a Germany poised for the kinds of transformations that the ideas of the text—especially about women's roles—were ready to offer.

In terms of reception, the Göttingen context supplied not only the advantages of a modern university but also an Enlightenment ethos of lay education and therefore of an engaged public. Haller's interest in the *Clarissa* translation was part of his larger support for Anglo-German exchange, but this was only one facet of his concern to create a vibrant university and university community. Along with founding the Academy of Sciences and editing the *Göttingische Anzeigen*, he initiated the botanical garden, the anatomical institute, and the first continental women's clinic. He engaged himself in constructing a building for the Reformed Church, of which congregation he was a member alongside Anna Vandenhoeck. Later in life he wrote three novels with the intention of depicting the advantages of different types of political organization: *Usong* (1771), *Alfred* (1773), and *Fabius und Cato* (1774). His poetry, particularly his most famous composition, *The Alps*, was translated into several languages. The tradition of Göttingen scholars' engagement in public education and popular culture—that is, intended for women and laypeople as well as academics—continued into the late eighteenth century, and not only via reviews in the *Göttingische Anzeigen*. Michaelis intended his biblical translations and annotations to benefit the laity ("*Ungelehrte*"). Georg Christoph Lichtenberg, the physicist and astronomer, wrote for periodicals and, tellingly, compiled a pocket calendar every year from the late 1770s to the early 1790s. Such calendars were fashionable, portable items to delight and instruct a broad public. The 1781 edition, for example, included not only lists of moveable feasts, phases of the moon, eclipses, zodiac signs, and the birthdays of the nobility but also historical anecdotes, anthropological observations, short essays about the placement of the universe, commentary on lifestyles, and amusing pictures of women's coiffures in Berlin, England, and Leipzig (as a way of both comparing and satirizing them).[17] Illustrations by the famous printmaker Daniel Chodowiecki offered comical depictions of men of different ranks and occupations proposing marriage. As I mentioned in chapter 1, Lichtenberg also edited a literary magazine with Georg Forster, published a book on Hogarth engravings, and acted as tutor to the British princes during their Göttingen residences. The interests of Göttingen professors were wide ranging, and university leaders such as Münchhausen and Haller encouraged the full pursuit not only of a variety of academic disciplines but also lay education and public involvement. That these activities were remunerative doubtless must have increased their attraction to professors who needed to multiply their sources of income: typically, for example, they had to charge students to attend their lectures and to board students at their houses. Connections between academic and public culture were therefore close and lively.

Regarding the context of Göttingen in the mid-eighteenth century, one sees that Johann David Michaelis participated in forcefully promoting a liberal agenda, in all its cosmopolitan and conformist complexity. With him, international, national, and personal impulses coincided, and a distinctive attitude toward gender and class took shape. Michaelis's translation of the English work *Clarissa*, though more literal than free, implied a vigorously pursued politics with protofeminist and bourgeois implications. His reluctance to translate the "Ode" in *Clarissa* did not emerge from anxiety, but as a genuine, if paternalistic, tribute to the accomplishment of a talented woman, with the intention of reorienting readers' ideas about women's potential. Therefore the evidence we have of Michaelis's own views of language, British culture, and women's education reinforce his centrist view of translation. His desire to foreground Elizabeth Carter's "Ode" by leaving it untranslated reflects a genuine appreciation for the strengths of Clarissa as a character, Carter as a female poet, women as readers and textual interpreters, and the German public overall as capable of valuing English poetry and song in the original.

2. *Göttingen Daughters and the Drive to Translation*

Michaelis's upbringing of his daughter Caroline corroborates this. Caroline Michaelis (1763–1809) lived in the magnificent house in which Michaelis taught classes and entertained luminaries. It was filled with student-boarders, some of whom became Caroline's tutors. She was therefore well educated for a girl of her time, regularly exposed to new ideas and accustomed to academic discussions. Michaelis's encouragement of his daughter was not unusual; Caroline was only one of a group of highly accomplished daughters of Göttingen professors who offered one another companionship as well as competition. The progressive nature of the university was thus extended into the professors' own homes without necessarily undermining the professors' substantial self-regard or assumptions about male superiority.

The best known of the Göttinger protégées, Dorothea Schlözer (1770–1825), was a daughter of the historian and political scientist August Ludwig Schlözer, who actually conducted an educational experiment on his bright firstborn child as a way of challenging the theories of German educationalist Johann Bernhard Basedow, founder of the famous "Philanthropic" school at Dessau. Contra Basedow, who followed Jean-Jacques Rousseau's ideas of sex-differentiated "natural" education,

Schlözer felt there should be an empirical basis for pedagogical theory, and he threw himself into his project. At the age of fifteen months Dorothea commanded "87 words and 192 ideas, if I have counted correctly," wrote Schlözer.[18] At eighteen months she was able to express herself clearly and was learning the ABCs via Schlözer's new method. Schlözer took pride in strolling around Göttingen with two-year-old Dorothea and astonishing passersby as they heard a toddler conversing as though she were six. At thirty-two months she learned the Low German dialect; she began to study German reading and writing at four years and two months. From there she studied English, Swedish, and Dutch. French and Italian were squeezed in; Latin instruction began when she was eleven years old; Greek commenced at fifteen (Kern, 52–53). At five and a quarter years she was taken to Schlözer's colleague Kästner for private instruction in mathematics (a field to which Schlözer felt himself unequal). In keeping with Schlözer's notions about practical education—as evidenced in the progression of modern, conversational languages—he took Dorothea on a number of trips, including an extended trip to Italy (fall 1781 to spring 1782), where she was expected, as an eleven year old, to perfect her command of Italian. He desired moreover to further her understanding of mineralogy through a six-week expedition to various German mines, a number of which she visited on her own in 1786 (Kern, 64–65). The study of literature was ignored entirely as a waste of time, though Dorothea was expected to acquire the feminine accomplishments of knitting, sewing, home economics, drawing, music, and dancing (Kern, 54). Even here Schlözer's program opposed that of Basedow, who, leaning on Rousseau, fostered in women attentiveness to masculine authority over practical accomplishments. Dorothea's upbringing, based on a belief in rationality and empirical outcomes, thus became an elaborate experiment in human development that was viewed in Göttingen as an unqualified success and that resulted in Dorothea Schlözer receiving in 1787 the first PhD awarded to a woman by the university.

The example of Schlözer demonstrates the intensity with which pedagogy and the education of girls were approached in Göttingen. Although Johann David Michaelis did not experiment with his children in the same way, his well-educated, independent-spirited daughter Caroline nonetheless became equally famous. She may sometimes have lamented the relentless rigor of Dorothea Schlözer's education, but what Caroline's life and the lives of her friends Therese Heyne and Meta Wedekind tell us are how the progressive Göttingen approach, its embrace of British culture, and their later revolutionary ideals shaped their experience and their thought, influenced their broader life choices, and appeared in their translations and other literary endeavors.[19]

Caroline Michaelis is better known today by her married names Böhmer-Schlegel-Schelling. Her first husband, the doctor Johann Franz Wilhelm Böhmer, died in 1788, four years after they were married; two of her three children died the next year. With her much-loved daughter Auguste she returned to live with her father in Göttingen and then with her brother in Marburg. In 1792 she moved to Mainz, which in the fall came under French control. There she took part in the circle of French revolutionary supporters, in particular Georg Forster and his wife Therese, born Heyne, her childhood playmate.

Therese Heyne (1764–1829) was the daughter of Christian Gottlob Heyne, a professor of ancient civilizations and director of the famous Göttingen University library. She and Caroline had an uneven childhood friendship, sometimes lively and involved and sometimes characterized by mistrust and competition. Perhaps growing up in the fishbowl of academic Göttingen contributed to this.[20] In 1785 Therese married Georg Forster. Forster had lived in England for many years and when he was seventeen years old, as assistant to his naturalist father Johann Reinhold, set sail on James Cook's Second Voyage; the publication of his *Voyage Round the World* (1777), which appeared in German as *Reise um die Welt* (1778–80), assured his fame. After that exploration he returned to Germany to secure employment. First he taught in Kassel; then he received a professorial position in Vilnius, at the time part of Poland. Therese joined him there and life was difficult, primarily because funds that Forster had been promised were not forthcoming. After searching about for alternatives, Forster was called to become librarian at the University of Mainz.

Given Forster's British upbringing, it is not surprising that life at the Forsters' house had an English flavor. He appears to have assumed the role of country gentleman or aristocratic host—perhaps he was also inspired by South Sea hospitality—entertaining many travelers for extended visits. Such guests commented on how the Forsters daily served high tea. Wrote one visitor: "One gathered at seven o'clock, after work was done, around a tea pot, according to English custom, and remained together until nearly nine o'clock."[21] Newspapers were perused and current events discussed. "At Forster's in the evenings one read the latest edition of the 'Moniteur' with news from Paris" (Siegel, 99). And Caroline wrote to a friend that "we are participating in a most interesting political era, and that gives me, in addition to the wise things that I hear evenings around the tea table, a good deal to think about."[22] Given the radical politics espoused by this circle, it is not surprising that Forster maintained contact with the British radical circle surrounding the publisher Joseph Johnson, whose books Forster brought back after a trip to London in 1790. He set those around him in Mainz the task of translating the revolutionary texts Johnson himself had promoted in England.

Georg Forster's most prolific translator was Meta Forkel (her chosen nickname and the surname of her first husband, Johann Nikolaus Forkel; sometimes she is listed under Margarethe Liebeskind, with the surname of her second husband). Another Göttingen daughter, Meta was born in 1765, a year after Therese and two years after Caroline. Her father was a professor of philosophy and a Protestant minister whose sermons preached a practical morality reminiscent of British essays in the *Tatler* and *Spectator*, which had been translated into German soon after their British publication. He addressed not only public issues but also discussed domestic questions such as housekeeping, medical remedies, and childrearing. He decried aristocratic excesses, women's enslavement to fashion, and the taste for French luxury, and Meta absorbed her father's enlightened bourgeois views. Nonetheless she became a controversial social figure because she separated from (and eventually divorced) the Göttingen music historian Johann Nikolaus Forkel; she came to Mainz and lived with Caroline, who wrote to a friend that she could not understand the outcry against this perfectly reasonable person.

Göttingen daughters and Germans in general enjoyed greater access to divorce in this period than the English did. In England divorce required a private act of Parliament, something only very wealthy men could afford and something pursued almost exclusively in cases of infidelity. By contrast in many parts of Germany there reigned a Protestant understanding of marriage as subject to natural right and, increasingly through the period, as a contractual arrangement that could be dissolved. Madame de Staël, visiting Germany in 1803–4, remarked on the ease with which women were able to divorce and remarry: "They change husbands with as little difficulty as if they were arranging the incidents of a drama."[23] In Göttingen, a city with a population of about eight thousand, 190 divorce cases were filed between 1740 and 1840. The majority of cases was brought by working-class women whose most frequent complaint was that their husbands were abusive and wasteful or even threatened their lives as a consequence of alcoholism. Men's general complaint was that women failed in housekeeping, wasted money, or cooked badly. In Berlin, according to one calculation, there were 1,020 divorced women around the year 1800.[24] Consequently, while divorce was rare, and while it still affected a woman's reputation negatively, it was an option that could be considered and invoked in extreme cases.[25]

The Göttingen daughters were all involved in divorce. Meta and Caroline saw their cases through and then remarried, and Therese began the process though Georg Forster died before she had completed it. In a 1794 plea to the University court to remarry, Meta Forkel wrote: "Meine Heyrath an den Herrn Doctor Forkel ist bekanntlich gleichsam in meiner Kindheit geschehen, wo ich noch keine hinlängliche Einsicht, und Überzeugung von der ehelichen Verbindung und deren Verpflichtung haben konnte. . . . Dagegen bin ich nun durch bittere Erfahrung zu besserer Überzeugung gekommen, und dadurch weiser gemacht, kann ich mich fähiger hoffen, bey einer anderweitigen Verheyrathung die Pflichten einer Gattin und Mutter zu erfüllen" (My marriage to Dr. Forkel, as is well known, happened virtually in my childhood, when I could not yet have an adequate understanding and conviction about the marriage bond and its obligations. . . . However now I have come to a better conviction through bitter experience, and, having been made wiser by it, I can hope to be more capable, in a future marriage, to perform the duties of a wife and mother).[26] Meta was sixteen years old when she first married, hence her emphasis on being a naive child as she entered matrimony with Forkel. In her plea she was forced to adopt a bourgeois embrace of housewifely duties, though her biography shows that she espoused a more progressive politics: her attempts to live independently through her work as a translator, and the radical ideas in the books she agreed to translate, suggest that she was animated by hopes of profound social and gender transformation.

Such a double view may appear contradictory today, but Göttingen's progressive environment simultaneously insisted on a solid bourgeois ethic, and divorce, though available, provoked scandal. The conjunction of the two competing tendencies can be illustrated in the life and writings of the poet Philippine Gatterer Engelhard (1756–1831), the third of fifteen children born to one of Göttingen's professors of history, Johann Christoph Gatterer (1727–99). Philippine displayed her emotions and expressed her opinions freely. Seventeen-year-old Caroline Michaelis, judgmental in evaluating her female cohort, wrote of Philippine, "for a woman she is too bold, thinks and speaks too freely," and Wilhelm Grimm commented much later that "she speaks bluntly."[27] Her first two volumes of verse were brought out by the Göttingen publisher Dieterich when she was twenty-two and twenty-six years old. She married a civil servant and moved to Kassel, where she remained the rest of her life, raising ten children. Other collections of her poetry appeared in 1787, 1789, and, after a long hiatus, in 1821. At age seventy-four she translated and published verses of the French poet Pierre-Jean de Béranger.[28] She was one of the best-loved German women poets of the eighteenth century, and while her verses tended to focus on subjective reflections, from time to time she considered the position of women in general, as in the 1779 poem "Mädchenklage" (The Girl's Lament), where she decries the limitations of gender roles: "Oft hab ich mit Thränen / Und innigem Sehnen, / Verwünscht mein Geschlecht! / Es fesselt fast immer / Mich Arme ins Zimmer—/ Wie frey gehn die Männer! Selbst Knabe und Knecht" (How oft with damnation / And tears of frustration / My gender I curse! / Its ban ever dooms / Us girls to our rooms; / How freely men move! Even youngster and serf.)[29] Therefore even a daughter with more conservative inclinations nonetheless absorbed the interest in gender politics prevalent in Göttingen and found a means of self-assertion and self-expression through print.

For her part, Meta Forkel's politics can be seen most clearly in her desire to translate for Georg Forster the most controversial texts produced in what has been called his "translation factory."[30] This expression was used satirically to describe the way in which German translations were churned out prodigiously, seemingly mechanically, by entrepreneurs at a time that saw an overwhelming interest in foreign literature. The increasing market for such works opened the possibility of independence for an educated woman like Meta Forkel, so that she could pursue what the figure of Clarissa modeled—a writing woman who, in a quandary concerning marriage, proceeded to make up her own mind in accord with her conscience. Forkel's translations can therefore be interpreted on levels both personal and political; her work measures the extent to which the market for intra-European translation in this period offered Göttingen daughters the means to avoid Clarissa's fatal end.

Indeed, translation became for the Göttingen women a textual means of liberation from financial distress, obscurity, sexual restriction, and political powerlessness. It offered a way of earning their bread respectably and participating in the republic of letters. The great demand in this period for books translated into German created a lucrative market, which resulted in the establishment of a translation infrastructure where translators, unable to keep up with the demand on their own, would subcontract translations and then correct the work, supplying also introductions and notes: hence the rise of the "translation factory."

The rapid increase in translation affected intra-European cultural transfer on many levels, including socioeconomic and political exchange, and increasing studies of this phenomenon have exposed weaknesses in reigning interpretations of European national ideas. Margaret Cohen and Carolyn Dever's edited volume *The Literary Channel: The Inter-National Invention of the Novel* (2002), for example, fundamentally contests most long-standing interpretations of "the rise of the novel." National paradigms have anachronistically been imposed on literary history, contributors to the volume argue; the novel actually emerged from a transnational, intercultural milieu that was affected but not determined by capitalist development. According to Joan DeJean, "No genre has had a history more closely bound up with nomadic conditions of production than the modern novel. To forget this and write the novel's history as though each national tradition were an entity unto itself, as though each had developed without the stimulus of foreign artists, is to blind ourselves to a particularly significant type of literary interconnection."[31] She discusses the "diasporic conditions" of many innovators of the novel and questions whether the country of their birth or the language in which they wrote ought to determine to which literary history they belong. Mary Helen McMurran points out that during the long eighteenth century, translations were omnipresent and central. She shows that in Britain from 1660 to 1770, "translations of French romances and novels constituted as much as 36% of the published prose fiction in a given year and hovered around 15–30% up to the late eighteenth century." From 1700 to 1740 four of the best-selling narratives were translations (*Télémaque, Don Quixote, Arabian Nights, Guy of Warwick*), and from 1750 to 1769, six out of the twenty most popular novelists were foreigners, two of them female authors: Marie-Jeanne Riccoboni, Voltaire, Jean-François Marmontel, Miguel de Cervantes, Rousseau, and Jeanne-Marie Leprince de Beaumont. Nor was the situation in France different. McMurran concludes: "Just as translations of novels in the eighteenth century did not represent a move from one cohesive nation and national literature to another (to the extent that an established cultural and literary value system inflected the translation, its reception, and its influence), the contact between France and Britain cannot be properly described as the simple intersection of two distinct others but was a more fluid interaction based on a history of cultural intimacy."[32]

Cohen and Dever's volume has greatly enhanced the discussion of translation's meaning for literary and cultural history; however, exchange moved beyond "the Channel zone" of France and England, and adding a consideration of German examples affords a fuller and more complex picture. James Raven, for instance, has offered the astonishing statistic that in 1776, 76 percent of the novels published in England were translated into German. Such a fact needs to be reflected in historical scholarship, and fortunately recent work such as Stefanie Stockhorst's anthology *Cultural Transfer through Translation* takes up this challenge.[33] In keeping with the essays of that volume, I consider not only the novel but also other literary genres, since the remarkable flow of texts between countries involved both established and emerging forms. Moreover, stylistic and aesthetic issues reveal significant ideological orientations; consideration of the cultural politics emerging within the context of the Personal Union allows us to expand beyond English-French relations and gauge the ongoing reformist content of women's participation.

3. Meta Forkel in Georg Forster's Translation Factory

Meta Forkel and Mary Wollstonecraft, born only six years apart, belonged to the same generation of progressive-minded bluestockings. Both faced anxious personal lives, with their first liaisons falling apart, children born out of wedlock, and a desperate need to earn a living. In order to do so, they entered the literary marketplace. Forkel published her first novel, *Maria*, in 1784; Wollstonecraft's first novel, *Mary*, appeared in 1788. Both books, containing autobiographical content, were also responses to Richardson's *Clarissa*, depicting sentimental heroines who wished to retain independence despite social pressures and gender roles that dictated marriage and customary behavior for women. Both authors were gifted with languages and completed translations. Both saw in the progressive movements around them possibilities of freedom; they attached themselves to revolutionary circles; they were motivated to publish in the interest of furthering radical political ideas.[34] Their lives and literary careers thus parallel each other in substantial ways. However, their approaches to translation reveal distinct radicalisms and demonstrate differences in how the French Revolution was received within the Personal Union; the ramifications were significant for women seeking reform, for gender politics, and for national self-definition.

Meta Forkel separated from her husband in 1788 to move to Berlin, where she studied literature and translation with Johann Jakob Engel and began her career. She needed to make money, and having from childhood been talented in languages she found in translation the most suitable means of earning a living. In 1789 she visited Mainz, where her brother Georg Wedekind was a doctor, and there she got to know Georg Forster, the university librarian, who was married to her childhood friend Therese Heyne. The Forsters were friends of her brother's—the Forsters and Wedekinds were godparents to one anothers' children—and she began to translate books for Georg Forster. Moving between Mainz and Göttingen, where she was seeking to find a solution to her marital problems with Forkel, Meta continued translation work all the while.[35]

Georg Forster had good connections, especially with the Berlin publisher Christian Friedrich Voß. Voß recognized that Forster would lend prestige to his publishing list, and he wished in particular to cash in on current interest in international travel literature by embarking on an entire series of voyage accounts. Forster had not only journeyed around the world with James Cook but he had also written several travel books of his own, had contributed countless articles and reviews to significant publications such as the *Göttingische Anzeigen* (a periodical he helped to edit for a time), and had lively, ongoing connections with British booksellers. He was a star on the literary and intellectual scene. Later, Alexander von Humboldt would estimate Forster's academic contributions highly: "Durch ihn began eine Ära wissenschaftlicher Reisen, deren Zweck vergleichende Völker- und Länderkunde ist. . . . Nicht etwa bloß in seiner trefflichen Beschreibung der zweiten Reise des Kapitän Cook, mehr noch in den kleinen Schriften liegt der Keim zu vielem Großen, das die spätere Zeit zur Reife gebracht hat" (Through him an era of scholarly travels began, whose goal is comparative ethnology and geography . . . Not only in his excellent description of Captain Cook's second voyage, but even more in the short writings there lie the seeds of many great things that later times have brought to fruition").[36] Voß was therefore willing to compensate him handsomely as editor of a series of travel accounts that Forster himself would select. For his part Forster harbored elevated literary ambitions; he wished not only to communicate to readers accurate, factual descriptions of newly explored parts of the world but also to offer well-edited travel narratives with literary merit.[37] Moreover, Forster needed the money. Never able to keep ahead of his personal expenses, he welcomed a second income and set up his translation factory. Voß paid Forster well, offering up to eight taler a sheet for the translations. With more work than he could undertake himself, Forster subcontracted translations to Forkel, Ludwig Ferdinand Huber, and others for about two to three taler a sheet, and then he would go over the translations, editing and supplying introductions and explanatory notes.

The work was undertaken in haste, since competition between publishers was fierce and the dates of the Leipzig and Frankfurt book fairs always loomed.[38] Fortunately Meta Forkel worked fast. Her husband Johann Nikolaus, she discovered, had used up her dowry buying music manuscripts and, when he saw Meta earning money for translating, he confiscated that income also. Forster therefore wrote to his father-in-law Heyne in Göttingen, asking him to advance pay directly to Meta so that Johann Nikolaus could not take it. As was the case with all of Forster's subtranslators, Meta's work needed editing; Forster valued her as his most productive subtranslator. Forkel rendered a number of travel accounts into German for Forster. She began with Mathurin Jacques Brisson's *Geschichte des Schiffbruchs- und seiner Gefangenschaft,* translated from the French, followed with Hester Lynch Piozzi's *Reise durch Frankreich, Italien, und Deutschland,* Maurice Benyowsky's *Reise durch Sibirien und Kamschatka,* as well as Thomas Anburey's *Reise in das Innere von Nordamerika.*

Most interesting, however, are the texts that most stimulated Forkel herself: revolutionary books that had first emerged from the circle surrounding Joseph Johnson, the liberal London publisher. These works not only represented ready money to Forkel; she felt they were important contributions to human thought and human freedom. With Forster and her brother, who also joined the Jacobin Club, she fully supported revolutionary ideals. She began with David Ramsay's *History of the American Revolution* and followed with Thomas Paine's *Rights of Man.* She went on to translate the novels of women in the radical British circle: Elizabeth Inchbald's *A Simple Story,* Charlotte Smith's *Desmond* and her later novel *Celestine.* (Mary Bell Price and Lawrence Marsden Price also list a 1795 translation of William Godwin's *Caleb Williams, or, Things as They Are* and a 1797 translation of Smith's *Marchmont,* though I have been unable to locate these).[39] The fictional works reinforce the kinds of social and gender questions that Meta Forkel pursued in her own novel *Maria,* so it is not surprising that she felt moved to translate these texts in particular. She also tackled the radical *Ruins* from the French of Constantin-François de Chassebeouf, the Count of Volney. After Meta divorced and remarried the civil servant Johann Heinrich Liebeskind in 1794 she moved to Königsberg and then Ansbach and other places associated with Liebeskind's commissions. Relocating frequently, finding publishers on her own, and less pressed financially, she translated fewer works, favoring titles that would instantly interest a bookseller and readily find a market: the gothic fictions of Ann Radcliffe, for example, and James Boswell's acclaimed *Life of Samuel Johnson,* works that despite their popularity nonetheless offered literary novelty and experiments in genre.

Meta Forkel's work on Thomas Paine's *The Rights of Man*, translated in revolutionary Mainz and first published in German in 1792, is especially interesting because Georg Forster did not dare to take on the translation of such a radical work himself. Writing to Voß in the summer of 1791, he explained: "Sie heißt The Rights of Man und ist wider Herrn Burke gerichtet. Vier Editionen sind schon vergriffen. Sie ist aber so demokratisch, daß ich sie wegen meiner Verhältniße nicht übersetzen kann. Madame Forkel übersezt sie und ich will sie ihr revidiren" (It is called The Rights of Man and is directed against Mr. Burke. Four editions have already gone out of print. But it is so democratic, that because of my circumstances I cannot translate it. Madame Forkel will translate it and I will revise it for her).[40] Unlike the normal practice, with Forster subcontracting the work, Forkel in this instance actually negotiated her translation fee directly with Voß. Such a circumstance suggests Forster's concern to distance himself from the controversial project in case there were legal repercussions. Forkel wrote to Voß: "Sie haben Herrn Forster sehr gütig geschrieben, ich möchte das Honorar für den Bogen bestimmen, allein Sie werden mir verzeihn, wenn ich das nicht thue. . . . Wäre ich nicht in der Lage, wo es mir Pflicht ist, meine Zeit auch in anderer Hinsicht einträglich zu benutzen, so würd ich ein ganz eignes Vergnügen drein setzen, diese Arbeit ohne jede Vergütung als die meines eignen Wohlgefallens daran, gemacht zu haben, so aber überlasse ich es ganz und gar Ihnen selbst, was sie an jenem Ersatz mir bestimmen" (You have very kindly written Mr. Forster that I should set the rate for the manuscript; however you will forgive me if I do not do that. . . . If I were not in the position, where I am obliged to use my time lucratively also in other respects, I would take a personal pleasure in having done this work with no more reward than that of my own enjoyment in it; as it is I will leave it entirely to you, what you determine my compensation to be). She knew the importance of the work and became impatient when at first Voß hesitated, for fear of retribution, to publish a book she viewed as something "das als Urkunde der Menschheit anzusehen ist" (that is to be viewed as a charter of humanity).[41] In the end Voß did issue the text and Forster contributed an unsigned preface.

Forkel contributed her own preface to the translation of Charlotte Smith's *Desmond*, an epistolary novel that takes the French Revolution as its theme and critiques both political and domestic tyranny. Publishing this text in 1793 was another risky venture for Forkel; however, she forestalls criticism in her preface by insisting (in a masculine voice) that readers are sophisticated enough not to mistake the views of characters with those of an author, let alone a translator:

> Das Publikum ist schon gewohnt, den dramatischen Schriftsteller von den Grundsätzen frei zu sprechen, die er seinen Personen in den Mund legt: sollte ein Uebersetzer sich denn nicht eine gleiche Billigkeit von seinen Lesern versprechen dürfen? Er fürchtet daher um so weniger, dass man die von ihm hier treu übersetzte hin und wieder mit verführerischem Schimmer aufgestellte Bemerkungen über die französische Staatsumwälzung für sein politisches Glaubensbekenntniss ansehen werde, wenn er gleich den Text durch keine berichtigende Note zu unterbrechen sich erlaubte.

> [The public is already accustomed to acquit the author of the principles that he puts into the mouth of his characters: shouldn't a translator be able to expect the same fairness from his readers? He therefore does not fear that one will interpret the observations about the French Revolution, that are here faithfully translated and that now and again shimmer seductively, as a statement of his own political beliefs, even if he has not allowed himself to interrupt the text with a corrective comment.]

Having conceded that she has not mitigated any of the enthusiasm expressed about the French Revolution, she goes on to suggest that many friends of humanity were drawn to a dream that was later shattered, not because the dream was unworthy, but because harsh experience has shown that the original principles—ones one could only admire—were not upheld. These are courageous words for a woman who was soon, as Germans retook the region in 1793, to be imprisoned for her support of the Mainz Republic.

Given the timeliness and importance of Meta Forkel's translations, not to mention the social repercussions that followed upon them, it is curious that her contribution has been largely ignored by scholars; moreover, the scant attention she has received has been paid to (mis) perceptions of error in her translations.[42] As I have suggested, circumstances imply that, while Forkel's translations may have needed the kind of editing that was typical for quickly completed "translation factory" products, they proved highly marketable and popular; they were frequently reprinted, and she was able to find work as soon as she sought it. In particular, Forkel's Paine translation was deemed solid enough to be reprinted as late as 1973 by the respected Suhrkamp Verlag in a "Theorie" series edited by Jürgen Habermas, Dieter Henrich, and Jacob Taubes. The editor and introducer of the volume, Theo Stemmler, insists that: "Bei objectiver Beurteilung ihrer Übersetzung gelangt man zu dem Ergebnis, daß diese Leistung durchaus anerkennenswert ist: Frau Forkel übersetzt auch schwierige idiomatische Wendungen in ein lesbares Deutsch, folgt meist genau dem Wortlaut des Originals, ohne jedoch pedantisch an der syntaktischen Konstruktion der Vorlage festzuhalten" (In an objective evaluation of her translation one comes to the conclusion that this achievement is perfectly commendable: Mrs. Forkel even translates difficult idiomatic expressions into a readable German; she generally follows the wording of the original without holding on pedantically to the syntactical construction of the model).[43] The perfunctory dismissals of Forkel's work would therefore appear to reflect not only a paternalistic attitude to a woman writer but also a general denigration of translation as a serious literary endeavor. And yet, translation was pursued, theorized, and lauded by the greatest writers of the time.

Indeed, most significant European authors of the period saw translation as central to literary life and many engaged in this type of cultural transfer.[44] Samuel Johnson expressed surprise at the rare author who could become eminent without doing translations, and the work of German translators was held in high esteem in Europe, witness Germaine de Staël's essay on translation, or Thomas Carlyle, who in 1827 would write:

> The Germans study foreign nations in a spirit which deserves to be oftener imitated. It is their honest endeavour to understand each, with its own peculiarities, in its own special manner of existing; not that they may praise it, or censure it, or attempt to alter it, but simply that they may see its manner of existing as the nation itself sees it, and so participate in whatever worth or beauty it has brought into being. Of all literatures, therefore, the German has the best as well as the most translations.[45]

Although Carlyle's laudatory words suggest a neutrality in German translation, the earlier practitioners studied here did harbor designs in their choices of texts and modes of translation. Forster's and Forkel's theories of translation followed on the type of modified literal translation offered by Johann David Michaelis and Luise Gottsched in the belief that Germans would benefit from adopting foreign ideas faithfully rendered

into the German. Gottsched had felt that German letters would improve;
Michaelis had, among other things, sought to increase the status of wom-
en; and Forster and Forkel wished to increase the liberty of Germans
overall. The benefits of a largely literal translation were thus perceived to
accrue on many levels, political, social, and literary. Meta Forkel's translation of Paine's *Rights of Man* or Smith's *Desmond* can therefore be said
to embrace English-language contributions to German culture and to
represent an international as well as protonationalist moment. Clearly
Forkel felt that certain ideas expressed in English contained force explosive enough to alter German political consciousness—the legal consequences to Paine's English publisher Joseph Johnson suggested this (he
was convicted and imprisoned for selling a seditious pamphlet), as did
Forster's and Voß's reluctance to handle the volatile text. Forkel saw
Paine's work as a document for all of humanity, an "Urkunde der Menschheit," whatever its national origin, and Smith's novel offered trenchant insight into revolutionary politics and domestic life. Embracing
cosmopolitanism, Forkel saw translation as a means of sharing mutual
human assets rather than breaching walls that separated cultures, even
if this occurred in the interest of improving German life in particular.

Sherry Simon has suggested, in keeping with a generally held view,
that the German Romantic attitude to translation contrasted with the
French—the free style in the tradition of "les belles infidèles"—and that,
conveyed to Madame de Staël by such thinkers as August Wilhelm Schlegel, Staël embraced it as she visited Germany in the early nineteenth century.[46] Although one can argue for a widespread German approach to
translation, I have been suggesting that this was not a nineteenth-century
Romantic phenomenon but one that had far earlier roots, a much longer history,[47] and that this timeline is significant not only for the study
of translation but also for our understanding of emerging nationalism
and the gender politics that shifted alongside it in the early nineteenth
century.

The universalist imperative coincided with the feminist impulse
Forkel sought to advocate; at this moment she perceived the advancement of women incorporated within a general vision of liberty and therefore as likely to profit from revolutionary change. Mary Wollstonecraft,
whose translation of Christian Gotthilf Salzmann's *Moralisches Elementarbuch* seeks explicitly to foreground *female* agency, surprisingly delimits
cultural transfer in the interest of an insularity she is reluctant to breach.
Wollstonecraft's focus on women in her translation from the German
paradoxically coincides with a retreat to particularities of sex as well as

nation, and this represents a different epistemology that has been tradi-
tionally associated with Romanticism but that is clearly inflected by the
different circumstances of late-eighteenth-century British politics and
gender politics. Considering Wollstonecraft's translation reveals how
two women, similarly positioned with like aims in two nonrevolutionary
countries, nonetheless were affected differently by the ideological forces
surrounding them.[48]

4. Mary Wollstonecraft's Translation of Salzmann

While German radicals such as Meta Forkel were interested in dissemi-
nating English ideas, so too English radicals were interested in German
ones. There was in particular a prevalent British fascination, as I have
suggested, with new German pedagogical theories: those theories led to
substantial experimentation on the part of the Göttingen political scientist August Schlözer with his daughter Dorothea, and also stimulated
the group of Rousseauian "Philanthropists," including Johann Bernhard Basedow (whom Schlözer challenged), Joachim Heinrich Campe,
and Christian Gotthilf Salzmann. These men founded institutions, ran
prolific presses, and composed many works on educational theory and
practice in the late eighteenth century. German influence on English
radicals can be discerned, among other places, in Wollstonecraft's translation of Christian Gotthilf Salzmann's *Moralisches Elementarbuch* (1783),
rendered into English as *Elements of Morality for the Use of Children* (1790),
an acclaimed German work that proved equally popular among English
readers: there were at least eleven editions published in England, Ireland, and the United States between 1790 and 1811.[49]

Christian Gotthilf Salzmann was born in 1744 in a town near Erfurt to
a Protestant minister. He felt his own schooling was rigid, and as a young
pastor increasingly concerned with the fate of the poor, he concluded
that much of the pain and suffering of the world was derived from people's inadequate education. He wrote a book about the best way to teach
children religion, but when this was rejected by his superiors, Salzmann
was happy to accept a position at the Philanthropist school founded in
1774 by Basedow, who was supported by the liberal Prince Leopold Friedrich Franz of Anhalt-Dessau.[50] There, still reacting against an education
he felt remained insufficiently experience-based, Salzmann developed
his ideas in various publications, including his *Moralisches Elementarbuch*,
and persuaded the liberal Duke of Gotha, Ernst II—like Friedrich Franz

a freemason—to support his purchase of an estate at Schnepfenthal, where he built his own school. He admitted his first pupils in 1785 and by 1800 there were fifty-eight students. Education was practical, and the curriculum included—along with academic subjects—gymnastics, sex education, music, and travel. In addition to Salzmann's many publications, his fellow teacher Johann Christoph Friedrich GutsMuths wrote a number of well-known texts on physical education: *Gymnastik für die Jugend,* discussed below, was translated into English and published by Joseph Johnson in 1800.[51] Christian Carl André became a teacher for girls, whose instruction took place in a separate building but enjoyed a parallel curriculum; he published books about their studies and especially the benefits of field trips to their development.[52] Henry Crabb Robinson, visiting Schnepfenthal in 1804, paid particular attention to the physical education and also noted that "[w]ith edifying improvements, Salzmann translated Mary Wollstonecraft's 'Rights of Women,' and he was in correspondence with her."[53]

Salzmann wrote dozens of educational texts for children, teachers, and parents, even issuing a periodical, "Der Bote aus Thüringen," for twenty-eight years at the Schnepfenthal press. The work translated by Mary Wollstonecraft, the *Moralisches Elementarbuch,* was his most popular; it remained in print until the mid-nineteenth century with several editions each decade, and appeared also in an amended version for Catholic youth. Salzmann's book was illustrated by the famed artist Daniel Chodowiecki, Germany's most prolific liberal book illustrator.

Mary Wollstonecraft's treatment of this work confirms the significance of British-German cultural transfer and at the same time shows how a translation of the revolutionary era reworked the aims of the earlier generation, imposed national binarisms, and shifted away from earlier forms of feminism. The book was offered as a new, English product. William Blake's role as illustrator reinforced the drive to reinterpret and re-present the text. He adjusted the composition of the original illustrations and even added some new ones to further a radical metaphysics that proved so significant to Wollstonecraft's version of this book.

Therefore while the literal translations of Michaelis and Forkel into the German were intended directly to effect sociopolitical change, the freer translation of radical Mary Wollstonecraft, I argue, paradoxically tended toward privatization and protonationalism. Adumbrating Romantic notions of authorship, Wollstonecraft offered simultaneously domestication and transcendence at moments that in the German original are presented as straightforward social and ethical concerns. As a result Wollstonecraft's translation limited the moral compass of the original text to highlight instead an omniscient, nearly omnipotent female figure whom I will call the mother-instructor, who reflects Wollstonecraft's own view of what ought to be women's new domestic sovereignty, with the home as microcosm of the polis and the mother as unacknowledged legislator.

In this, then, she adopts an "ultra-radical" epistemology, to use Barbara Taylor's characterization, that jumps from the domestic to the transcendent in an abrupt move uncharacteristic of other contemporary feminist approaches, whether liberal, conservative, or even radical. Barbara Taylor writes that the political ambitions of "most 1790s radicals . . . were limited and pragmatic," but that the millenarian influence of Richard Price lent to Wollstonecraft's thought a utopian thrust, an "unwavering faith in divine purpose that, suffusing her radicalism, turned anticipations of 'world perfected' into a confident political stance."[54] Wollstonecraft's unusual apocalyptic view is shown, via a comparison to the German text, ultimately to undermine her radical aims. The focus on gender questions becomes here, in the Romantic ferment of the French Revolution, a privatizing move despite her claims to a freer and more feminist approach.

Mary Wollstonecraft's earliest works, *Thoughts on the Education of Daughters* (1787) and *Original Stories from Real Life* (1788), reveal an author fiercely involved with issues of morality and women's education, and it is therefore not surprising to find her at this time taking up Salzmann's collection of tales about the Herrmann family concerned with the moral development of children. Salzmann's own practical theories of pedagogy pervade the stories of the *Elementarbuch*. Despite Wollstonecraft's political and epistolary links with Salzmann, however, she makes meaningful if subtle changes in her version of Salzmann's treatise. Critics have tended to follow Ralph Wardle by emphasizing Wollstonecraft's addition of a story about Indians and her attention-getting remark in the preface (actually translated directly from Salzmann) that children should be told matter-of-factly about human reproduction.[55] But there are more significant aspects to Wollstonecraft's translation that shed a brighter light on her writing career and politics in general; her *Elements of Morality for the Use of Children* (1790) finally moves away from the bourgeois German book not only to deepen the role of the mother, called Mrs. Jones in her version, but also to demonstrate Wollstonecraft's views on the advancement of civilization, the need for a reformation of manners to facilitate such advancement, and the ways the mother in particular can lead civilization to its perfected state.

Wardle has been the only Anglophone scholar to take a close look at Wollstonecraft's "Englishing" of Salzmann. He briefly analyzes some of her modifications but does not consider changes in the role of the mother. Instead he focuses on the subtle ways Wollstonecraft reveals her radical opinions on class distinctions by diminishing the material possessions of the wealthy.[56] On the Continent, German scholar Ingrid-Charlotte Wolter has concluded that Wollstonecraft adjusts the original by foregrounding personality development over Salzmann's emphasis on social morality.[57] In my view the "Englishing" tendency on the part of Wollstonecraft needs to be examined more closely, since it highlights how questions of gender and nation are intertwined. Wollstonecraft significantly terms this process one of "naturalizing" the text.

> I term it a translation, though I do not pretend to assert that it is a literal one; on the contrary, beside making it an English story, I have made additions to, or altered many parts of it, not only to give it the spirit of an original, but to avoid introducing any German customs or local opinions. My reason for naturalizing it must be obvious from this—I did not wish to puzzle children by pointing out modifications of manners, when the grand principles of morality were to be fixed on a broad basis.[58]

Wollstonecraft worked from the German original aiming to offer something specifically English, with the paradoxical goal of conveying transcendent principles. Adhering to national—"natural"—customs will simultaneously allow readers to avoid the distractions of national difference.

To complicate this strained argument, national difference, to Wollstonecraft, appears to be defined to a significant degree by French culture. Wollstonecraft in the preface actually praises the German text for its non-Frenchness: "Though I have not copied, I have endeavoured to imitate the simplicity of style and manners which I admired in the original. If it had been a French work, I should, probably, have had to curtail many smooth compliments, that I might not have led my little readers to the very verge of falsehood."[59] Behind Wollstonecraft's concern to transcend nation by invoking it rests the abiding British obsession with French character and culture. As did Samuel Johnson, she scoffs at French influences, leaning heavily on unflattering stereotypes.

At the same time she may be convincing her readers that she is not translating from a French version but from the German original. Since in this period some British translators of German works actually retranslated French versions, Wollstonecraft by contrast wants to emphasize that she had worked from Salzmann's own text.[60] She says she undertook the translation from the German in order to improve her language skills; she asked Joseph Johnson to send her a German grammar book;[61] and she includes sections from the German work—notably the "Introductory Address to Parents"—that do not appear in the existing French translation.

Oddly enough, however, if she had adhered to the French version of this text, she might have remained closer to the German. Wollstonecraft evinces a more national stance toward the German text than does her French-language counterpart. Where the translator into the French pointedly *avoids* "Frenchifying" the text (by introducing French characters in a French context), Wollstonecraft "Englishes" the text in precisely this way because, as we have seen, she believes it will be more "natural." The French translator explains his reasons for retaining the German setting and characters:

> Les personages de ce livre sont la plûtot part Allemands, parce que l'auteur a principalement écrit pour sa nation. Je les ai laissés tels, en ne changeant rien à leurs moeurs, à leur façon de penser, ni à leur ton. Cela sera plaisir à des lecteurs qui, exempts de préjugés nationaux, aiment à connaitre d'autres caractères et d'autres moeurs que celles de leur nation.[62]

So the French translation consistently hews to the German text. Interestingly, the French translation appears to have been undertaken by a German translator (Johann Christoph Schwab) and published in Leipzig by Siegfried Lebrecht Crusius beginning in 1785. Salzmann or his translator may have desired less to influence the Francophone market across the border (teaching the French German ways) than to reach an aristocratic one within the German principalities (i.e., teaching Francophilic German aristocrats bourgeois German ways). Wollstonecraft by contrast "Englishes" and domesticizes her text so that her work becomes a proto-Romantic translation resting on an assumption of cultural difference rather than claiming to participate in a cosmopolitan endeavor as is asserted by the (German) French translation.

Therefore, while critics have suggested that Wollstonecraft chose to offer an adaptation rather than a literal translation because she was just learning German and was therefore incapable of exact translation, I am arguing instead that her translation, generally remaining faithful to the original, purposefully veers from her source at specific junctures in order to promote the feminist and national project Wollstonecraft favors. Wollstonecraft's entrenched views of national character—especially in light of the French version's consistent faithfulness to Salzmann's original—are exposed in her "natural" aims at "Englishing." Despite her interest in and admiration for Salzmann's German text, she harbors a sense that it is too foreign and that this difference has a deeply gendered basis.

Already in the introduction she changes the German focus on the boy to "children" in general. Her concern to naturalize involves careful attention to sex, but this becomes part of her larger project to address "grand principles" and articulate these on a "broad basis." Englishing and naturalizing her text involve magnifying the moral significance of everyday events, creating a continuum between inner and outer landscapes, and muting the physical, demonstrative nature of the characters while intensifying their self-consciousness. Even her apparently intermittent and merely descriptive alterations ultimately serve to push a quintessentially material Enlightenment original toward a more metaphysical Romantic and British expression. I will argue that her emendations reveal a determinist conception of history as well as a sense of poetic transcendence that finally undermine any pragmatic aim of social transformation, something clearly the goal of the practical German text. Ironically, then, even as Wollstonecraft rearranges the book to put women at the center, she unwittingly contributes to their ultimate marginalization. Like a number of her other writings, the *Elements of Morality* demonstrates how Wollstonecraft envisions the home as metaphor for the polis, depicting women as self-scrutinizing governors of their families who take up their deserved place as the unacknowledged legislators of an ideal nation.

5. *"Englishing" the* Elements of Morality

Wollstonecraft's views do not shift significantly over the course of her short career. In the *Original Stories*, for example, one of Wollstonecraft's earliest works, Mrs. Mason's moonlight reverie about improving the world despite personal tragedy leads directly to the kind of pronouncement in the *Letters Written During a Short Residence in Sweden, Norway, and Denmark*

(1796), published the year before Wollstonecraft's death, where Wollstonecraft's "favorite subject of contemplation" is "the future improvement of the world." The ideas we see distilled in Wollstonecraft's alterations to Salzmann's *Elementarbuch* demonstrate the consistent nature and means of that improvement: progress depending on the behavior of a mother who acts as teacher, poet, and prophet. Unfortunately, this "mother-instructor" can finally operate only via metaphor to effect social and political change; by relying on synecdoche Wollstonecraft ultimately undermines her own revolutionary aims.

Numerous subtle but consistent modifications go a long way to reveal Wollstonecraft's agenda in her translation. As a way of adapting the German story for her British readers, Wollstonecraft alters the accoutrements and routines of daily life, for example. She consistently changes descriptions of meals: in the German, the curate's family eats cheese for supper, but Wollstonecraft substitutes bread; while the Germans consider meat as well as soap necessary household expenses, Wollstonecraft leaves out the meat. One detects Wollstonecraft's distaste, not merely for heavy meals, but for overindulging in general: "gluttony." That deadly sin occasions the most vehement of Wollstonecraft's inserted diatribes. In Salzmann's version a servant, caught snatching food, is simply told by the mistress of the house, "Was kann ich denn dazu, daß ihr eine so häßliche Gewohnheit angenommen habt? Wenn ihr euch nicht selbst bei Ehre erhalten wollt, so kann ich es auch nicht" (How can I help it if you have cultivated such an ugly habit? If you do not wish to be honorable, then I cannot do it for you).[63] Wollstonecraft, by contrast, has Mrs. Jones lash out at the maid:

> But is it my fault that you have acquired such an hateful habit? I have once or twice reproved you gently; now, since you have not listened to me, I must expose you to the family, to see if that will cure you. Nay, the pimples on your face expose your gluttony; we should seldom look ugly, or be obliged to take nasty medicines, if we did not greedily overload our stomachs; and if we forget our duty in private, and cheat our fellow-creatures of their share, it is but just that we should be laughed at in company, and called what we really are, gluttons. (II:35)

Far from committing a simple fault to be amended, the servant has revealed a disease that must be cured and a duty to others that has basely been abandoned. In the German version the offense is merely taking snacks ("naschen"), not gluttony; Wollstonecraft wishes to escalate the action to a religious and moral crime.[64] Further, Wollstonecraft manipulates by means of shame and guilt. She has Mrs. Jones descend to derision of the servant's physical appearance as well as threaten to "expose" the servant to the ridicule and laughter of the family. Leaning on theories of physiognomy, Wollstonecraft reveals that her aims are broader and metaphysical in contrast to the practical German goals of behavior modification.[65] According to Wollstonecraft, one's small, private actions must pass muster in the larger scheme of things.

Repeatedly Wollstonecraft raises the moral stakes in what would appear to be less than earthshaking events. When the Jones family returns after a feast, their moderate eating habits are contrasted with those of the other guests, who have overindulged in "artificial high-seasoned dishes" and are now feeling ill. "Is it possible that such a hodge-podge should digest, or that such artificial compositions should not injure the blood, *and interrupt the simple course of nature?*" I have emphasized Wollstonecraft's addition; again she heightens the moral stakes, taking Salzmann's straightforward point about health and the simple life and extending it to encompass cosmic concerns. "Nature" itself is upset as artificial foods infect the blood of the people, who are after all the blood of the nation and the world. Everyday events, ones as mundane as meals and digestion, have far-reaching consequences, not only for the well-being of the characters but also for the function of nature itself, for the very workings of the universe. Thus Wollstonecraft establishes a link between body and state, as each citizen's blood, via synecdoche, fuels a larger world; the duty to eat right takes on exaggerated ethical and political significance.

Given the metaphorical links between people and their natural, social, and political world, Wollstonecraft's further alterations to the German text—delineating a way of life that is less active, demonstrative, and violent than that in Salzmann—have broader implications as well. For example, instead of amusing children at a party by setting up a game involving the shooting of birds, Wollstonecraft wants to entice the young with cherry-picking and a walk through the garden. While in the German Herr Heilberg's house suggests baroque effusiveness by containing large paintings by the greatest artists of elaborate rural scenes and lively ancient myths, along with costly mirrors and sumptuous furniture, Sir William's place in the English version (note the elevated social rank absent in the German) reflects symmetry and restraint, with cool "pillars of fine marble" and "beautiful statues." Wollstonecraft shares a pride in heightened English sensitivity and prefers a refined neoclassical interior.[66]

Such delicacy, as Wollstonecraft portrays it, has sexual as well as national implications. While Salzmann suggests that a woman is a prostitute, has disreputable men coming and going, Wollstonecraft omits it. In Salzmann a bad innkeeper slaps his wife across the face, while in Wollstonecraft's version he merely throws a handful of cards at her. This appears to suggest a greater tolerance among Germans for violence, but even positive emotions are more vehemently expressed: when, in Salzmann, the main protagonist Herrmann feels overcome by admiration for a virtuous innkeeper, he throws himself around the man's neck and gives him a big kiss, whereas in Wollstonecraft "Mr. Jones was so full of respect for this good man, that he shook him heartily by the hand." Wollstonecraft's version lacks the vigor and perhaps the realism of the German original. Commotion and tumult are internalized in Wollstonecraft; vitality and agitation remain largely mental events.

Thus, though Wollstonecraft insists in her preface that "all the pictures are drawn from real life" (I:iv), she does not wish that life to look too harsh or physically unrestrained; the enhanced inwardness and physical restraint she introduces not only spare female characters violent encounters and abuse, they also make of an energetic German Enlightenment model a muted English Romantic copy: they shift the arena of action from the robust and rugged world (to which Salzmann wished to introduce his pupils) to the minds of the characters and readers. There are repercussions. In Wollstonecraft, thousands of infinitesimal activities of the body—eating, drinking, walking, playing—are given profound weight, and the inner mental and physiological events of a contained body come to constitute determining world occurrences. Wollstonecraft creates a synecdochic link between inner and outer world—self and nation—and suggests that events in one significantly affect events in the other.

Given the links between inner and outer worlds, a mother, especially one who eats correctly and maintains self-control, simultaneously gains command of social circumstances by virtue of her dominion over self and family. Wollstonecraft's feminism, seeking to expand the sphere of women's power, paradoxically takes a turn that will have antifeminist repercussions. In Salzmann's "Introduction to Parents," for example, he explains how a mother who employs his storytelling system will be rewarded by having better-behaved children:

Grosser Lohn wartet deiner, wenn du dich diesem Geschäfte unterziehen wirst. Es wird dir bey deinen übrigen Geschäften die ange-

nehmste Aufheiterung geben. Die Gesellschaft deiner Kinder, die dir
vielleicht sonst so lästig war, wird dir nun, wenn sie immer gehors-
amer, thätiger, gefälliger werden, mehr Vergnügen schaffen, als ir-
gend eine andere. (xviii)

[Great reward awaits you, if you will undertake this task. It will most
pleasantly brighten your other tasks. The society of your children,
which was otherwise perhaps a burden to you, will now—as they
become ever more obedient, busy, and obliging—supply you with
more pleasure, than any other.]

Wollstonecraft, by contrast, focuses solely on the mother and her frame
of mind.

If you have sufficient resolution to persevere, you will be amply recom-
pensed for the trouble this employment gives you, and it will become,
after you have acquired a taste for your duty, your most agreeable
relaxation. The society of your children, which was, perhaps, sometimes a little troublesome to you, will soon, when you are anxious to
improve them, become your dearest enjoyment. (II.11)

Only the mother's frame of mind, not the children's behavior, is changing in Wollstonecraft's sentences, in contrast to Salzmann's. Mothering
becomes more enjoyable because of the mother's own "resolution to
persevere," words not used in the German, where it's simply a job to be
done. In Wollstonecraft it is the mother's new "anxious" desire to do her
"duty"; moreover the focus falls on the mother's improving the children,
rather than, as in Salzmann, on the children themselves becoming obedient, busy, and obliging.

Indeed, Wollstonecraft consistently emphasizes duty in a way Salzmann does not, and again this is because of the social, national, and
cosmic implications Wollstonecraft reads into the performance of one's
vocation. She has the father of the family in the text, Mr. Jones, laud a
farmer's industry by saying, "not only a good harvest will be the reward
of your labour, but you will have health and cheerfulness whilst looking
forward to it, and doing your duty in the station in which God has placed
you" (II.7). Salzmann makes no mention of God and the duty dictated
by one's God-given social station.[67]

Even though the seemingly random addition of a single phrase would
appear beneath notice, it again demonstrates the depth of Wollstone-

craft's agenda when taken in the context of her other works. Fulfilling the duty of one's station recurs as a theme throughout her writings, and it is particularly pronounced in the *Vindication of the Rights of Woman* (1792). Many commentators have analyzed Wollstonecraft's depiction of the active citizen mother,[68] but I would emphasize how the mother's "doing the duty of her station" has millennial implications. Wollstonecraft's citizen mother studies history and political science to learn her natural place; she breastfeeds her children and creates a neat and happy home.

> I have . . . viewed with pleasure a woman nursing her children, and discharging the duties of her station with, perhaps, merely a servant maid to take off her hands the servile part of the household business. I have seen her prepare herself and children, with only the luxury of cleanliness, to receive her husband. . . . Whilst my benevolence has been gratified by contemplating this artless picture, I have thought that a couple of this description, equally necessary and independent of each other, because each fulfilled the respective duties of their station, possessed all that life could give.[69]

As in the example of the farmer from the *Elements of Morality*, whose hard work not only brings a plentiful harvest but also justifies his place in the larger scheme of things, so too does the mother justify her existence in the moral universe by "fulfilling the duties of her station." This phrase takes on a millennial quality when Wollstonecraft links it to the prophecy of Isaiah:

> [T]hough I have compared the character of a modern soldier with that of a civilized woman, I am not going to advise them to turn their distaff into a musket, though I sincerely wish to see the bayonet converted into a pruning-hook. I only recreated an imagination . . . supposing that society will some time or other be so constituted, that man must necessarily fulfil the duties of a citizen, or be despised, and that while he was employed in any of the departments of civil life, his wife, also an active citizen, would be equally intent to manage her family, educate her children, and assist her neighbours.[70]

The father and mother fulfill their duties in good bourgeois fashion. Isaiah 2:4 prophesies that "they shall beat their swords into plowshares, and their spears into pruninghooks." Richard Price, Wollstonecraft's mentor, had delivered and published a sermon drawing on this millennial passage, preaching it to the "Supporters of a New Academical Institution among Protestant Dissenters." The millennial and educational context of Wollstonecraft's own sentences suggests Price's influence, and she had in fact written the *Vindication of the Rights of Men* to defend Price from Edmund Burke's attacks; the *Vindication of the Rights of Woman* followed from that earlier polemical work.

Characteristically, Wollstonecraft superimposes the millennial vision onto her model of social existence, so that Isaiah's prophecy becomes, via Price, a vision of civic life as a representation of God's millennial order. As mothers and fathers fulfill the duties of their station, Wollstonecraft will read out of their behavior a moral progress indicating the days of plowshares and pruning hooks. This direction in her thinking is later overtly articulated in the *Historical and Moral View of . . . the French Revolution* and the *Letters Written During a Short Residence in Sweden, Norway, and Denmark*, where she spells out her theory of the advance and eventual perfection of civilization. Time and again she speculates about the necessary ingredients for achieving social felicity, and the central ingredient consistently remains individual morality. Hence the focus of her travels is to observe "the present state of morals and manners, as I trace the progress of the world's improvement."[71]

Although Wollstonecraft retains a focus on the mother-instructor's multifaceted role, she moves increasingly toward an elevated analysis in which she considers larger systems and ties them to larger solutions. This may appear to be politically more efficacious and more feminist; however, it also becomes more removed and conceptual. Wollstonecraft refines the imagined link between individual, family, and nation: "man has been termed a microcosm; and every family might also be called a state." She spells out her metaphorically linked concentric spheres, with the model mother-instructor, governor of a microstate, at the center. Fulfilling the duty of her station, this mother acquits herself simultaneously in all spheres: within her microcosmic disciplined self, within the well-run family, within the state composed of active, dutiful citizens, and from the perspective of the macrocosmic millennial order.

Wollstonecraft's alterations to Salzmann's *Elementarbuch* offer her system in distilled form. For instance, when the Jones family receives an invitation from Sir William, little Mary is not allowed to go along because her bonnet is dirty. In Salzmann's German version, by contrast, the daughter Luise's entire dress is covered with beer and grease stains. The draconian punishment—missing what turns out to be half a week's outing—corresponds to some extent with the magnitude of the crime. Moreover the explanation for the punishment is more straightforward. Luise's father will not allow her to go along, he says, because Luise's dreadful appearance would reflect badly on her mother's reputation as a housekeeper; she might be thought "eine unordentliche Frau" (a disorganized woman) by her peers. The other children will also not want to play with "ein so schmutziges Mädchen" (such an unkempt girl) (8).

In Wollstonecraft's version, by contrast, it is the mother rather than the father who denies Mary the pleasure of going along. And, as if to emphasize the mother's authority, Wollstonecraft has the denial proceed from the mere dirty bonnet rather than from a completely unpresentable dress. Wollstonecraft also increases the amount of guilt Mary feels: Mary's appearing in the dirty bonnet would shame her mother rather than simply reflect on her housekeeping skills; moreover, by not being allowed to go, Mary is diminishing the pleasure of her mother in the party:

> I must leave you at home, because I should be ashamed to let you appear in company such a dirty figure. I shall not enjoy half the pleasure I expected, now I am obliged to leave you at home. (I.9)

And of course it is all Mary's own fault: "But remember, that the disappointment entirely arises from your own thoughtlessness, and your not paying proper attention to my example, who always keep my clothes in order" (I.9).[72] Little Mary must pattern her behavior on the ideal mother-instructor's example.

Later in the book both Luise in the German and Mary in the English version have learned the lesson that they must keep their clothes clean. Their mothers look into their closets and smile approval at the order they find there. Little Luise tells her mother:

> ich will auch immer so ordentlich seyn, liebe Mutter, daß Sie mir gut seyn können, und ich nicht wieder so weinen darf, wie letzthin—ach, da hat es mich gar zu sehr gedauert, daß ich zu Hause bleiben mußte! (246)

> [and I always want to be so neat, dear Mother, so that you can be pleased with me, and I do not have to cry again, as before—oh, I felt so unhappy that I had to stay at home!]

Again, Wollstonecraft makes subtle but significant changes:

> I will never be careless again that you may always look at me as you
> do now, and that I may never cry as bitterly as I did when I saw the
> coach drive off—Oh!—that was a sad day, I shall never forget it!—no,
> never! (II 160)

The "dear Mother" is tellingly left out, the mother's powerful gaze is
emphasized ("that you may always look at me as you do now"), and the
relentless repetition of "never," the acute pain expressed in Mary's cry-
ing "bitterly," the coach driving off in front of her face, and the repeated
dashes and three exclamations suggest Wollstonecraft's desire to height-
en the drama of this didactic moment.

But Wollstonecraft goes even further. She adds a full paragraph, not
found in Salzmann, to explicate and justify the governing power of the
mother:

> All my commands have the same tendency, said her mother; I assist
> your weak mind, and I am endeavouring to make you wise and happy,
> when I deny you any present pleasure: for you are yet too young to
> know what is really good. (II 160)

Not only does Wollstonecraft's mother-instructor offer a perfect example; with her elevated mind she is in touch with the Good and therefore
owns the authority and the power to control her daughter's life in its
minutest detail by denying pleasures. Even the smallest event shapes the
mind, reflects on large moral questions, and therefore must be scrutinized if the child is to develop into a highly evolved, civilized, and civiliz-
ing force like her mother.

Wollstonecraft's emerging Romantic view is expressed in this transcendent turn. Increasingly discouraged by the failures she encounters in instructing people in her own life, Wollstonecraft leans less on
demonstrable causality and more on metaphorical, concentric links that
are to empower the mother-instructor. As with characters in Wollstonecraft's earlier writings—the governess Mrs. Mason, the schoolteacher
Anna Lofty, and Mary—it is their dignity of manners that attests to their
mental strength and wherewithal to fight depression and exist independently: one needs to "have in this uncertain world some stay . . . and
this stay it is, which gives that dignity to the manners, which shews that a
person does not depend on mere human applause for comfort and sat-

isfaction."[73] Having experienced the inevitable harms of the world, these women have learned to avoid the most painful sensations by demanding little but by controlling the people in their sphere. In particular, directing the mental development of girl children represents a form of self-renewal and self-discipline that prepares the mother-instructors for eternity. Unfortunately the act of translating did not offer Mary Wollstonecraft herself the kind of self-renewal that would have filled her sails or her coffers. To George Blood she wrote, "I am so fatigued with poring over a German book, I scarcely can collect my thoughts or even spell English words."[74]

6. Anti-French Reaction

Despite Wollstonecraft's personal fatigue, her influence on her German translator, Georg Friedrich Christian Weissenborn, was vigorous and direct. Weissenborn had just joined Salzmann's faculty as instructor for classical and modern languages and had been educated at the universities of Jena and Göttingen.[75] He married one of Salzmann's daughters and was clearly a Wollstonecraft aficionado. After completing the translation of *A Vindication* he translated the *Original Stories* (1794) and edited the English version of the *Elements of Morality* (1796), which he used in his classes to teach the English language. In addition, in 1799 he published a translation of Godwin's *Memoirs of the Author of A Vindication of the Rights of Woman* (1798) as *Denkschrift auf Mary Wollstonecraft Godwin, die Vertheidigerin der Rechte des Weibes.* He wrote a feminist essay, "Über den Richterspruch in der Sache des weiblichen Geschlechts gegen das männliche" (On the verdict in the case of the female sex against the male) in 1800, which called on women to demand their rights: "Suchet das zu werden, was Ihr seyn sollet; und man wird gezwungen seyn, Euch das zu geben, was man Euch schuldig ist! Lernet Eure Pflichten kennen: und man wird Euch Eure Rechte nicht vorenthalten können!" (Seek to become that which you ought to be, and one will be forced to give you what you are owed! Become familiar with your duties and one will not be able to deny you your rights!).[76] Such a sentiment strongly echoes Wollstonecraft's own language in the *Vindication* and attests to the views prevalent in progressive circles in this period.

However, Salzmann, for his part, added an introduction and footnotes that tend to mitigate and alter Wollstonecraft's most radical pronouncements in that book—most notably in his support for the aristocracy (introduction, 124). These are what Henry Crabb Robinson had described as Salzmann's "edifying improvements." Perhaps this was done to avoid offending a patron or students' parents. In any case, while Joseph Johnson had hired Wollstonecraft to translate Salzmann's text aiming to further liberal ideology by teaching English readers progressive German approaches, even those German educationalists succumbed to nationalist tendencies in the early years of the nineteenth century in reaction to French incursions in the Napoleonic wars. Salzmann came to see education as a means of teaching love of the fatherland to defend against French aggression.

The upshot of the Terror and the Napoleonic wars was no less unsettling and vehement for the Göttingen professors' daughters. Caroline Michaelis-Böhmer and her daughter Auguste, along with Meta Forkel and her mother, were arrested and imprisoned in the Königstein fortress as they sought to escape Mainz, which had been recaptured by the Germans in 1793.[77] This incarceration became particularly dangerous when Caroline found she was pregnant by a French soldier, since the assumption of her captors would be that the traitor, Georg Forster, known to be a friend, was the father of her child. So she needed to find a timely way to be released, which was fortunately arranged by her brother and an acquaintance from Göttingen, August Wilhelm Schlegel.

As has been suggested, not only Caroline but most of the Göttinger daughters joined their fellow male radicals in believing in sexual freedom, and they bore children out of wedlock: Meta became involved with and ultimately married Ferdinand Liebeskind, having earlier given birth to his son, Adalbert, in 1792. Therese Forster became the lover of houseguest and translator Ludwig Ferdinand Huber, whose continued presence in their home was tolerated by Forster. Therese was beginning divorce proceedings when Forster, having traveled to Paris in early 1793 to seek annexation of Mainz, died there in January 1794. Therese married Huber in April.

After three months' incarceration at Königstein Caroline was released, but she was banned from the Rhein provinces and could not return to Göttingen either. Schlegel arranged for her to come under the protection of his brother Friedrich near Leipzig. Realizing she needed a protector, and perhaps out of gratitude for Schlegel's concern for her, she agreed in 1796 to become his wife and moved to Jena to join him. There she hosted a lively salon of progressives, including her husband, Ludwig Tieck and his wife Amalie, Novalis (Friedrich von Hardenberg) and his fiancée Julie von Charpentier, Friedrich Schelling, Johann Gottlieb

Fichte, and Friedrich Schlegel and his mistress and future wife Dorothea. She helped her husband with the translation of Shakespeare and contributed to the *Athenäum*, the literary periodical edited by the Schlegels that came to define early Romanticism. Georg Wilhelm Friedrich Hegel came to reside in the same house in 1801. It is this spirited intellectual atmosphere that Henry Crabb Robinson describes as he enrolled at the University of Jena, attended lectures by Schelling, met famous writers and visited Goethe, Schiller, Wieland, Herder, Kotzebue, and others in nearby Weimar, translated German poetry, and published explanations of Kantian philosophy, especially for a British journal, the *Monthly Register*.[78]

Schlegel and Caroline separated and in 1803 finally divorced; Caroline, having been involved with Friedrich Schelling, married him and lived with him, mostly in Würzburg and Munich, until her death in 1809. Caroline Michaelis-Böhmer-Schlegel-Schelling thus lived a tempestuous life, one characterized by many of the same conflicts we see not only in her childhood friends but also in Mary Wollstonecraft. Wives, mothers, lovers, writers, critics, translators, republicans: their lives register changes in the horizons of women's expectations and roles that emerged as possibilities in this period, but that were thwarted not only by antirevolutionary backlash—the most common explanation—but also by the very ideologies that should have offered independence and freedom.[79]

7. Joseph Johnson and the Anti-Napoleonic Fitness Fad

The kind of interiority and transcendence that Mary Wollstonecraft lent to her writings was not prevalent in all the German translations published by Joseph Johnson; indeed, her "ultra-radical" approach, as I have suggested, was first and foremost a response to her perception of woman's untenable gender position in that period. After the French Terror and the fall of Maximilien Robespierre, the increasing military power of the French called forth other styles of response. I would like to draw attention to one in particular, a text that carried substantial ideological force despite its focus on physical culture: the exercise manual *Gymnastik für die Jugend*, published by the Schnepfenthal press in 1793 and brought out by Johnson in 1800 as *Gymnastics for Youth*.[80] After initially supporting the French Revolution and suffering disappointment in the excesses of the Terror, Johnson sought through this translation to promote progressive scientific approaches to physical culture in England even as he joined an international effort to promote fitness as a means of countering increasing French encroachment. British interest in German publications, so often seen around the year 1800 solely in terms of philosophical writings, is shown to have a broader scope and wider range of impulses.

Johnson had ongoing continental connections, and his noteworthy interest in translating German books was most influenced by his close association with Henry Fuseli, a Swiss artist and writer who became a trusted literary consultant and lifelong friend from the 1760s on.[81] Fuseli maintained ties to Swiss authors, for instance the physiognomist Johann Kaspar Lavater, whose *Aphorisms on Man* he translated for Johnson in 1788. Johnson brought out Goethe's *Iphigenia in Tauris* (1793) and Schiller's *Fiesco; or, the Genoese Conspiracy* (1796) as well as works by less celebrated but popular authors. Johnson's connections with the Hamburg booksellers James and William Remnant, for instance, led to the publication of Leonhard Wächter (pseudonym Veit Weber) and Wieland; he supplied Samuel Taylor Coleridge with a letter of introduction to William Remnant—along with an order for books—when Coleridge traveled to Hamburg in 1798.[82] All the while Johnson published notices about German literary productions in his critical periodical the *Analytical Review* (1788–98).

After Johnson brought out the *Elements of Morality,* the Schnepfenthal press reciprocated by translating Wollstonecraft's *Vindication of the Rights of Woman*, which Johnson had published in 1792, as *Rettung der Rechte des Weibes* (1793).[83] These reciprocal translations reveal a mutual effort undertaken between Johnson's circle and the instructors of the Schnepfenthal institution to promote transnational reform through progressive pedagogies. Surprisingly, however, far from being interpreted as promoting a liberal sociopolitics and influencing supporters of women's self-reliance, GutsMuths's exercise book has been viewed by some historians as a harbinger of reaction in the Napoleonic period and beyond. It therefore becomes helpful to evaluate the historiography surrounding GutsMuths and the translations of his *Gymnastics.* To determine the meaning of Johnson's publication, it is necessary to "follow the actors" in the vein of Latour; this helps us to dodge a restricted, nation-based evaluation of this text that otherwise leads to an inevitable story about the construction of not only German but also British national identity.

Indeed, GutsMuths's text has been evaluated narrowly, most recently being pegged as launching German fascination with sports training, a fascination, as Michael Sosulski and others have argued, that led to Nazi youth programs and the athletic obsessions of the German Democratic Republic. Sosulski defines his historical and narrative trajectory by considering GutsMuths not merely the grandfather of school gymnastics, as commentators have long claimed, but also the grandfather of German national identity-building, concluding that, "Whether we consider East German athletic pride and win-at-all costs mentality regarding the Olympics, National Socialist promotion of amateur sports and the accompanying fetishization of the well-toned human physique, or the [Friedrich] Jahn-inspired gymnastic festivals that continued throughout the nineteenth and well into the twentieth century . . . the idea of constructing, recovering, or strengthening nationhood through physical exercise and achievement has inarguably been characteristic of German attempts at self-definition throughout the modern era."[84] Kai Reinhart and Michael Krüger similarly lay at GutsMuths's and the Philanthropists' door the idea of sports as a means of inculcating the discipline, bodily strength, and obedience necessary for sustaining dictatorship. Reinhart and Krüger engage the theories of Michel Foucault regarding discipline and the state to discuss Hitler and then to focus on late-twentieth-century East Germany.[85] These interpretations therefore identify GutsMuths's book as a contribution to a German *Sonderweg* or "special path." I will not discuss *twentieth-century* German history or enter the long-standing debate about whether a *Sonderweg* existed in the period of World Wars I and II; it is beyond the scope of this study. I do, however, wish to suggest that for a discussion of GutsMuths's 1793 book, the notion of the special path is too narrow and a look at transfer suggests why.

Although there are passages in GutsMuths's book that support ideas about the disciplinary power of gymnastics, and while there is no doubt of his influence on later German proponents of gymnastics, selective use of the text and of isolated quotations constitutes a unidimensional and therefore ultimately incomplete evaluation of GutsMuths. Moreover it encourages in readers a prejudgment of GutsMuths's text based on subsequent events. Perhaps responding to this reading, and to what are perceived as tendentious interpretations, opposing historians have sought to raise GutsMuths's reputation through sunnier but equally narrow interpretations: they argue that GutsMuths's book promoted a generous cosmopolitanism, spurred democratization, and encouraged peaceful competition inspired by ancient practices, ultimately lending impetus to the revival of the Olympic Games.[86]

A broader survey of the cultural impacts of GutsMuths's gymnastics book, a view of the *terrains vastes*, enables a more nuanced interpretation that finds a route between debunking and deification. GutsMuths's activities and writings had a multivalent impact, and, seen embedded in the context of European and American events, demonstrate shifts in ideas about politics, gender, and nation for which we ought to account. Although GutsMuths is a figure crucial to the history of gymnastics, and while his methods were central to the adoption of physical education in much of the Western world, it would be precipitate to call *Gymnastik für die Jugend* a spur to reactionary political activity or even to class his early work with that of the nationalist "exercise father" Friedrich Jahn in generating German paramilitary organizations.

GutsMuths's *Gymnastik für die Jugend* inspired modern gymnastics programs across Europe and America. It was grounded in Lockean psychology and Rousseauian ideas about natural education, and these were developed in Germany among the Philanthropist pedagogues. GutsMuths practiced this pedagogy at the famous Schnepfenthal school founded by Salzmann. He taught physical education there and published *Gymnastik für die Jugend* based on exercises he undertook with the pupils. GutsMuths's program aimed to increase the strength of different muscle groups, promote balance and mobility, refine eye-hand coordination, expand the breath, improve the circulation, and above all render the body capable of the exertion that daily life might demand of it.

Henry Crabb Robinson, the British writer, visited the Schnepfenthal school in 1804. He commented:

> Salzmann has made himself generally known by the very elaborate and solicitous attention he pays to the gymnastical part of education, by the anti-disciplinarian principles, and by the universal tendency and direction of the studies. I saw that the boys were healthy, happy, and courageous. And Salzmann seemed to have succeeded in the difficult task . . . of giving liberty and repressing licentiousness. The boys are on no occasions struck,—this is a fundamental law. Another is to give them freedom in everything not obviously dangerous. They botanize and study natural history, and take long journeys with their preceptors on foot over the mountains. They climb trees, jump over hedges, swim, skate, &c., &c., and, as far as general culture of the active powers is concerned, there is much to be applauded, but I fear solid learning is neglected.[87]

Crabb Robinson was only one among many prominent visitors to Schnepfenthal interested in its progressive pedagogy.

Given its contemporary status as a progressive document, how is it that GutsMuths's *Gymnastics for Youth* has been described as reactionary, protonationalist, and militaristic? This conclusion is largely based on subsequent events, particularly Napoleonic occupation and the activities of Friedrich Jahn, called "Turnvater Jahn" or the father of German exercise. Jahn was a visitor to Schnepfenthal in 1807; perhaps inspired by GutsMuths he developed his own ideas that he wrote up nine years later in *Die Deutsche Turnkunst* (*The German Art of Exercise,* 1816). But there was no contact between the two men for the rest of their careers, and while they occasionally expressed respect for each other's work in public, they consistently sought to promote their own different visions of physical culture and education.[88] Jahn's version was decidedly more militaristic. Under Jahn's influence gymnastics indeed became a nation-building enterprise in the early nineteenth century: Jahn rejected the foreign term gymnastics and instead used the old German word "Turnen." He organized a system of clubs, called *Turnvereine,* and staged gymnastics meets at his outdoor exercise grounds at the Hasenheide where participants numbering in the hundreds would demonstrate stunts. Jahn's energetic organizing, his missionary zeal, and his attention-getting gymnastics events lent a crusading aura to the activity. By 1819, after one of Jahn's gymnasts murdered the conservative writer August von Kotzebue, aristocrats felt threatened; they blamed post-Napoleonic social unrest on Jahn's operations and on the activities of the *Burschenschaften* or fraternities, who were often involved in the gymnastics programs. Jahn was imprisoned and on probation for five years and the organizations were banned—in Prussia the Turnen movement was in abeyance for twenty-three years.[89] Jahn thus represented opposition to the reactionary forces of the aristocracy.

Nonetheless, as scholars have argued, he buttressed nationalism since, as Teresa Sanislo argues, the gymnastics movement fed into militarism and nationalist ideology in the Napoleonic period: "The new gymnastics [became] a training ground for manly citizen-soldiers. . . . Propaganda, designed to stir patriotic sentiment and sacrifice, along with the Prussian king's call to arms in 1813, put heroic manliness at the center of the 'liberation' project."[90] Heikki Lempa has described how certain guerrilla warfare units within the volunteer militia of Major von Lützow were formed from Jahn's gymnasts, whom Jahn had trained to be "active, brutal, and tribal male[s] fit for guerilla attacks."[91] Jahn's organization, the fervor with which it was pursued, and its close ties to anti-Napoleonic combat fed into German militarism. It is worth noting, at the same time, that even Jahn's nationalist activities take on another aspect when seen in a transnational and colonial context: for instance, it was he who inspired the American Turnvereine and school gymnastics programs, which were first introduced in 1825 at Massachusetts's Round Hill School and then at Harvard by followers of his. He was, moreover, wooed unsuccessfully to head Boston's first public gymnasium.[92] His work was clearly viewed at that point in America as a way of successfully furthering national liberal-democratic aims, though its ultimate purport there remains to be evaluated.

GutsMuths's book, generated well ahead of Jahn's activities, was part of a dynamic process of transfer that changed its meanings and its impacts, for better or worse, so that it is best interpreted in a context that goes beyond mere German identity formation. Indeed in the Napoleonic period the text was seen as a means of preparing populations to resist invasion and occupation. *Gymnastik für die Jugend* was widely translated: into Danish (1799), into English (with a London edition in 1800, and a Philadelphia edition in 1802), French (1803), Dutch (1806) and Swedish (1813), as well as into Italian (1825) and Greek (1837).[93]

Following upon the translations, different nations developed their own institutionalized versions of GutsMuths's program, or they imported someone to develop such an operation for them, and these undertakings were generally housed in educational and military establishments, as a quick survey will demonstrate:[94] In Denmark, for example, Franz Nachtegall (1777–1847), inspired by GutsMuths's book, opened a private gymnasium, and he was then made the first director of the Institute for Military Gymnastics in 1804; subsequently as national director of gymnastics he devised the first systematic mandatory gymnastics program for schools. Pehr Ling (1766–1839), having studied gymnastics in Copenhagen with Nachtegall, moved to Sweden and developed a gymnastics system that spanned educational as well as military and medical aims. He opened the Royal Central Institute of Gymnastics in 1813, wrote manuals on gymnastics and bayonet fencing for the army, and is credited with developing Swedish massage. Ling moreover inspired massive gymnastics demonstrations called Lingiads, which took place in the 1930s and '40s and were then replaced by international Gymnaestrada festivals in 1953 that still convene every four years. In England an American-born Swiss man, Phokion Clias, was invited by the king to develop GutsMuths-inspired gymnastics programs in 1821. He taught at the royal military and naval schools as well as at the Charterhouse public school. His text *Anfangsgründe der Gymnastik oder Turnkunst* (1816) was rewritten for the English as *An Elementary Course of Gymnastics Exercises* (1823, fourth edition 1825), and Clias prefaced it by saying, "It has never been our wish to make any secret of our mode of instruction, and gratitude to the English nation especially, from whom we have received such liberal encouragement, makes us anxious to impart to them, as extensively as possible, these advantages, which have been highly appreciated on the Continent."[95] In Switzerland GutsMuths's ideas influenced Johann Heinrich Pestalozzi, who founded a famous school at Yverdon in 1805 where he taught Guts-Muths's exercises before devising his own strategies. Pestalozzi in turn inspired the Spaniard Francisco Amoros, who headed an academy in Madrid and then, after the fall of Napoleon, moved to France. There Amoros opened an outdoor gymnasium in the style of Jahn's Hasenheide and trained students, firemen, and soldiers. In 1820 he was made director of the "Gymnase normal militaire"; he published the *Manuel d'Éducation physique, gymnastique, et morale* (Paris 1830).

Such a short survey clarifies how gymnastics training, spurred by GutsMuths's method, looks remarkably similar from country to country. The British response is therefore typical. Nations in the early nineteenth century—following on the American and French Revolutions and during the Napoleonic wars—predictably desired a strong youth and a ready military; they systematized physical education in institutions that often spanned military and civilian missions. Gymnastics became an international fad that saw experts visiting foreign institutions to study methods, founding gymnasiums and school programs, devising apparatuses and new exercises, and publishing and translating texts. GutsMuths's book thus launched a far-ranging movement that, for one thing, explains why we have all grown up taking mandatory P.E.

Whatever militaristic upshot GutsMuths's book inspired among governments, however, he himself intended it as a spur to individual liberty in the Philanthropist vein. He dedicated his book to the Danish prince Fredrik, "the defender of human rights," who "with a mildness friendly to humankind broke the shackles of slavery in north and south." (Denmark in 1792 had legislated, though not yet enforced, an end to the slave trade.) Ideas of freedom for women followed. While German Philanthropist pedagogy included girls from the start,[96] and while Guts-Muths's book cursorily addressed the issue of their physical education, it was his followers who devised programs specifically for women and these were particularly notable in the British and colonial context. Phokion Clias composed a book on women's gymnastics based on his English experience, *Kalisthenie oder Uebungen zur Schoenheit und Kraft fuer Maed-chen* (1829). He inspired the work of J. A. Beaujeu and his wife, who settled in Dublin, opened a gym, and published *A Treatise on Gymnastic*

Exercises, Or Calisthenics for the Use of Young Ladies (1828). Madame Beaujeu then moved to the United States and, under the name Mrs.
Hawley, opened a Gymnasium in Boston at the corner of Tremont and Bromfield
Streets, and then moved on to New York and opened another gym on
Eighth Street. There were also French and German books on women's
exercise.[97] These texts advocated rigorous exercises for women with
the clear intention of making them agile and strong. Jan Todd writes
of Beaujeu's text: "In addition to the unusually high strength levels his
exercises required and produced, and to his apparently egalitarian attitude toward women, Beaujeu's small textbook is noteworthy in another
way. He appears to be the first author to recommend [in print] a distinct
gymnastic costume for women. . . . The available evidence suggests that
Beaujeu was *not* alone in his egalitarian approach to exercise."[98] Inspired
by these developments Catharine Beecher, in the United States, actively
promoted exercise for women at her Hartford Female Seminary in the
1820s and eventually published a volume devoted entirely to it: *Physiology and Calisthenics: For Schools and Families* (1856), which broadened its
domestic and institutional application.

Consequently a view of GutsMuths's *Gymnastics for Youth* and its repercussions allows one to reach a number of conclusions that shed light on
British-German cultural transfer at work within Euro-American movements. First, it draws attention to the ways in which most Western nations
functionalized GutsMuths's work. They systematized physical training
across their schools (before Germans did) in order to further their own
educational and military goals, which they then tailored to their own
perceived needs. Second, we see that it is problematical, in the context
of cultural transfer, to argue that GutsMuths's book supplies stepping-
stones for a late eighteenth-century German *Sonderweg*. GutsMuths wrote
not only for Germans; moreover, other nations, inspired by him, promoted athletic bodies with the calculation that, given certain political
necessities, those bodies could be switched into fighting ones. A careful parsing of transnational political valences becomes crucial. Although
in the twentieth century Nazi youth movements certainly drew on the
by-then long tradition of German gymnastics and physical education,
nonetheless, a close look at the early nineteenth century reveals how military programs with careful physical training existed across the Western
world, and in those countries fitness found its way into daily life. Organizations promoting exercise proliferated. YMCAs in the United States, for
example, took inspiration and sometimes even derived real estate from
the German American Turnvereine, which had been inspired by Jahn's

more explicitly militaristic exercise program. Physical fitness became integrated into a larger economic and moral project intended to counteract the negative, deracinating effects of capitalist expansion, as young men leaving the country to seek work in the cities were offered not only equipped gyms but also housing and Bible study. Far from a German *Sonderweg*, we see European and American nations creating parallel programs that communicated across borders and across the years.

Third, a German-only view of GutsMuths leads to a proliferation of European *Sonderwege*, most notably a British one. The bifurcated understanding of British "sports" versus "exercise," for example, needs to be interrogated in this context. Given the transfer history revealing the role played by Phokion Clias and others in contributing exercise elements to British training, the touted British preference for sports and games over calisthenics should not be viewed as a clear dichotomy and a British *Sonderweg*, as has been suggested.[99] Significantly, the desire to define Britishness via physical culture has resulted in privileging the one term over the other. Thus the rugby-playing public schoolboy conveys a singular and appealing British identity: a "sport," like rugby, becomes something healthful and desirable, good clean fun, while "exercise," by the logic of the binary, comes to represent the unfun activity of the Other—that is, the compensatory striving of girls, the wannabe pastime of the middling classes, or the driven drudgery of Germans.

But of course "sport" existed in Germany too; the nation did not limit itself to dreary exercises, and we should resist the unhelpful reinscription of national stereotypes. In 1796 GutsMuths himself published a book on games called *Spiele und Erholung des Körpers und des Geistes* (*Games and the Recuperation of the Body and the Spirit*). He also produced a text on swimming, *Kleine Lehrbuch der Schwimmkunst* (*Little Textbook on the Art of Swimming*), that appeared in 1798.[100] In 1801 he brought out a book on making things by hand, *Mechanische Nebenbeschäftigungen für Jünglinge und Männer* (*Mechanical Avocations for Youths and Men*). These later books supplemented the *Gymnastics* by furthering types of physical culture endorsed in Philanthropist theory and they demonstrate the broad view that GutsMuths maintained throughout this period about what constituted physical mastery. GutsMuths also published a second, fully revised edition of *Gymnastik für die Jugend* in 1804, probably in the hope that his system, which had met with such widespread application abroad, would finally be adopted at home. And in 1817, twenty-four years after the first publication of *Gymnastik für die Jugend,* two years after Napoleon's defeat, and one year after the publication of Jahn's popular *Deutsche Turnkunst,*

GutsMuths himself published a book called *Turnbuch für die Söhne des Vaterlandes* (*Exercise Book for the Sons of the Fatherland*, 1817). This nationalistic book nonetheless represents an attempt to distinguish between Jahn-inspired *Turnen*, which he calls a preparation for soldiers, and *Gymnastics*, a practice of general physical education that he argues can serve as a preparation for *Turnen* without depriving students of their human right to free individual development ("ohne das heilige Jugend- und Menschenrecht der freien Entwickelung zu verletzen"). Even while furthering the new nationalist tone, then, GutsMuths would appear to be making a space for individualist Philanthropic approaches. In any event, GutsMuths's writings after *Gymnastik für die Jugend* did not have the same international impact. Though GutsMuths wanted to make money on sequels (he needed to finance a daughter's dowry), and though he felt that these works encouraged as yet unexplained categories and strategies of movement, international readers were not interested to the same extent. Apparently *Gymnastics for Youth* had already done the cultural work those international readers required: it had supplied ways of systematizing physical training for schools and soldiers.

Consequently I question the readiness of historians to interpret GutsMuths as paving the early nineteenth-century German *Sonderweg*, as leading the way in defining early nationalism, and as aiming to initiate a masculinist and militaristic German identity. As I have shown, a consideration of cultural transfer suggests that a similar story could be told for Britain and any number of other European and American nations, ones that applied GutsMuths's methods before Germans did, continued on to create intense athletic-training programs, promoted sports through cradle-to-grave organizations, and staged spectacular athletic festivals. Historiography becomes skewed if GutsMuths's work is viewed narrowly in a confined national context, and if questions of gender are left unaddressed. His determined focus on physical mastery combined with the idea of the human rights of the individual theoretically left a space for the development of women and people of all classes, something later writers interested in physical culture took into account. By looking at the *terrains vastes*, by "following the actors" in the manner of Latour, and by considering decisions that appear to have dead-ended, the historian sees broad European and American trends, with the result that local challenges are set in relief, historical shifts are brought to the fore, the road theoretically conceived but not taken until later—women's nonmilitary participation, for example—alters the frame, and realignments in GutsMuths's thinking during the Napoleonic period, as evidenced in his later publications, come to light and alert us to ideological shifts. Recognizing these contingencies adds depth to our understanding not only of Guts-Muths but also of Philanthropist pedagogy, the place of sport and exercise in nation-building projects across the developed world, the involving role of women, and the tricky ideological shifts between progressivism and reaction as well as internationalism and nationalism in the period.

Johnson's translation of GutsMuths was dedicated to Thomas Beddoes, a fellow supporter of the French Revolution before the Terror, an author of antiwar pamphlets in the 1790s, a man who had studied at the University of Göttingen, and founding director of the Bristol Pneumatic Institution, where he conducted experiments with gases in an attempt to find treatments for lung ailments.[101] Patients afflicted with consumption were particularly to benefit from a gymnastics program. Johnson's translation of GutsMuths's text thus promoted enlightened scientific and educational ends, sought to enhance human development by cultivating individual well-being and autonomy, even as the book itself, an actor in a Latourian network, became an international player in a project for public health and national strength.

* * *

Mary Wollstonecraft and the Göttingen professors' daughters, attempting to get beyond personal difficulties, also became part of a larger network. First energized by the French Revolution, they positioned themselves within liberal circles that allowed them to publish their feminist visions of social change. Cultural transfer in the form of translation facilitated the articulation of their favored political alternatives. With the Terror and the Napoleonic wars, however, they became deeply disillusioned and were constrained to seek spaces of equilibrium and safety—German lands were literally overrun by the French, and Wollstonecraft sought metaphysical transcendence. In both Germany and Britain, faith in the consequences of the American Revolution nonetheless remained undiminished for many, and the recently created United States came to represent a place of potential freedom that beckoned some to move there and start afresh, sometimes in utopian experiments that could be undertaken in a republican context. Thus travel offered an alternative way of moving beyond European troubles, of conceiving of different modes of being, and travel literature, discussed in the next chapters, allowed writers a discursive ground on which to examine the consequences of the strongly gendered, militarized culture created through the wars of Napoleon and by those determined to stop him.

CHAPTER 3

Representing Vesuvius

Northern European Tourists and the Napoleonic Culture of War

The volcano would appear an irresistible metaphor for social upheaval, but it came to denote political eruption generally only in the late eighteenth century with reference to the French Revolution and the Napoleonic wars. Writers talked about a "political volcano" that "had broken out in France, and was sweeping over Europe like a sea of lava"; "Um jene Zeit war Frankreich namentlich ein fortbrennender politischer Vulkan"; "L'Europe . . . savait bien que la France est le volcan politique du monde."[1] The comparison was employed both by those for as well as those against political and armed conflict. On the one hand the volcano metaphor was used to incite soldiers and convince the public of the need for battle, of the excitement of a sublime display of might, of the natural, periodic quality of eruption, and of the renewing and regenerating consequences of those released powers.[2] Georg Forster, representing the Mainz Republic, wrote from Paris: "The lava of the Revolution flows majestically and no longer spares anything"; "You see the volcano is not yet silent; the earth still quakes under our feet."[3] With the bloodshed of the Terror, the massacres of the Vendée, and the slaughter of the Napoleonic wars, such radical and liberal thinkers became deeply disillusioned. However, the language of eruption had entered the European vocabulary and came to be used in various political contexts throughout the nineteenth century. It even made its way to Latin America, where Simón Bolívar, after the defeat of Spain, termed the oppressed masses "a great volcano [that] lies at our feet."[4]

Even as the volcano metaphor conveyed excitement, it served as criti-cism. It expressed indignation at the violence, chaos, and unpredictable and uncontrollable forces unleashed in battle, resulting in social tur-moil, destruction, and death, with future eruptions always to be feared. A late nineteenth-century commentator concluded: "FRANCE has been the political volcano of Europe. . . . The lava-torrents of human blood that have accompanied its frequent eruptions have, each in its turn, either destroyed one system of government or marked the inauguration of another. . . . Is the volcano extinct, or is it smouldering still?"[5] In 1842 a British traveler to Germany judged that "France has been from age to age . . . something more than leaven; it has been the political volcano of Europe, hurling forth on all sides its burning cinders and scalding lava. No country has felt this so much as Germany: it is probable that none is destined still to feel it more."[6]

Vesuvius in particular came to be associated with the Napoleonic wars, since Naples was an important flashpoint.[7] In 1799, the French general Jean Étienne Championnet attempted to create a "Parthenope-an Republic" of the Kingdom of Naples, which resulted in a gathering insurgency that later reunited and feistily opposed Napoleon's inroads from 1806 to 1810. As punishment entire villages were burnt and the inhabitants ruthlessly slaughtered, in a pattern that had been employed a decade earlier to squelch the rebellion in the French Vendée.[8] Nea-politans themselves were compared with their eruptive terrain: "the most dreadful revolts of the Italians against foreign occupation took place in those torrid regions, where it seems that the force and brutal riot of men vie with the subterranean fires and ruinous tremors of the earth and sea"; "Neapolitans, like their volcanic country, are never in a state of repose."[9]

Susan Sontag's popular novel *The Volcano Lover* (1992) took up the theme of Neapolitan explosivity, using Vesuvius to weave together images of eighteenth-century political, scientific, affective, aesthetic, and military eruptions with a focus on William Hamilton, British envoy to Naples from 1764 to 1800, who avidly studied earthquakes and volcanoes, completed nearly a hundred ascents of Vesuvius, and eagerly collected antiquities. He published *Observations on Mount Vesuvius, Mount Etna, and Other Volca-noes* (1772) as well as *Campi Phlegraei* (1776), a fantastic folio volume illus-trated by Pietro Fabris with fifty-nine hand-colored copper engravings, an extravagant forerunner of the modern coffee-table book. Sontag's novel explores the erotics of Hamilton's obsessive volcano-observation, artifact collecting, and active role as host to travelers of all nationalities.

He regularly displayed his vases and also his wife, Emma, who performed "Attitudes," solo tableaux vivants representing moments from ancient myths by using as props only a shawl and her long hair.[10] Emma Hamilton took as a lover Lord Horatio Nelson, the celebrated hero of the Battle of the Nile (1798) who later commanded the victorious Battle of Trafalgar (1805) in which he was killed. Exploring the full range of the volcano metaphor, Sontag thus included not only the sexual passions of the protagonists, the obsessive hunt for rare antiquities, and the risky pursuit of geological knowledge, but also the bloody counterrevolution in Naples and the pitched sea battles involving Admiral Nelson.

Sontag consciously followed in the footsteps of Swiss author Germaine de Staël, whose travel-novel *Corinne, or Italy* (1807) demonstrated how Vesuvius as symbol could critique Napoleon's dictatorial, military culture as well as the social inequity and gender-role oppression bred by it. The volcano provides the dramatic setting for the turning point of the novel.[11] There the main characters, Corinne and Oswald (the British Lord Nelvil), finally reveal their backgrounds and confess their secrets. Oswald's is sorrow: a French woman's betrayal and the death of his father, with consequent guilt and remorse making it impossible for him to marry Corinne. These dark feelings are attributed to excessive paternal authority and oppressive social norms that inevitably debilitate a sensitive and decent person, and they are likened to the relentlessly encroaching lava the pair sees killing everything in its way. "The river of fire which was flowing down from Vesuvius . . . had a keen effect on Oswald's troubled imagination"; it revealed "a funereal colour . . . dark, like the picture of hell in one's imagination."[12] Vesuvius represents deadly sexual politics, the forging of a gender ideology suffocating to Oswald, stifling to Lucile (the proper young English girl he marries), and fatal to Corinne.

Napoleon exiled Staël, who used her ten-year period of banishment to gain knowledge, write, and make friends and allies on her travels; "I became European," she said. Angelica Goodden has recently viewed Staël's biography in terms of her exile and her challenges to Napoleon: "At Coppet she assembled a group of friends whose limited real power was belied by their ability to goad and incite; in Germany she put together an intellectual and artistic arsenal (later given literary form in *De l'Allemagne*) that seemed to threaten Bonaparte's imperialist ambitions; and she turned Italy into a living denial of his hegemony."[13] The use of Vesuvius in *Corinne* thus formed part of a larger transnational political project. It is a deadly obstacle at the center of the novel's landscape; it

represents forces with which the characters try to cope but which ultimately control and stifle their lives. Corinne the character, representing
Italy, portrays the devastation following revolution; *Corinne* the novel,
offering a tour through the country, displaying the admirable monuments of antiquity, argues the need for sound rule and just institutions
as the way of creating a truly free people. The emphasis is on civilization
over eruption, reform over revolution, as in women's and society's best
interests.

1. Situating Travel Accounts

Indeed, Staël's novel—both fiction and travelogue—employs Vesuvius in
ways similar to nonfiction travel accounts of Naples at the end of the eighteenth and the beginning of the nineteenth centuries. In this chapter I
will consider these travel narratives within the *terrains vastes* to show how
British-German transfer was affected during the unsettling Napoleonic
period and after. Differences between the two northern countries reced-
ed as mutual opposition to French aggression and occupation came to
the fore. British and German tourists, able to travel again following the
end of hostilities, moved in a landscape that announced their place in
a new order whose strict economic, political, and gender organization
as yet had no name but could be felt, absorbed, and inscribed. Consequently, as in Staël's novel, the travel accounts of Naples offer strikingly
gendered discussions of Vesuvius. They point to disparate understandings of power and agency and query the place of affect in a changing
sociopolitical and economic context. Travel writers employ Vesuvius to
address simultaneously the personal and political: British and German
men and women register their distinct responses to international and
sexual politics in the context of the increasing masculinism, militarism,
and nationalism of their time. Cultural transfer in the form of travel
writings about Vesuvius in this period therefore reveals meanings that
go well beyond individuals' experience of Italian antiquity and *la dolce
vita* to analyses of individual, national, and gender identity within the
turbulent power politics of a restive Europe.

The volcano in general gained its political meaning in consequence
of what David A. Bell has termed Napoleon's culture of "total war": "a
kind of warfare whose scale had little or no precedent, whether in the
mobilization of population and resources, the ambitious and ill-defined
war aims, the demonization of entire enemy populations, or the threats

to the French leadership in case of defeat. It was a perceived war to the death."[14] Women were rendered peripheral to the masculine military culture formed in the period 1794–1814. Earlier, in the aristocratic culture of combat, women actually played a part. Men were urged "to fight bravely and gloriously but also with restraint, with self-control, with honor"; rulers were first and foremost warriors, who led their men in battle and recognized advantages to limiting the scope and damage. As a common occurrence, war was viewed as an ordinary part of the social order, and women were active supporters and even muses: aristocratic officers carried on amours, wrote their lovers poetry about battlefield valor and conducted epistolary flirtations between skirmishes, while wives, with their servants, followed the troops to help sustain the war effort. Bell reports that General John Burgoyne's defeat at Saratoga in the American Revolution was sometimes blamed "on the 2000 women who accompanied his 4700-man army."[15]

If women became peripheral to the new culture of total war (except, as Napoleon told Staël, to birth soldiers[16]), they were also relative newcomers to the Grand Tour and were certainly a minority among climbers of Vesuvius. This meant, however, that they had some space to innovate in their travel reports and to formulate critique, since expectations were not well defined. Men apparently found less room for maneuver. Despite their varied nationalities and political persuasions, male travel-narrators, perhaps in the way of soldiers compelled to fight in Napoleonic conflicts, generally ended up employing the modern tactics and modes necessary to prevail: in their narrative accounts of Vesuvius they grasped for the romantic sublime.

It should be noted that though I am suggesting that gender differences in the travelogues trump national ones, I am concentrating on writers' specific responses to the volcano in its Neapolitan setting at a particular point in history. Although scholars have carefully analyzed Grand Tour travel narratives in general with regard to questions of gender, they have not come to a consensus on the meaning of differences between male- and female-authored travel accounts. This is not surprising, given the enormous geographical and temporal scope of such analyses; however, scholars do agree that the accounts record gender differences. Barbara Korte says that female and male authors "share many characteristics" but that women "associate journeys with an escape from 'normal' life" and that their narratives "express a counter-discourse to this life."[17] In *Ladies of the Grand Tour* Brian Dolan anatomizes women's responses to the many issues they confronted—education, fashion, politics, manners,

art, health—and concludes that overall "men's travel accounts are preoccupied with conquest, connoisseurship and domestication of the wild,
[while] women's narratives record more diverse experiences concerned
with individual growth, independence and health."[18] Chloe Chard notes
that female travelers could "claim an additional authority by reference
to their gender" as they enjoyed a "privileged opportunity to enquire
into female manners," and she argues that a "conjunction between the
antique and the feminine" was established; however, she ultimately sees
male and female authors operating within the same discursive template,
which shapes their responses to the extent that foreign women become
general "metaphors for difference, unfamiliarity and mysterious other-
ness."[19] Elizabeth Bohls argues that female travelers, unlike men, were
empowered by class but disempowered by gender; they "did not fit the
traveler's image as heroic explorer, scientist, or authoritative cultural
interpreter," and as a result their travel accounts were "deeply divided."[20]
Focusing on Italy, Mirella Agorni takes note of political differences; wom-
en's "images of Italy . . . [seem] to be used instrumentally to foreground
the possibility that their egalitarian claims . . . could be legitimized by
the culture of their time."[21] I agree with Agorni that a focus on specific
subjects rather than broad responses to travel in general best allows one
to analyze how gender might work within travel narratives. Consequently
I highlight a single location at a critical sociopolitical juncture to facilitate comparison between travelers' entanglement in the discourses of
eruption.

The rhetoric of the volcano, including its use as a metaphor for political conflict and war, affected the experience and discourses of Grand
Tourists; their travel accounts reveal the mountain as means of both reinforcing and critiquing transnational cultural norms and gender roles.
That is, militarized culture inspired travel narratives that reinscribed or
challenged the gendering of Vesuvius representations, deepening the
period's obsession with sex and gender. More broadly, as Gary Kelly has
argued, such literary moves sought to define what kind of subject was to
populate the emerging liberal state, a point to which I will return below.[22]

A comparison of two related poems by Felicia Hemans, Britain's most
popular early nineteenth-century poet, will serve to demonstrate the
thematic link between the Napoleonic wars and Vesuvian eruption even
as it shows vividly the clear gender distinctions that emerged from the
encounters. "Casabianca," Hemans's best-known poem (1826), describes
a dutiful boy who stands amid shell fire on a burning ship, waiting for
his father to command him to leave his post during the Battle of the

Nile (1798). "The boy stood on the burning deck, / Whence all but him had fled; / The flame that lit the battle's wreck / Shone round him o'er the dead" (lines 1–4). Not knowing that his father has been killed, the boy persists though all others have left, and he is blasted away when the flames reach the ship's store of gunpowder. So it is not enemy fire that ultimately kills him, but "friendly" powder, a circumstance that adds to the poem's irony and pathos. On the one hand, the verses celebrate the boy's innocent loyalty to his father and his patriotism to his country; on the other hand, and more emphatically, they represent a waste of valuable life and love, as the last lines suggest: "But the noblest thing that perish'd there / Was that young faithful heart" (ll. 39–40).

Hemans's 1827 poem "The Image in Lava" likewise takes up a historical subject; it concerns the archaeological discovery at Herculaneum of the impression of a woman grasping her child, unearthed remains of the Vesuvian eruption of 79 AD. The volcano here creates a "monument," but one "cast in affection's mould" (ll. 35–36). Hemans contrasts the "human love" of the powerless mother and child, an emotion in which one can have faith, with the fleeting fame of mighty men and their institutions, epitomized by the image of the phallic "temple and tower": "Temple and Tower have moulder'd, / Empires from earth have pass'd, / And woman's heart hath left a trace / Those glories to outlast! / And childhood's fragile image, / Thus fearfully enshrined, / Survives the proud memorials rear'd / By conquerors of mankind" (ll. 5–12). Hemans's reflection on mother love came in the year her own much-loved mother died, with verses on misplaced trust perhaps recalling how her husband, a military veteran, abandoned her, pregnant with their fifth son, and moved to Italy in 1818. Her mother then helped her care for her family. Indeed men in this poem do not participate in "human love" at all; men's love of women proves as untrustworthy as men's love of fame (see esp. lines 26–28, 39–40). Hemans deploys a resonant image of a woman, not to avoid probing the actual costs of catastrophe, but in order to expose them, in order directly to critique a masculine drive for mastery that renders mother love so vulnerable.

Significantly, the poem ends on a question. The speaker asserts mother love to be "immortal" and thereby apparently only a more permanent memorial than the "temples and towers" of the conquerors. But at the same time such love gives off an "earthly glow," not a heavenly one, and it is the "ashes" that exude its "holiness." The images are surprisingly untranscendent. The speaker cannot ultimately be certain of the immortality of human love, though she desperately wishes it: "Love, human love! what art thou? . . . / Immortal, oh! immortal / Thou art, whose earthly glow / Hath given these ashes holiness—/ It must, it *must* be so!" (ll. 41–44). Susan Wolfson has noted that a Hemans poem often contains "unexpected surprises" and can be "at war with its lesson."[23] Grant Scott has suggested, "If it were not for the last line, 'The Image in Lava' might be seen as an anti-monument poem that nonetheless appropriates the rhetoric of monumentality to celebrate the immortality of its subject. But," he concludes, "the final stanza reveals a hint of skepticism."[24]

Hemans introduces a moment of skepticism shared by female travelers who visited Herculaneum. Vesuvius's threat to civilization lay not simply in its capacity to overwhelm the "temples and towers" but to wipe out the human connections that those towers existed to defend in the first place. In a down-to-earth calculation of costs, Hemans privileges human emotion and human ties and implicitly rejects the quest for transcendence. Therefore while both "Casabianca" and "The Image in Lava" depict a failure on the part of parents to protect their children (and themselves) from deadly forces, the failure in "Casabianca" is one of utter loss, the destruction of innocent life through a ruinous masculine war that, in a bitter irony, dispatches a father who cannot do his duty to his own dutiful son. "The Image in Lava" in contrast conveys heroism in the mother's final embraces of her child and explicitly condemns the masculine forces that pretend—but fail—to sustain civilization. Hemans is by no means the only writer to make this argument; a similar theme is simultaneously and extensively treated by Mary Shelley in *The Last Man* (1826), in which natural catastrophe exacerbated by war nearly wipes out human civilization.[25]

Gary Kelly implies the comparison with Shelley's novel as he helpfully contrasts Felicia Hemans's aim of limning a "Romantic death" that is meaningful in the face of the "mass death" of the Revolution and Napoleonic Wars:

> Romantic death . . . was increasingly set against and in relationship to several other figures. These include natural cataclysms such as storm, flood, and volcanic eruption; biological disaster such as pandemics; and historical catastrophes such as the fall of empires and the disappearance of entire peoples and civilizations into the abyss of oblivion. These figures were deployed in literature and culture mainly in relation to forms of mass death; they embodied widespread anxiety about the process of history as read through the prolonged global crisis of Revolutionary and Napoleonic disruption and violence, which was

perceived at the time as an unprecedented and profoundly transformative world-historical event. Romantic death was figured as meaningful death and set against the meaninglessness of mass death, which
in turn was widely used to summarize or represent the Revolution and
the Napoleonic adventure.[26]

Kelly sees Hemans's depictions of good, Romantic death "serving the
liberal ideology of the autonomous sovereign subject,"[27] in contrast to
the illiberal implications of mass death, but this view is complicated by
the insistence on human connection that recurs consistently in women's
writings: the sovereign liberal subject is not an individualist one nor even
simply independent. The mother's heroism in "The Image in Lava" con-
sisted in the loving embrace of her child, not independent defiance of
overwhelming power. The sublimity required for representing the sovereign self tends not to be forthcoming in women's works, as they seek to
redefine heroism. Both Hemans's poems and Shelley's long novel were
written after Napoleon's death but in the midst of a British crisis leading
up to the Reform Bill of 1832 that threatened to unleash revolutionary
activity if social change were not forthcoming.[28] These female authors
were concerned to warn against and forestall the development in Britain
of a culture of combat that could result in mass violence. Their position, however, was problematical since the figures of bonding sentiment
and harmonious domesticity used to counter brutal images of violence
and death failed to introduce a hoped-for era of communal peace, and
instead circumscribed the authors' social influence through domestication and privatization and finally led to their devaluation as writers altogether. The effect of their work was indeed, as Gary Kelly has argued, the
delineation of the modern liberal subject, even though, I would suggest,
they had harbored hopes of a communal, utopian end.

2. Containment versus Instrumentalization

Prerevolutionary accounts of Vesuvius foreshadowed many of Hemans's
and Shelley's concerns with loss and destruction, so that pressing postrevolutionary themes regarding war, bravery, and death dovetailed easily with and could supplement the treatment of disaster brought up
by images of the volcano. In the earlier, prerevolutionary accounts we
see contrasting sublime versus sentimental experiences of Vesuvius following upon Edmund Burke's analysis of the sublime and the beauti-

ful and William Gilpin's popular notion of the picturesque. Employing these discourses, many female travel writers sought to debunk myths of a feminine nature, which they contained—framed and distanced—via the picturesque, while the majority of male Grand Tourists engaged in self-fashioning via the sublime. Consequently Vesuvius, after the revolution, became a natural locus for debating the concatenation of politics and sexual politics, with containment of the mountain's threat emphasized on the one hand and its instrumentalization stressed on the other.

The volcano offered a climax to the Grand Tour. Naples generally represented the southernmost point of the journey, after which tourists turned around to head home, and the ascent of Mount Vesuvius was the culmination. In 1786 British tourist Hester Lynch Piozzi began a typical ascent of Vesuvius, which involved being strapped up and carried by porters. Usually visitors stopped halfway up the mountain at the Hermitage, a hostel that provided welcome refreshment: a wine called Lacrimae Christi, grown on the slopes of Vesuvius in the superb volcanic soil. Piozzi, a sociable woman, was pleased to find that one of the so-called monks at the Hermitage was a Frenchman who had been a hairdresser in London. She hoped to prolong her conversation with him, but she had to accompany her group to the crater. And she was not impressed. Like many other women, Piozzi found a way to deflect the force of the volcano—in her case, through a worldly wise attitude: "That the situation of the crater changed in this last eruption is of little consequence; it will change and change again I suppose. The wonder is, that nobody gets killed by venturing so near, while red-hot stones are flying about them so."[29]

By contrast most male tourists actually hoped to witness an eruption firsthand and perhaps to absorb the power of the mountain. It was a means of self-fashioning, which of course had been one of the traditional purposes of the Grand Tour for generations of young gentlemen. Maximilien Misson, already in the late seventeenth century, observed male travelers who sought to enhance blasts by carrying gunpowder up to the crater, where they "dug mines to have the pleasure of blowing up bigger rocks."[30] John Moore reported that there were "young English gentlemen betting, who should venture farthest, or remain longest, near the mouth of the volcano."[31] Proximity to the largest possible explosions of the volcano was clearly the lure. Johann Wolfgang von Goethe explained tourists' desire for proximity: "a present danger has something attractive about it and encourages people's spirit of contradiction to defy it."[32] It offers an invigorating sense that one might be a match for nature's power, able to contend successfully with it hand to hand.

Goethe spoke the language of the sublime, long viewed as capable of enhancing a sense of self. In *A Philosophical Enquiry into the Origin of our Ideas of the Sublime and Beautiful* Edmund Burke drew on (pseudo-) Longinus to point out that "[w]hatever . . . tends to raise a man in his own opinion, produces a sort of swelling and triumph that is extremely grateful to the human mind," and this kind of self-consciousness is especially derived from the sublime experience, where "the mind always claim[s] to itself some part of the dignity and importance of the things which it contemplates."[33] Burke gendered the sublime as masculine, identified by strength, depth, and extent; it possessed the power to invoke terror and concerned self-preservation. In contrast the beautiful, with smooth curves and soft colors, inspired love, reassured, concerned the social, and was viewed as feminine.[34] Burke influenced the writings of not only Goethe but also Kant, Schiller, Coleridge, and others, who posited that the sublime elevated the human soul through contact with the infinite. An individual observing nature or art would overcome the initial awe by identifying with the creative power that formed the object.[35] On one ascent Goethe timed the pauses between eruptions and ran to the edge of the crater planning to exit before the next blast. He lost count, however, and he and his guide, with stones flying about and noxious fumes choking them, nearly failed to clamber out.[36]

The postrevolutionary period brought a heightened and more explicitly gendered rhetoric. For no one was the desire of proximity to the volcano greater than for Percy Shelley, who traveled to Naples with Mary Shelley and Clare Clairmont in 1818. Mary was depressed when she visited Naples, which explains why she did not say much about it in her journal or letters. The illness of Percy, she wrote, "[took] away from our gusto for this place." However, Percy himself ignored his pain and reveled in the "impressive exhibition of the energies of nature." To him, the hardened lava was "an actual image of the waves of the sea, changed into hard black stone by enchantment"; the summit showed "the most horrible chaos that can be imagined." Only in conclusion did Percy admit that he felt terribly ill: "I should have enjoyed the scenery on my return, but that they conducted me, I know not how, to the hermitage in a state of intense bodily suffering."[37] After pages of sensory wealth Percy spoke of his pain as though it were the expected concomitant of the tortured landscape he had just witnessed. Even his illness united him with the powerful mountain. As in his poem "Mont Blanc," Percy's experience was a sublime event in which, in tune with Kantian notions, natural energies came to elevate the poet's status: "And what were thou, and earth,

and stars, and sea, / If to the human mind's imaginings / Silence and
solitude were vacancy?" ("Mont Blanc," ll. 142–44).

The literary critic Marlon Ross suggests how mountains supplied sublime elevation to Romantic poets. Climbing, he notes, tests

> the power and limits of self, it stresses the solitude of self-questing
> and pits the self against nature's power. The height of the mountain
> represents both the ever-spiraling ascent of imagination and the ever-
> present threat of falling, the loss of self-identity, the reabsorption into
> nature's overriding power. It is from mountains that prophets pro-
> claim their truth; for the poet-prophet the mountain symbolizes the
> necessary solitude of the leaders of men and the necessary stance of
> truth—its transcendence, its elusiveness, and its immense might. It is
> another metaphor of masculine potency, which, through association,
> reinvests the poetic vocation with power and influence.[38]

The identity conferred by the mountain is consistently masculine and,
in the late eighteenth- and early nineteenth-century travel accounts,
bestowed upon a male subject. Consequently it makes sense to invoke
the concept of a "masculine sublime" in this context.

By contrast Mary's reactions on the mountains they toured consistently differed from Percy's. Social events and social ideas emerged for
Mary from the trip to Chamonix that inspired "Mont Blanc," whereas
for Percy "the glaciers" represented forces of nature to be tapped by the
solitary poet.[39] Writing about that trip, as Meena Alexander points out,
Mary "consciously maintain[ed] the fabric of shared life" in her journal account: the Mer de Glace was not simply barren, frozen ice but
was surrounded by vegetation, and she and Percy joined the substantial tour group ("beaucoup de monde") for a picnic. Moreover, in the
Mer de Glace scene in *Frankenstein*, when Victor meets the monster, he is
called upon to "Remember, that I am thy creature," that he has responsibility for the being he has placed on earth and cannot continue in
his self-absorbed, removed state. Naples, despite the lack of enthusiasm
expressed for it in Mary's journal and letters, became a significant location in her fiction. *The Last Man* begins there, with the narrator's visit to
the cavern of the Cumaean Sibyl. There "Sibylline leaves" and pieces of
bark, inscribed with verbal fragments, provide the material translated by
the narrator to create a story of natural disaster and cultural devastation.
Verney, the central figure, may be alone at the conclusion of the novel,
but it is far from the artist's apotheosis Percy fantasizes; he wanders aim-

lessly around the ruins as Mary, depressed, must have paced Pompeii and Herculaneum. He visits libraries where poetical productions are rendered meaningless without readers. Mary Shelley's use of her travel experiences is, as in *Frankenstein,* utterly distinct from the ways her husband channeled those adventures.

Percy Shelley's view also differed from that of the naturalists. Marlon Ross has explained how, on the one hand, the Romantic poet identified with the quest of the scientist since he "searches for laws that he takes to be natural and universal, and, as inventor, he originates powerful ways of applying these laws to transform the material conditions of society." An emerging group of geologists followed William Hamilton and measured the volcano's crater after every blast in the hope of fathoming it, and many gentleman virtuosi carried along various instruments— thermometers, stopwatches, quadrants—to enhance their climb.[40] However, on the other hand, the poet wants more. While scientists are restricted "by the limitations of material cause and effect . . . the poet's power is limited only by his own capacity for self-possession. . . . To use Shelley's terms, to follow scientists instead of poets is to become enslaved to the material conditions that we want to control."[41]

Hester Lynch Piozzi's account demonstrated a concern about material conditions more akin to that of the scientist and lay naturalist; she displayed no interest in Percy Shelley's type of enchantment. Piozzi and the scientists shared a realistic assessment of the mountain's danger. But unlike scientists Piozzi questioned the extent to which human beings could prevail. What was the point of pursuing knowledge in the face of overwhelming destructive power? she asked. By pointing to the ever-changing nature of the mountain and the inevitable red-hot stones, Piozzi called into question the efficacy of scientific observations as a way of ultimately controlling a phenomenon that always had and always would threaten human life.[42]

Other female travel-narrators, whether British or German, described more mundane attempts than Piozzi's to repel the impact of the uncontrollable mountain. Though expressing different levels of interest, they ultimately, literally or figuratively, also turned away from the chasm: Elisa von der Recke retreated, fighting the smoke.[43] Mariana Starke tersely recalled her ascent; in three sentences she rerouted attention from the volcano to proper supportive equipment: "a stout stick and a pair of boots" are what is needed to complete the climb, she points out.[44] For Lady Morgan redirecting attention from terror was fortuitously supplied by others. Expecting "a strong sensation . . . of meeting Nature, all solitary and sublime" at the crater, she instead came across "a group of English dandies" who gossiped about last night's party and allowed her easily to be distracted: "a sacrifice of the sublime to the agreeable!"[45] Friederike Brun purposely moved her attention away from the crater and attached it to the graves at the Hermitage. There she romantically indulged "noble thoughts of immortality" and of "the inseparability of moral beings," the communication of souls. Vesuvius itself, she said, looked dead to her; not the dried lava but the life that forced its way through warranted attention: "What is moving is the timidly sprouting young plant life in the old lava masses."[46] Again Staël's fiction coincided with the factual accounts; she depicted Corinne, on Vesuvius, comparing the volcano negatively with other peaks and finding it decidedly unromantic: "By drawing us near to heaven, all other mountains seem to raise us above earthly life, but here I feel only anxiety and fear. . . . This is certainly not the abode of the righteous."[47] Vesuvius represented only threat: physical, material, and untranscendent, and British and German female travel-narrators shared the aim of reinforcing this point for their readers.

This most common response of women—of redirecting their attention away from the mountain—implied an understanding that the mountain could not be vanquished or its energy tapped for the self in the way Percy Shelley and other male travelers desired. It was an object not to be instrumentalized but left to be what it was: a menacing feature of the landscape with which one had to come to terms. As Staël concluded of the erupting mountain, "nature has no longer any relationship with man. He can no longer believe himself to be the dominating power."[48] Women's responses explicitly evaded the sublime and transcendent, even as they called scientific mastery into question: we witness the transnational development of a particular, gendered epistemology.

Percy Shelley's style of response is nonetheless often ascribed to a general Romantic drive to reenchant nature following the empirical emphasis of Enlightenment science. For instance, Chloe Chard has discussed Romantic travel overall as a way of satisfying "individual desires, demands, needs and impulses," saying that this supplanted an earlier Enlightenment quest "for acquiring and ordering knowledge of the world" via "observation and comparison."[49] But Vesuvius accounts complicate the story; they suggest that both qualities—satisfying individual impulses as well as ordering knowledge of the world—are simultaneously present. Moreover, they go beyond mere ideological or aesthetic concern to grapple with the material and physical experience of the climb,

with the volcano's flying red-hot stones, its rumbling and hissing nois-
es, its choking, sulphurous emissions, its encroaching, flaming lava, all
recalling the sensations of fiery conflict in a population that had experienced the period of Napoleon's military dictatorship, the slaughter and
destruction, and the legacy of total war. They reveal a clash of values that
has been described by Marshall Brown. Brown has pointed out that the
terms "Romanticism" and "Enlightenment" are complex and shifting,
and it is a mistake "to take Romantic values as the new and Enlightenment values as the old" when in fact we may be "dealing with a clash of
contemporaneous values" that "need to be referred to their contemporary context in order to be understood."[50] Analysis of visits to Vesuvius,
I suggest, offers an example of such a clash. Approaches to nature and
power, to life and death, to war and military culture, are revealed in representations that on the one hand mythologize the mountain as a way for
the narrator to incorporate its force and emerge victorious, or, on the
other hand, to compartmentalize the destructive power of the volcano in
an attempt to preserve human life and affections.

3. Aesthetics and Desire

Whereas pragmatic northern European female travel-narrators thus
expressed and even urged a different view of Vesuvius, the predominant
ideological and aesthetic habits of interpretation nonetheless loomed
large. As I have suggested, most tourists' incorporation of the volcano's
power occurred via the sublime, fueled by an overwhelming desire. Upon
arrival in Naples many male tourists' first impulse was to scramble up to
the crater and to tap the vigor of the erupting mountain for themselves:
"The smoking peak of the volcano had beckoned to me; the desire to
approach it defeated the exhaustion of a slow and uncomfortable trip
from Rome," wrote Lorenz Meyer.[51] The erotic aspect of the encounter,
as Marlon Ross had suggested of mountains in general, was not lost on
them: John Moore, who was on the Grand Tour as a tutor, mocked weak
young men who did not pace themselves on the climb and arrived "panting and breathless at the top; like those young men who, having wasted
their vigour in early excesses, and brought on premature old age, link
themselves to some ill-fated woman, who drags them, tormenting and
tormented, to the grave."[52]

Johann Gottfried Seume, popular and radical author of the *Spaziergang nach Syrakus im Jahre 1802* (*A Walk to Syracuse in the Year 1802*),

frames his story of the Vesuvius ascent with female figures who offered an opportunity for a kind of consummation. Seume fortuitously met an Italian woman and her cousin, and they decided to climb together. At the point when they got off their mules "what was to be expected happened: the lady . . . could not proceed on foot and remained behind, and I was so ungallant as not to trouble myself about it." Seume climbed farther despite the resistance of a tired porter, exploring the dormant crater despite the oppressive heat. As he describes the quick descent, the brisk slide down ash and sand, Seume comments on how he had sought water everywhere on the dry mountain; now, at the top of the vineyards as if by magic a charming, sweet young woman brings a full jug. Seume indicates that his sexual desire matched the need for a drink: "As thirsty as I was, the girl was nearly more welcome than the water: and if I were to stay here longer, I almost think I would often visit the volcano on precisely this path maybe without a guide." In Seume's next sentence the first lady, the tourist, appears with some Lacrimae Christi wine to refresh her cousin and Seume, but she is a disappointment by comparison with the young woman: "the water was preferable" as was the first "Hebe," an allusion to the daughter of Zeus who was cupbearer to the gods—a reference that places him in appealing superhuman company. Seume is rewarded for his manly effort by the services of not one but two women, the younger of whom becomes an object of fantasy. Even though the older lady gives him the address of her lodgings when they part, he again says he does not have the time to bother with her. Instead, for the whole evening his mind returns to the top of the mountain, and he composes a poem about a violent eruption that fills the gulf with its fireflood. Such a terrifying poetic consummation has a relaxing effect: "With these fantasies I fell asleep peacefully." Where there was no actual eruption Seume supplied his own in poetic form.[53]

Seume's narrative draws on an aesthetic recommended by fellow radical Georg Forster and promoted by Forster through translation of a travel narrative of Charles Jean-Baptiste Mercier Dupaty. Dupaty's description is particularly notable because it was selected by Forster both for review in the *Göttingische Anzeigen von gelehrten Sachen* and for presentation in his group of translated travel narratives. Indeed, the importance of this text as an object of transfer would be hard to overestimate, as it helped inspire Forster's own innovative and influential mode of travel description that was lauded by Alexander von Humboldt (see chapter 2). In the review, which appeared on 7 February 1789, Forster emphasizes the novelty of Dupaty's account, which unlike previous travel descriptions does not draw on chronicles and topographies, nor does it depict streets or buildings or meals or local dialects or governments. Instead, Forster says, the writer chooses to describe "what was striking to him, what interested his heart and his mind," paying greater attention to "the relationship of his spirit to things than to the things themselves."[54] Forster praises Dupaty's ardent but also tender "understanding of the beauties of nature and art" and singles out his unusual description of Raphael's painting, *Incendio del Borgo*, in which Dupaty pretends to be a part of the action of a city fire and only at the conclusion of the experience admits that it is not an actual occurrence but an involving pictorial representation. "No one before our author has possessed to this high degree the gift of making a picture of the description of a picture" (227–28). Forster likewise expresses admiration for "the philosophical penetration and right feeling" (227) of the author's political observations. Though the text was to Forster an anonymous one, the author was rumored to be Dupaty, "the upright, passionate advocate, who uncovered the shortcomings of the French criminal justice system and saved three innocent men who were condemned to torture on the wheel" (229).[55] Two months later, in the preface to his German translation of Dupaty's work, dated 23 April 1789 and less than three months before the storming of the Bastille, Forster heightens Dupaty's political importance. Not only is he "the most vociferous opponent to the shortcomings and horrors of the French penal laws," but he has also contributed "to the great ferment in his nation," by means of which "an enlightened people should also become a free people."[56]

As a result of Dupaty's influence, Forster's own travel writing combined political and artistic observation, social and aesthetic aims. In 1790, the year following the review and translation of Dupaty, Forster set out with young Alexander von Humboldt on a trip through Holland and Belgium and England, and they returned to Germany via Paris, where they witnessed preparations for the first anniversary celebrations of Bastille Day. Forster's book about that trip, titled *Ansichten vom Niederrhein* (*Views of the Lower Rhine*), was praised for its innovative tone; it was, according to Thomas Saine, "of great influence in the history of describing art works and as a model of what a modern travel book could become."[57] In other words, it innovated in precisely those ways Forster commended in Dupaty. Concerning the contemplation of works of art Forster says in *Ansichten*: "In my opinion one accomplishes one's goal better by telling what one felt and thought in the presence of a work of art, that is, how it affected one, and what kind of effect it had, than by *describing* it at length. . . . Through this reproduction of feelings we can get an inkling—not of how the work of art was really constituted—but at any rate, of how rich or poor it had to be in order to give expression to one force or another."[58] Forster adopted Dupaty's method to the letter. Though Forster did not specifically discuss Dupaty's Vesuvius description in his review of the book, he justified the omission by saying that he would not spoil readers' pleasure by divulging the contents of the visit to Naples and the ascent of the volcano; moreover, "this is why these entertaining letters are worth a translation,"[59] something he himself then provided within two months. Forster thus whetted readers' appetites for a book he knew he would soon offer for sale. And given Dupaty's strong influence on Forster, his book could well have spurred Forster's prolific use of the volcano metaphor, quoted at the outset of the chapter, as it occurs in Forster's discussions of the inevitability and desirability of political renewal.[60]

Dupaty's *Lettres sur L'Italie* was also translated into English in the revolutionary year, 1789, within a year after it appeared in French. Dupaty, like Seume, conveys the desire inspired by his experience. Based on travel from 1785, the narrative moves in a sexualized arc through the phases of increasing stimulation, creative eruption, and denouement. The volcano grants (pro)creative powers that allow Dupaty to beget both literary and physical progeny: "I have traced these few lines on the top of Mount Vesuvius, by the light of its eruption. I have in a certain manner struck a medal to attest my journey; to recal one day to the mind of such of my children as may one day wish to be present at this wonderful conflagration, this epoch of their father's life."[61] Because of Vesuvius Dupaty can mint his coin, create a self that, anticipating the ambition of Mary Shelley's Victor Frankenstein, will garner the veneration of coming generations.[62] Like female travelers, and unlike other male ones, Dupaty mentions his children, but they are not so much flesh-and-blood dependents as phantom children whose future adulation promises his own immortality and glory. The isolated hero of the scene (though in reality he did not travel alone), Dupaty impresses upon the reader the simultaneous terror and thrill through repeated exclamations that form the climax of his account: "Behold me at length arrived at the crater. . . . The fiery gulph begins to growl within.—Hark! How dreadful and horrid the crash!—Behold that immense whirlwind of flames striking across that thick shower of blazing ashes!—Millions of sparks ascend into the air—millions of stones, distinguished by their black colour, are hissing, falling, rolling, and falling again" (II:149). "Quite in extasy," he does not want to come down from the heights but would prefer to remain with his fiery mistress: "I could have wished to pass the night near such a conflagration . . . but the wind, that blew very cold, had already frozen my limbs; I descended, but alas! with what regret!" (II:151). Dupaty comes down and makes a plea for his progeny, the conduits of his immortality: "Farewell again thou ignivomous mountain. . . . If it is written above, that thou art to bury under thy ashes those palaces, those villages, or that city, oh! let it not happen when my children are there!" (II:151).

If male travelers reveled in the sublime and used it to experience and depict both personal and political enhancement, female travelers tended to emphasize the picturesque. Anna Jameson, who was as thrilled as any of the men with her climb of Vesuvius, ultimately interpreted it via the picturesque in her *Diary of an Ennuyée* (1826), published in the same year as Hemans's "Casabianca" and Shelley's *The Last Man*, and inspired by Staël's *Corinne*.[63] Like Dupaty, she undertook a thrilling nocturnal ascent of Vesuvius; like Dupaty, she was nearly hit by flying fiery stones. But, as with Dupaty, her account became self-consciously gendered. The men in Jameson's party greeted the eruptions with exclamations, as did Dupaty: "As we approached, the explosions became more and more vivid, and at every tremendous burst of fire our friend L** jumped half off his seat, making most loud and characteristic exclamations,—'By Jove! a magnificent fellow! now for it, whizz! there he goes, sky high, by George!' The rest of the party were equally enthusiastic in a different style; and I sat silent and quiet from absolute inability to express what I felt" (IV:143). In contrast to Dupaty, for whom the sublimity of the experience initially brought on ecstatic, participatory exclamations but ultimately rendered him silent after the descent, Jameson's initial muteness turned into speech once she had returned to the desk at her hotel: "I am not in a humour to describe, or give way to any poetical flights, but I must endeavour to give a faithful, sober, and circumstantial account of our last night's expedition, while the impression is yet fresh on my mind" (IV:142). Even though she finds the work difficult, struggling with the sublimity of it—"the whole scene around us, in its romantic interest and terrible magnificence, mocked all power of description" (IV:146)—she nonetheless overcomes the hurdle by seeing the vista "with a painter's eye."

Jameson invokes the discourse of the picturesque, I would argue, as a way of framing and thereby gaining a measure of control over the landscape. She seeks critical distance in order to offer a realistic, "faithful, sober, and circumstantial account," and at the same time struggles to find her place in the event. In evaluating the scene, she does not participate in a (pro)creative and self-immortalizing happening, but incorporates desire differently; she views the scene from the outside, as an observer (as well as appreciator) of masculine absorption, a quality supplied by soldiers gathered around the crater: "Great numbers of the Austrian forces, now occupying Naples, were on the mountains, assembled in groups, some standing, some sitting, some stretched on the ground and wrapped in their cloaks, in various attitudes of amazement and admiration: and as the shadowy glare fell on their tall martial figures and glittering accoutrements, I thought I had never beheld any thing so wildly picturesque" (IV:147). As had many travelers, Jameson had absorbed the work of William Gilpin, the English writer who did the most to popularize picturesque landscape aesthetics. Although Gilpin generally viewed human figures as mere "appendages" to a landscape, nonetheless special characters could "further some idea of greatness, wildness, or ferocity."[64] Among these are soldiers, but, as Gilpin insists, they must be dressed for the part: "not in modern regimentals; but as Virgil paints them,—*longis adnixi hastis, et scuta tenentes*" (leaning on long spears and holding shields), figures who, like gypsies and banditti, "add a deeper tinge to the character of the scene."[65] Jameson's "cloaks" and "glittering accoutrements" supply the antique effect Gilpin requires. Jameson is as thrilled as Dupaty by her experience, but her gaze shifts away from the crater to the attractive viewers of the crater. Like the other women she diverts her attention. Gender would appear to position Jameson differently vis-à-vis the sublime terror of the volcano. Importantly, her account pacifies military culture, with lounging soldiers as aesthetic objects who add color to the scene. In the framed artistry of the picturesque, then, she is able to make sense of her experience and to communicate priorities. In chapter 4 we will see how she goes further and uses military uniforms not only to distance and objectify soldiers but also to critique their modern mechanistic slaughter in comparison with what she sees as the bloody but naturally motivated raiding of Native American warriors.

British and German women travelers thus shared a response emanating from a socially constructed gender position that drew attention to the similarities within their class. Indeed, transnational continuities of women's lives in general during the early modern period have been outlined by Olwen Hufton, whose overview of western European women's history shows how their lived experience, their practical, everyday reality, was more differentiated by class than by nation. Wealthy women in Britain and Germany (as well as France), and especially those literate ones writing travel accounts, had more in common with each other than they had with their servants.[66] Female travelers of similar privileged backgrounds, when faced with the enormity and violence of Vesuvius, drew on a substantially shared ethical, religious, physical, educational, literary, and sentimental repertoire. They lived under similar legal and social disadvantages. Their responses to the mountain remind us that many of them were brought up with limited exercise, so they became exhausted when they climbed; some stopped partway. Their clothing was often pulled tight, so they could not breathe in the sulphurous smoke. The vogue of sentimentalism in the late eighteenth century, especially among their class, and for most, a shared Christian ethos whether Protestant or Catholic, encouraged dwelling on themes of death and fear and elicited sympathy for those killed by the volcano. Since they did not set out to create a cabinet of curiosities, they usually did not collect samples of lava as many men did.[67] Women with the energy and curiosity to climb Vesuvius were confident, strong, and unafraid of being viewed as "unfeminine." And in the new culture of total war, where such strong-willed women were made peripheral to the military-political regime, they felt everything from ennui to anger. The conflicted position of women vis-à-vis the volcano remained beyond the Napoleonic period. In revolutionary 1848, French satirical cartoons featured "Les Vésuviennes," female warriors who, though alluringly dressed in military clothing, carrying guns, and smoking, were ultimately more concerned about their hair and makeup. According to Laura Struminger, "The rhetoric of the Vésuvienne brought revolutionary ideas to male-female relations while keeping them at a safe distance from the realities of the bloody barricades"; the image was "both a conserver of the *status quo* and a spur to action."[68] Thus the volcano, decades later, continued to retain its strongly gendered associations. Confronting this mountain presented an occasion wherein cultural definitions of masculinity and femininity were formed or reinforced.

Women may have sensed this and decided it was likely to work to their disadvantage. In the prerevolutionary context, the mountain represented the loss and destruction of natural catastrophe. Therefore even before the early-nineteenth-century era of Napoleonic clashes, a confrontation with a mountain of sublime, fiery conflict might be approached with ambivalence, since women lacked sufficient protection on both material and symbolic levels. The mountain could mean very real disaster. In the introduction to her edited volume *Gender and Catastrophe*, Ronit Lentin points out that while one cannot essentialize women as "a unitary victim group" of disasters, women are nonetheless, because of their cultural location, affected differently than men by catastrophes, and that "for the gendering of catastrophes not triggered by political military manoeuvres, such as famines and 'natural' disasters, which cannot be simplistically linked to the construction of gender in society [as she argues is the case in military interventions], we must look at the targeting of women as mothers, unpaid domestic labourers, chattels, sexual objects, repositories of family and national honour and the symbolic representational trope of the nation."[69] The function of "femininity" even in the face of natural rather than human-made disaster can consist in underscoring representations of females that work counter to the interests of actual women. Margaret Kelleher, for example, has shown how women became the figure for the mid-nineteenth-century Irish famine, and that those images of dry-breasted or dead mothers, while giving expression to the "unspeakable," could serve to hide the sociopolitical catalysts and meanings of the disaster; "the affective response thus generated" could lead to "passivity and fatalism which works against real understanding."[70] Women could help the culture to represent horror, then, but those images could draw attention away from structural problems and inequalities that exacerbated disaster and required reform.

My sense is that prerevolutionary eighteenth-century women understood the sexual politics of disaster: the repercussions of a Vesuvian eruption likely, disproportionately, and on many levels would affect women and those for whom they were responsible, and female travelers therefore viewed the mountain with hesitation or impatience. They sensed the ideological implications of their fear. They respected the emerging scientific wish for empirical evaluations of natural phenomena insofar as they desired a down-to-earth assessment of the dangers and human costs of catastrophe. Their aim to deflect power implied both recognition of a larger force and the belief that they could attempt to live alongside it even if it could not be incorporated via the sublime. Female authors sought to evade the physical enormity and threat of the volcano and viewed it instead as a feature of the landscape that complicated the meaning of quotidian existence, whether this had to do with physical needs or metaphysical insights.

Eighteenth-century women also implicitly asked: Why glorify catastrophe when there is enough chaos and pain in the world? What male travelers valued as extraordinary in Vesuvius, women tended to view as part of life's eternal landscape. Their accounts suggest they were unconvinced that people would necessarily prevail. Reports of another prerevolutionary disaster, the Calabria earthquake of 1783, underscore this point succinctly. The Princesse de Gonzague judged that disaster "a terrible example of the instability of human affairs" and she reproached the philosophes for believing they could master nature: "What would become of their philosophical chatter, watching the earth tremble, the cities disappear!"[71] Hester Lynch Piozzi met a woman who was lamenting the loss of a fifteen-year-old son. He had rescued her but was then apparently crushed by crowds or falling debris. Asked whether she would take up the king's offer of premiums to resettle in Calabria, the woman replies, "No, no; that's a curst place; I lost my son in it. *Never, never* will I see it more!"[72] Moved by the story, Piozzi empathizes with the woman's grief and understands her refusal to return. She dwells on her own emotional response, on the tears welling up in her eyes and on the need to move away to another part of the room to compose herself. In doing so Piozzi deploys the rhetoric of sentimental narrative to raise a very practical question: Why put one's self at the mercy of trauma-inducing forces?

Lorenz Meyer, by contrast, uses a woman's response to the Calabria earthquake to come to a very different conclusion about virtue in distress. Instead of the female authors' skeptical stance he invokes sublime terror with the aim of reinforcing notions of masculine heroism and conduct-book femininity. Meyer tells of "a young pretty wife" who, nine months pregnant, is buried under her house for thirty hours when her husband, expecting a corpse, dramatically digs her out alive. When asked what she was thinking during those hours, she responds, "'*I waited*'." Meyer might have wondered why the young wife did not pray, fear for loved ones, or find reconciliation to God's will, but instead he concludes: "Need one comment on this most beautiful panegyric to feminine character?—" To Meyer, waiting represents the height of feminine virtue. Passivity in the face of fear is even more praiseworthy, apparently, than the wife's successfully giving birth just hours after her rescue.[73] The moment of masculine sublimity creates the hero—the rescuing husband desperately digging through the ravaged landscape—with the wife as waiting recipient. Meyer underscores the period's sexual politics of disaster, where the social construction of gender is reinforced to the disadvantage of actual women.

Lest this analysis of gender and disaster appear unrepresentative, I offer a more recent example to convey the urgency felt by a twenty-first century Iranian woman about such an antifeminist process: it offers striking parallels to eighteenth-century European women's views of revolution and disaster. A report by Roger Cohen from Tehran during mass demonstrations protesting the 2009 election loss of Iranian reform candidate Mir Hossein Mousavi takes up the very same subject.

I asked one woman about her fears. She said sometimes she imagines an earthquake in Tehran. She dashes out but forgets her hijab. She stands in the ruins, hair loose and paralyzed, awaiting her punishment. And she looked at me wide-eyed as if to say: do you understand, does the world understand our desperation?[74]

This woman's response to the current unrest in Iran, as reported by Cohen, reveals the same understanding of gender and disaster displayed by eighteenth-century European women. Fear is the emotion that leads the woman to an explication of her double bind, to an apprehension of the impossible situation in which she lives: even if she can manage to save herself from natural disaster, a patriarchal cultural code may well do her in. The requirement to wear the hijab and all it represents will not be lifted even under extraordinary circumstances. Notwithstanding an exhilarating movement for reform and a time of calls for greater social freedom, the very real possibility exists that oppressive patriarchal ways will be reinforced rather than eliminated. In this case the earthquake, the disaster, becomes a metaphor for social upheaval. And though a popular uprising, a political earthquake, is a quickening event that can bring the woman outdoors with hair loose, apparently finally free, she may simply end up standing in ruins, unable to move. In her imagination, then, a popular earthquake may not lead directly to liberation: the ruins may signify not the pulverization of a repressive regime but the loss of civilization, the rise of a new rigidity and another occasion for subjection. The constellation of concerns and perceptions of this Iranian woman, viewing her position in patriarchal culture through the lens of disaster, significantly resembles the analysis of European women at the end of the eighteenth and beginning of the nineteenth centuries. We obviously cannot *equate* the day-to-day experiences of a twenty-first-century Iranian woman with Enlightenment northern European women, especially via an account interpreted by an American reporter; however, we can *compare* them: the epistemologies revealed to make sense of their experiences in patriarchy, encompassing fear, critical perception, and an awareness of the ideological stakes of upheaval, do resemble each other and suggest recognition and a critique of symbolic patterns that reinforce the social construction of gender.

It helps to clarify why European female travel writers of the late eighteenth century felt inclined to turn away from sublime self-fashioning as well as from the other side of that coin, the passivity it implied for women. Male visitors to Vesuvius tended not to concern themselves with the consequences of a potentially catastrophic eruption; they commonly delighted in the mountain, focused on observations and self-enhancement, and enjoyed the emotional charge that an experience of the volcano could supply. Even more so in a postrevolutionary, militarized era could male and female visitors register distinct reactions or else be forced to interpret an atypical response as unsuited to the requirements of their gender.

Such difference accounts, then, for the distinct epistemology evinced by Jameson's response to the volcano. Jameson's use of the picturesque in her Vesuvius description reveals a hybrid approach, what I would like to call "critical apprehension." She drew on a social aspect of the picturesque, explained by David Marshall as a "double consciousness." By viewing a scene "with a painter's eye," Jameson, according to Marshall, "identifies with another beholder, experiences someone else's point of view, mediates [her] perception of the landscape through a double perspective that is divided between a sight and someone else's view of it."[75] Unlike the usual male travel-narrator, who depicted his sublime experience with the volcano as utterly solitary, Jameson both acknowledges the participation of others in the event and uses the picturesque to ensure recognition for and understanding of her interpretation of the brilliant soldiers. Picturesque aesthetics allows her simultaneously to deflect the threatening physical and symbolic force of the erupting mountain while offering a way of expressing need and emotional investments. Jameson's aesthetic corresponds with what some feminist critics have called the "feminine sublime" that favors the social, rejecting masculine sublime isolation and instead forging links. The "feminine sublime" helps to explain the strong gendering of aesthetic categories, and this buttresses the nonessentialist historical and sociopolitical arguments I wish to make.[76] Women understood the sublime,[77] but in narrating the Italian volcano they consciously deployed a different epistemological category, one that simultaneously embraced apprehension, emotion, and pragmatism. Their "critical apprehension" informs Piozzi's 1789 account, Staël's 1807 *Corinne, or Italy*, as well as Jameson's 1826 *Diary of an Ennuyée*.

4. Art and Archaeology

The artistic record offers more evidence of this lasting approach. A comparison of Angelika Kauffmann's *Pliny the Younger and his Mother at Misenum* (1785)—which represents one of the very few images of a blasting Vesuvius painted by a woman for public display—with renderings of "Eruptions of Vesuvius" by Michael Wutky, Joseph Wright of Derby, Jakob Philipp Hackert, and others, demonstrates this with particular clarity.[78] Wutky's depiction of the 1779 eruption, for example, was painted a half a decade before Kauffmann's, but in contrast to Kauffmann's neoclassicism, his picture demonstrates the Romantic sublime at its most dramatic (figure 4). Small human figures in poses of amazement stand at the lip of the crater, dwarfed by a mountain that is shooting out bright orangered lava, lighting up the black of the night. Such popular landscape paintings continue to do well at auction and enjoy top billing in exhibit catalogs and on posters. In the late eighteenth and early nineteenth century they catered to the popular interest in emerging scientific study of volcanoes even as they thrilled viewers with special lighting effects.[79] Indeed, Wutky (Austrian), Wright of Derby (British) and Hackert (German) belonged to an extensive international group of male artists painting such dramatic Vesuvius scenes, which included also the Dane Johan Christian Clausen Dahl, the Frenchmen Pierre Jacques Volaire, Charles François Lacroix de Marseille, and Pierre-Henri de Valenciennes, and the British artist J. M. W. Turner.[80]

The contrast between Kaufmann and the male painters of the sublime reinforces Marshall Brown's notion of dialectics within the Enlightenment and Romanticism, for Kauffmann compartmentalizes and frames the volcano no less than Jameson or Piozzi, both through the architectural setting and the theme itself (figure 5). She uses a historical subject to gain temporal perspective and to redefine heroism. As Wendy Wassyng Roworth reminds us, history painting "represented heroic or tragic human actions through narratives" based on history and literature, with the goal of providing "moral instruction through the representation of uplifting scenes of noble deeds."[81] This was precisely Felicia Hemans's aim in "Casabianca" and "The Image in Lava." Here it is the seated pair—mother and son—who convey heroism, "stille Grösse" in Johann Joachim Winckelmann's terms, in the face of tragedy. Indeed the mother, not the mountain, is at the center, and the picture's emotion is not terror. Although women in the background certainly express distress, the picture focuses on the proximity of the son to his mother and his sense of responsibility to his uncle's fame and posterity—he studies historiography, takes extracts from Livy—conveying the method by which he will inscribe himself and his uncle into the annals of history through his letters to Tacitus.[82] Kauffmann represents words, gestures, and even writing. Characters speak to each other, both in the foreground and mid-

FIG. 4. Michael Wutky, *The Summit of Vesuvius Erupting* (1779). Courtesy of the Akademie der Bildenden Künste, Vienna, Austria.

dle ground. Young Pliny, at his mother's side, links the characters of the painting, future readers of his historiography, and the viewer (modeled by the response of the male figure at the right) into a community, who recognize the vehemence and threat of the eruption, but who privilege the claim of future generations.

One can productively contrast Valenciennes's dramatic depiction of Pliny's death, where the historical subject merely serves to complete a representation of total devastation: nature overwhelms culture as the collapsing buildings and the small, unindividuated dying man in the foreground succumb to the power of the mountain spewing lava and ash from the background (figure 6). No didactic or redeeming message is conveyed but, as with Wutky, the goal remains overpowering sublime effects. Though Kauffmann's representation may differ from the more common men's Vesuvius representations in terms of genre (historical painting versus landscape), style (neoclassical versus Romantic), and perhaps market (academic versus popular), the combination of subject, aesthetic orientation, and theme still reinforces the implications I

FIG. 5. Angelika Kauffmann, *Pliny the Younger with His Mother at Misenum* (1785). Princeton University Art Museum / Art Resource, NY.

have been describing concerning gender in the travel literature. Women writers, as was Kauffmann, were not oblivious to the sublime; they were intrigued by it. But when it came to recording their own perceptions, they privileged a distancing, framing rhetoric because it better suited their priorities.

It is not that women lacked interest in the volcano or even in the representations of artists such as Wutky and his colleagues; indeed, they held strong opinions about the ways the mountain ought to be represented. Piozzi above all wanted a realistic depiction of the volcano, something for which she praises Volaire, famous among Vesuvius painters, because he represents Vesuvius without "that black shadow" (II:5) artificially employed by so many others as a contrast to the flames. Like Anna Jameson, Piozzi wants to take in the wildness of the scene—she recognizes its sublimity—but this does not mean a need for exaggeration or overdramatization of elements through mythologizing and self-

FIG. 6. Pierre-Henri de Valenciennes, *Eruption of Vesuvius on the 24th of August 79* (1813). Valenciennes depicts the death of Pliny the Elder in the foreground, as it was described in the letter of Pliny the Younger. Toulouse, Musée des Augustins, photograph by Daniel Martin.

aggrandizement. The point is precisely not to heighten the mystery of the mountain but to represent it in ways that readily expose its menacing relevance. In this respect, then, Kauffmann's seemingly restrained neoclassical picture models a characteristic female traveler's response, despite its academic and historical focus, since it suggests that the proper way to look at this phenomenon is by incorporating it within a human story. Kauffmann's representation does not avoid the fact of death—it alludes to that of Pliny the Elder—but it does seek to express the social meaning and consequences of his demise, and it insists above all on the centrality of women and human communication.[83] To this extent it represents what the women might well have considered a more "realistic" picture than those wild, lava-dominated ones painted by the men who ostensibly portray the volcano "as it was."

The gendered difference in response to the effects of Vesuvius before the 1830s is evident not only in representations of the mountain itself but also in apparently less spectacular responses to the archaeological findings at Pompeii and Herculaneum. These cities were destroyed in the year 79; archaeological digs began in earnest in 1738 and 1748. During the late-eighteenth and early-nineteenth centuries the outdoor theaters were the primary, unearthed sites for tourists to visit. Again, the commonest focus for male visitors was self-fashioning. At the theater in Pompeii, Percy Shelley praised the greatness of ancient poets and marveled at how they benefited from performances in open-air settings. Winckelmann focused on the dimensions and purposes of the theater's architecture, while unsentimental Goethe could not help but admit the intellectual pleasure derived from witnessing ancient scenes of death: "Much evil has happened in the world, but little that would have given descendants so much joy. I cannot easily conceive of anything more interesting."[84] More emphatically, Lorenz Meyer, though he also admits to being moved by the fate of the unlucky inhabitants, muses that Pompeii and Herculaneum were actually meant to be buried so that enlightened scientists could get the most out of their excavation. The cities were "preserved for the rediscovery of a century that knew how to draw advantages from this important discovery, which the centuries of ignorance would have scorned. In this way the world gained ten-fold compensation for the devastation of a small strip of land by the firefloods of Vesuvius."[85] Like Goethe he relishes the paradox that loss brings gain; moreover, the destruction is justified because of the advantages to be gleaned from it by modern historians. Perhaps the definitive nine-volume *Voyage d'un François en Italie, fait dans les Années 1765 & 1766*, compiled by Jérôme Lalande, had inspired such a view: "this lava of Vesuvius was a happy defender against the ravages of time and the plundering of the barbarians."[86]

Most female travelers, not interested in finding ways of recasting a destructive mountain as the paradoxical preserver of civilization, were above all motivated by themes of loss and pain. Visiting the theater at Herculaneum, Hester Piozzi reflected on "the scene of gaiety and pleasure, overwhelmed by torrents of liquid fire! . . . such a scene may be all acted over again to-morrow; and . . . we, who to-day are spectators, may become spectacles to travelers of a succeeding century."[87] Piozzi's experience inclined her to ponder the situational irony that could emerge if the volcano erupted during her own tour of Naples. She thus invoked simultaneously critical distance (ironic detachment), emotional proximity (empathy), the social ("we"), and an extended time frame that was not simply a past leading up to the triumphant, "happy" present, as in Meyer's and Lalande's accounts, but that imagined the future as well ("travelers of a succeeding century"). Although Dupaty had acknowledged the possibility of a further eruption killing human beings, he could not imagine *himself* dying; instead it was his progeny he cried out for, the carriers of his name and fame: "If . . . thou art to bury under thy ashes those palaces, those villages, or that city, oh! let it not happen when my children are there!" (II:151).[88]

Piozzi, by contrast, viewed from the position of victim and invoked space and time accordingly, with critical apprehension. And this was no less true of Kauffmann's painting despite its ancient subject, as it shifted in perspective between human foreground and natural background and privileged the activity of young Pliny, who would tell the story of the eruption and Pliny the Elder's death to people far away and to future generations. Even Anna Jameson thematized her own struggle to interpret her experience by recording how she sought distance, reflected, and wrote out her narrative at her hotel.

While the antitriumphalist view is prevalent in the work of Piozzi and Kauffmann before the Revolution, late Romantic women are particularly effusive on this score because, as I have argued, the Napoleonic wars foregrounded themes of death, militarism, and catastrophic threats to civilization. Mary Shelley's *The Last Man* (1826), as I have suggested, illustrates the focus on loss emphatically, as does Felicia Hemans's poem "The Image in Lava." All these works convey the extent to which catastrophe and gender are mutually implicated in a context of violent clashes, whether natural or human-made. Like the nonfiction travel writers they exhibit critical apprehension, an epistemology characteristic of women's accounts that acknowledges not only their fear—their apprehension—but also a double understanding on their part: a perception about coping with fear as well as an understanding of the ideological ramifications of that emotion. Vesuvius represented a limit, nature in its most destructive form, and Napoleon offered a human counterpart.

* * *

The travel literature I have analyzed suggests that Naples, though often characterized by the phrase "dolce far niente" (sweet idleness), was not uniformly the effeminizing place, or at least effeminizing in the manner that late-eighteenth-century critics of the Grand Tour claimed it to be. The warm south may have offered northern European travelers the chance to relax, but the majority of men's writings suggests that visits to Vesuvius, far from depleting energies, renewed them; in this sense the

FIG. 7. Auguste Desperret, *Troisième éruption du volcan de 1789*, from *La Caricature* 135 (1833), Planche no. 29. Huntington Library, San Marino, California.

volcano bolstered virility and thereby facilitated the traditional purpose of the Grand Tour, that of creating masculine leaders to set the tone for their generation and to supply warriors for armed conflict. Women, as newer partakers of the Tour, appear to have been ignored in this regard, assumed not to be threatened by southern sources of emasculation and unlikely to benefit from the volcano's charge.

The use of Vesuvius as symbol did not end with the Congress of Vienna or the exile or death of Napoleon. In an arresting cartoon image of 1833, Vesuvius was employed to champion an explosive "Liberty" that erupts from the revolution-volcano (figure 7). Oddly, the lava moves selectively, past the settlement representing France but gobbling up the monarchies whose flags dot the sides of the mountain, and the only people threatened appear to be the monarchs' soldiers—surprisingly there are no civilians, no women, no children. The culture of total war has succeeded in separating masculine militarism from the quotidian concerns of common life. The soldiers flee past the only ruined edifice, a foreground structure that was damaged by a previous eruption. That earlier blast had toppled the building stones of "divine right" that a viewer sees scattered over the landscape. Such an expression of excitement at the volcanic explosion combined with the fantasy of selective, limited destruction that will result in life-giving effects reveals a lasting trace of revolutionary and late Romantic belief in Vesuvius's sublime rewards.

In the revolutionary and Napoleonic era, women's travel accounts tended to reject the myth of the mountain; many insisted on a realistic view of the very substantial threat that this natural phenomenon could pose to human beings. Their accounts of journeys to Naples revealed an approach, critical apprehension, that challenged the sublime. Having witnessed the volcano and its crater, having seen the destroyed cities of Pompeii and Herculaneum, women writers tended to prefer a long view via the picturesque. Napoleon's imperial battles elicited a revulsion not only to the violence and death of combat but also to the constructions of gender initiated by the new system of total war. A threatening Vesuvius on evocative classical ground therefore inspired travel narrators of that era to either critique or confirm distinct gender roles, to reinforce or oppose the masculinized culture of war instigated by the French Revolution and Napoleon's rule. Vulcanism became a trope in political language and war itself a naturalized, looming presence in the landscape of Europe.

CHAPTER 4

Travel and Transfer

Anna Jameson and Transnational
Spurs to European Reform[1]

A study of transatlantic travel in this chapter will allow us to view British-German transfer within an even broader geographical scope; movement into the colonial contact zone provided Europeans with ideas for restructuring European society and those notions then became part of intra-European cultural transfer. The New World, imbued for Europeans with boundless possibility, promised models of social improvement, and European travelers took away impressions both positive and negative and developed ideas for reform. Ali Behdad has pointed out how travel in this period "is not just a search for the exotic and the erotic. Rather, it is an instructive activity that not only completes the traveller's formal education, but also benefits the general public by raising awareness of the public's own religion, government, and moral and cultural values. . . . The more Europe learns about other cultures, the better it understands itself."[2] Thus travel allowed a greater definition of what was specifically European. Behdad emphasizes that such self-understanding implies "self-recognition and self-realization," with the implication that a greater confidence attends metropolitan subjects upon surveying, knowing, and contrasting themselves with the Other. Such a contrast can, however, also demonstrate European failings and shortcomings. As Steve Clark has pointed out, while postcolonial criticism has usefully drawn attention to travel writing's "racialist and imperialist guises," bringing this hitherto underappreciated genre into the scholarly limelight, the purposes

of travel writing have always been multiple, and it would be an oversim-
plification to reduce the "cross-cultural encounter to simple relations of
domination and subordination."[3] These certainly existed and may well
have predominated with many travelers, but they were accompanied by
other forms of knowledge, and it is some of these to which I turn in this
chapter. More specifically, I will emphasize how a female traveler, Anna
Jameson, carried to Canada utopian aspirations gleaned from Enlightenment feminist forebears and was consequently primed to cull New World
ideas for reform. In particular First Nations practices concerning gender
and economy, witnessed on a visit to the frontier, informed her transnational communications, shaped her political activism, and eventually
inspired calls for changes in legislation. Consequently, while postcolonial scholars have probed the impact of travel and exploration on imperial expansion and the transculturation evidenced by colonial subjects, I
will consider how the contact zone could furnish to Europeans ideas for
social renewal, particularly to those inclined to view society from below.

1. Reform and Nonrevolutionary Britain and Germany

Britain and Germany, after the bloody Napoleonic era, were countries
weary of conflict, yet the impact of the wars spurred social and economic
shifts that in turn demanded moves toward sociopolitical restructuring.
British unrest culminated in the notorious Peterloo Massacre of 1819,
in which people who had gathered at Manchester to protest the first of
several onerous Corn Laws and to demand greater parliamentary representation were attacked by the cavalry. It is estimated that fifteen or
more people died; hundreds were injured. After years of protests, riots,
and vociferous political debate, the first Reform Bill was finally passed
in 1832; the Birmingham Political Union and the Chartist movement
ensured that questions of the expansion of the franchise and representation remained in the forefront of British political discourse and activity. In Germany, French occupation had introduced reforms that were
rarely realized. "Military power and bureaucratic control, not political
participation and civil liberties" characterized occupied regions; there
was a significant "distance between aspiration and accomplishment that
can . . . be found throughout Napoleonic Germany."[4] After the Congress of Vienna observers such as G. W. F. Hegel lamented that "these
eternally restless times of fear and hope" were likely to "go on forever";
a subsistence crisis led to protests across the land, including antisemit-

ic riots, one of which in Frankfurt led to the use of federal troops to check the turmoil. Regional protests continued throughout the 1820s. Vast demographic changes, increased bureaucratic control, combined with industrialization and the expansion of infrastructure, resulted in calls for political liberalization that crested in the revolutions of 1848. One entrepreneur in the 1840s wrote that "the locomotive is the hearse which will carry absolutism and feudalism to the graveyard."[5]

These countries that had avoided revolution and managed to shake off Napoleonic dominion on the Continent were threatened with internal eruption during the first half of the nineteenth century. What did external travel, especially in the New World, add to reform-oriented discussions and activities before 1848? What transfer can be registered in this direction, and how was it shared among Europeans in the early nineteenth century?

Images of the New World often inspired *utopian* ideas, especially among anti-Napoleonic advocates of social change. Where the French revolutionary and Napoleonic model came to be shunned by all but a small number of diehard supporters, that of the American Revolution was still able to inspire hope, despite observers' criticisms of slavery and anxiety about the fate of Native Americans. This added significantly to the period's interest in transatlantic travel accounts. Alexis de Tocqueville's *Democracy in America* (1835, 1840), for example, emerged from this European moment; it represented the most famous attempt of a European to find in America ways to approach Old World problems. Tocqueville and his travel companion Gustave de Beaumont were on a fact-finding mission from 1831 through 1832 to seek means of improving prisons, and they did produce a report on this topic, *On the Penitentiary System in the United States and Its Application in France* (1833); however, the upshot of their journey ultimately far exceeded that limited aim. Harriet Martineau traveled to the United States in 1834 because she "felt a strong curiosity to witness the actual working of republican institutions" and published *Society in America* in 1837. Although most European immigrants to the United States sought greater economic security as well as political and religious liberty for themselves and their families, some, such as Robert Owen, his son Robert Dale Owen, and Frances Wright, founded utopian communities; Wright's biracial Nashoba community intended to ready African slaves for freedom. Whereas spiritual ends had motivated earlier immigrants such as Ann Lee, George Rapp, or Christian Metz to form experimental communities in America, the new projects of the early nineteenth century were based largely on sociological principles with the goal of realizing the aims of liberty, equality, and fraternity that the French Revolution had promised but failed to deliver, and to reverse the detrimental effects of industrialization, capitalist development, and imperial expansion.[6]

By comparison South American travel accounts, according to Pratt, were dominated by the drive for economic development, with a European "capitalist vanguard" seeking to "reinvent América as backward and neglected" in order to justify exploitation and transform the continent into "a scene of industry and efficiency" that would convert its people "into wage labor and a market for metropolitan consumer goods."[7] However, at the same time, as Pratt shows, there were female travelers such as Flora Tristan and Maria Callcott Graham who also derived utopian images and ideas from their South American sojourns, and these in turn had significant repercussions in their writings and in Europe. Tristan's travels in Peru, detailed in *Peregrinations of a Pariah, 1833–34*, transformed her into a political activist who agitated until her death in 1844 on behalf of women's and workers' rights in France and England and wrote travel books that critiqued the social systems of both countries; Maria Graham's *Journal of a Residence in Chile during the Year 1822* followed volumes on travels she had taken to India and to Italy. In their works Tristan and Graham offered realistic narratives, couched in nonsentimental novelistic language, to critique injustices and to celebrate the "feminotopias" promoted by the women they met in Latin America.[8] The colonial and international context in which Europeans were embedded therefore influenced not only the production of travel narratives but also the relationships and reformist discourses that linked Europeans across national borders.

My interest in this chapter will be in probing the progressive ideological materials derived from transatlantic travel and their European implementation. Of course, despite the liberal aims of these efforts, the Old World projects initiated could redound back upon the colonies in the form of greater European control and coercion. I do not claim that the efforts to find new systems were universally beneficial or innocuous. I argue instead that by viewing areas of concern that loomed large for subordinated groups in Europe, especially women, one recognizes how such interests were translated into reform rhetoric and political activity that ultimately had lasting effects. The impressions of travel and travel narratives went beyond the simple consumption of scenes of foreign life and manners and souvenirs as a means of differentiating national and cultural identities; they contributed to the circulation of discourses and materials—the creation of a Latourian actor-network—that addressed pressing transnational political and social issues.

Again, my focus is on Anna Jameson, whose visit to Vesuvius I discussed in the last chapter. She is by no means the most prominent figure to travel to the New World, but her apparent conformity, obscuring the deeply reformist impulses of her writings, makes her an illuminating example. Certainly the popularity of her books and articles underscores the wide interest and approbation she enjoyed. Her three-volume account, *Winter Studies and Summer Rambles in Canada* (1838), which will be the main focus of my discussion here, has been appreciated by readers in Britain as well as in Germany, Canada, and the United States in over a dozen complete editions published from the book's first appearance, as well as in numerous excerpts, abridgements, and anthologizations reprinted to this day.[9]

Surprisingly, though Jameson has received increasing critical attention, she nonetheless remains a noncanonical author. It is no longer her sex that has kept her in the second or third tier, I would argue, but the fact that she was a *transnational* writer rather than a *national* one. She spent much time out of England and she often expressed a preference for the customs and institutions of other nations. In her travel accounts, criticism, art guides, memoirs, and other nonfictional works she often critiqued rather than trumpeted British ways. Her method and her message therefore unfitted her for the national project of English studies, and she has only in the last decades been taken up by feminists and postcolonial scholars who recognize that her writings offer a telling counternarrative. Jameson is therefore an excellent subject for talking about cultural transfer.[10]

2. Anna Jameson's Transnationality

Jameson's transnationality appears at every period and level of her life. Born in Ireland to a Protestant Irish father and an English mother in 1794, she moved to England in 1798 because her father, Denis Brownell Murphy, an artist by trade, sought commissions for miniatures in Britain. (It has been suggested that he was associated with the United Irishmen and sought to escape repression in the year of the Rebellion, but I have found no evidence of his participation, and Anna Jameson's own views were decidedly against the rebels, whom she called "louses."[11]) Murphy never earned much, however, and Anna realized early that she would need to support her parents and younger sisters. Educated by a strict governess for a few years, she was nonetheless largely self-taught. She read widely, sneaking literature considered inappropriate for her age, like Shakespeare's plays, which she had fully digested by the age of ten. She later wrote an important book of Shakespeare criticism that took up the question of his female figures: *Characteristics of Women: Moral, Poetical, and Historical* (1832). She was sufficiently trained in art to make accomplished sketches and watercolors during her travels, to create etchings to illustrate her publications, and to become by the 1840s one of England's most popular art critics and historians.[12] For over a decade in the 1810s and ´20s she worked as a governess for the Marquis of Winchester, the Rowles family (with whom she visited Italy), and the Littletons. In 1825 she married Robert Jameson, but from the start their relationship was troubled; he was sent as a legal envoy to Dominica in 1829 and to Upper Canada (what is now southern Ontario, including Toronto) in 1833, but Anna did not accompany him. Instead she traveled to Germany in 1833 and 1834–36 and met significant personages there, especially Ottilie von Goethe, the daughter-in-law of the renowned author. She visited Ottilie frequently and when apart they corresponded on average once a month for their whole lives. Jameson published *Visits and Sketches at Home and Abroad* (1834), which gave a detailed account of her German travels, before being called by Robert to join him in Upper Canada. He wished to be promoted to vice-chancellor, and her presence, suggesting married stability, would aid him in this endeavor. For her part, Jameson felt compelled to make the trip to Canada, either to reconcile or, if not, to finalize financial arrangements for a separation.[13] She sailed to New York, up the Hudson, then in the cold of December crossed upstate New York to Lake Ontario and traveled by steamship from Niagara to Toronto, arriving just before the end of 1836.

Winter Studies and Summer Rambles in Canada makes clear just how reluctant Jameson had been to leave Germany and how much of her heart remained there. For one thing, Germany offered a way of life for women that struck her as less constricted than the British and more rational than the Canadian. In 1833 Jameson lauded what she perceived as the easy interaction between the sexes. The German system allowed women to behave in a way she called "natural," meaning emotionally more spontaneous, socially less impeded, more at liberty, a chance for women to express their "character." In her account of those travels, *Visits and Sketches at Home and Abroad*, she observed:

I thought the German women, of a certain rank, more *natural* than we are. The moral education of an English girl is, for the most part, *negative*; the whole system of duty is thus presented to the mind. It is not "this you must do;" but always "you must not do this—you must not say that—you must not think so." . . . The idea that certain passions, powers, tempers, feelings, interwoven with our being by our almighty and all-wise Creator, are to be put down by the fiat of a governess, or the edict of fashion, is monstrous. . . . Now, in Germany the women are less educated to suit some particular fashion; the cultivation of the intellect, and the forming of the manners, do not so generally supersede the training of the moral sentiments—the affections—the impulses; the latter are not so habitually crushed or disguised; consequently the women appeared to me more natural, and to have more individual character.[14]

Illustrating this idea are her observations on a boat trip up the Rhine, a telling example of how, for Jameson, women's freedom of motion and claims to space are integral to their claim to human rights. She contrasts an English family, who put up a "fortification of tables and benches" (VS, I:4) around them to hold others away so the daughters can sketch, with carefree German girls who are traveling with an aunt and a brother. The German girls

> walked up and down the deck, neither seeking nor avoiding the proximity of others. They accepted the telescopes which the gentlemen, particularly some young Englishmen, pressed on them when any distant or remarkable object came in view, and repaid the courtesy with a bright kindly smile; they were natural and easy, and did not deem it necessary to mount guard over their own dignity. Do you think I did not observe and feel the contrast? (VS, I:6)

English girls are immured and repressed where German ones can walk about and act on an intellectual and sexual par with men. True, German women are "much more engrossed by the cares of housekeeping than women of a similar rank of life in England," but even this evidence of lesser prosperity is ultimately not problematical; Jameson decides that "more of the individual character is brought into the daily intercourse of society—more of the poetry of existence is brought to bear on the common realities of life" (VS, I:163, 162).

What mattered therefore was not transcendence of the quotidian but the opposite, an embrace of it. An idealist character would have struck Jameson as ungenuine or forced. In this orientation Jameson furthered the anti-Romanticism of the Young Germans with whom she had contact there. "I have been asked twenty times since my return to England, whether the German women are not very *exaltée*—very romantic? I could only answer, that they appeared to me less calculating, less the slaves of artificial manners and modes of thinking; more imaginative, more governed by natural feeling, more enthusiastic in love and religion, than with us." To Jameson, German women's upbringing allows them to take full advantage of both the material and metaphysical realms in their claims to freedom; there is no need for escape in lofty transcendence or exaggerated materialism. In this then she parts ways with Mary Wollstonecraft, whom she otherwise admired; transcendence appeared an undesirable and ineffective alternative to her. She would be happy to give up English luxuries "for the cheap mental and social pleasures—the easy intercourse of German life" (VS, I:174).

Jameson's reflections on achieving human freedom via more liberal gender socialization in Germany are therefore a measure not only of the influence of German political ideologies but also of what she regards as the decline of renowned Enlightenment British liberty for women.[15] According to conjectural histories like those of John Millar in *The Origin of the Distinction of Ranks* (1778), a society's level of progress could be calculated via its treatment of women. As the community moved from savage ways to civilization, women's development away from drudgery reflected the society's level of refinement. Jameson was familiar with such theories, but she invoked them only to call them into question. European women's position to her mind had both expanded and diminished since the late eighteenth century, to the extent that national roles were now reversed: Germany, despite lagging behind Britain in material wealth and industrial development, became a model for what she hoped would bring increased British women's social freedoms and human rights. And a comparison of European females with First Nations women in Canada would go even further to complicate simplistic theories of historical progress.

3. Transnational Literary Production

Jameson arrived in Toronto in December 1836, just before Christmas, and felt cold, isolated, and miserable. She communicated her feelings to a journal that she then turned into *Winter Studies and Summer Rambles*. The first part of the book concerns Jameson's reading. Cooped up and sick at home, with the glass of water by her bed frozen solid each morning, Jameson studied, translated, and commented on German literature. Christa Zeller Thomas has argued that this activity served her as a way of maintaining her sense of identity as a cultivated European in the frosty, isolating wilderness. Where Canada was terra incognita, Germany was a known land to which she clung, sustained by cherished memories and relationships.[16] Jameson devotes much space to Johann Peter Eckermann's account of his conversations with Goethe, which she began to translate from a prepublication copy of the book she had received in Weimar.

In this activity she was inspired by the work of Sarah Austin, a prolific translator from the German and a woman she had met in 1834 and greatly admired. The two authors shared their interest in German letters and became good friends. Austin had just published a three-volume work, *Characteristics of Goethe* (1833), which included translations of and commentaries on Goethe's works, exactly the mode that Jameson herself came to favor. At the time of their first meeting Austin was translating Victor Cousin's reports on Prussian public instruction, with the hope of furthering progressive approaches in Britain.[17] It is these pages that Jameson brought to Canada and wished to introduce in order to encourage more profitable discussions on national education.

It is worth considering Jameson's concern with educational theory, as it sheds light on her ubiquitous and enduring desires to advocate for subalterns by instructing and reforming; on her constant transnational orientation; and on her frustrations with the styles of political discourse among the people in Toronto. The primary issue that led to the 1837 unrest in Upper Canada was the inequitable appropriation of lands, and, in particular, the monopoly of the church over property revenues that "by far the most numerous" of settlers, according to Jameson, felt should be applied toward education.[18] Jameson was astonished at the low level of discourse on the issue, "the strange, crude, ignorant, vague opinions I heard in conversation, and read in the debates and the provincial papers." If Canadians could only read the preface of Cousin's report on Prussian education, translated by Sarah Austin, then, Jameson thought, the settlers might come to sound conclusions:

> It struck me that if I could get the English preface to Victor Cousin's report (of which I had a copy) printed in a cheap form, and circu-

lated with the newspapers . . . it might do some good—it might assist
the people to some general principles on which to form opinions;—
whereas they all appeared to me astray; nothing that had been promulgated in Europe on this momentous subject had yet reached
them; and the brevity and clearness of this little preface, which exhibits the importance of a system of national education, and some general truths without admixture of any political or sectarian bias, would,
I thought—I hoped—obtain for it a favourable reception. But, no;
cold water was thrown upon me from every side—my interference in
any way was so visibly distasteful, that I gave my project up with many
a sigh, and I am afraid I shall always regret this. (WS, I: 35–36)

Jameson, apprised of theories that might propel the discussion, felt powerless in Canada to spur sociopolitical change. The people were wary
"of the 'authoress'," who was "anything but popular"[19]; her voice in this
wilderness counted for little.

Even as they displayed an aversion for a theoretically informed debate
on education, the Canadians evinced, to Jameson's mind, a misguided
belief in the inequitable, cutthroat systems of political economy. She felt
they ignored helpful theories and embraced problematical ones. She
witnessed a fire on King Street, and some said that the blaze would be
a benefit, because a brick house would be built in place of a wooden
one. But Jameson turned consideration of this point into a discussion
about viewing things from the emotional perspective of the individual
and the individual loss rather than the calculating, utilitarian perspective of political economy: "In these days of political economy, it is too
much a fashion to consider human beings only in masses. Wondrous,
and vast, and all-important as is this wide frame of human society . . . is
it more important in the sight of God, more fearful, more sublime to
contemplate, than that mysterious world of powers, and affections, and
aspirations, which we call the human soul?" (WS, I: 111). As in Jameson's
analysis of Vesuvius, the circumscribed personal picture must trump vast
sublimity in the context of disaster. Utilitarian projects and Malthusian
calculations, she felt, could lead to cruel and ultimately wrong policy
decisions.

Jameson was nonetheless aware of both the positive and negative
power of thinking in masses. On the one hand, when the intention was
to corral people unthinkingly into bloody or coercive actions such as
war, she found thinking in masses repugnant. She reports how Colonel
Fitzgibbon, a romantic youth who wanted to be a chivalrous soldier, was

shocked to find the battlefield totally unlike the image he harbored: "He then described . . . his utter astonishment and mortification on finding the mechanical slaughter of a modern field of battle so widely different from the picture in his fancy;—when he found himself one of a mass in which the individual heart and arm, however generous, however strong, went for nothing—forced to stand still, to fire only by the word of command—the chill it sent to his heart, and his emotions when he saw the comrade at his side fall a quivering corse [sic] at his feet" (WS, I:129). The new style of war represented to Jameson the clearest example of the heartlessness and irrationality of the modern system. Utilitarianism and political economy were simply other manifestations of the same tendency.

It was the absence of feminine influence, Jameson was convinced, that had brought Europe to this undesirable pass. The separation of the sexes allowed masculinity to run rampant, uninfluenced by any feminine principle. Jameson would later insist that "whatever be the system selected as the best, it should be carried out by a due admixture of female influence and management combined with the man's government." To be sure, Jameson appears to endorse traditional sex roles, but she was nonetheless convinced that only women's and men's cooperation, what she termed "the communion of labour," would lead to "the more humane ordering" of national endeavors.

Observations on gender pervaded Jameson's analysis of Canada. Jameson found that the Native peoples on the frontier, in facing issues over land, subsistence, and broken agreements, experienced quandaries of self-determination just as did settler and European women. In the summer months she was finally able to leave Toronto and travel west on her "Summer Rambles," which were to inform the second part of her book. Her principal goal, she said, was to evaluate questions of gender, "to see with my own eyes the conditions of women in savage life."[20] What emerged was an overwhelming sense of a parallel in status and exploitation between First Nations people and European and settler women.

If, in this rapidly expanding industrial and imperial economy, changes in custom and social policy were not forthcoming, then the dilemmas faced by the Native peoples on account of the white men could speak to the long-standing issue of European women's fates. Visiting Detroit, for example, she surveyed the situation of the Wyandots, who long had made claims concerning land. Jameson in her account lets these Hurons speak for themselves, reproducing a five-page petition and concluding, "Is there not much reason as well as eloquence in this appeal?" (WS,

II:325). She doubts whether the colonial legislature will do justice to the Native peoples, "seeing that the interests of the colonists and settlers, and those of the Indians, are brought into perpetual collision, and that the colonists can scarcely be trusted to decide in their own case. . . . The poor Indian seems hardly destined to meet with *justice*, either from the legislative or executive power" (WS, II:329). Consequently she understands and praises the efforts of Tecumseh and Pontiac to rally the various tribes to oppose the Europeans, and laments the futility of their "noble and fated race, to oppose, or even to delay for a time, the rolling westward of the great tide of civilization. . . . Wherever the Christian comes, he brings the Bible in one hand, disease, corruption, and the accursed fire-water, in the other; or flinging down the book of peace, he boldly and openly proclaims that might gives right, and substitutes the saber and the rifle for the slower desolation of starvation and whisky" (WS, II:240, 250).

There is tension here between Jameson's recognition of overwhelming European power—to colonize, industrialize, and "civilize"—which she both supports and criticizes, and her estimation of its efficacy, which she laments. That is, though Jameson everywhere lauds economic development and the Europeans' efforts to make the land west of Toronto productive, she simultaneously recognizes the terrible cost of this, and she finds its fatal consequences to the Native peoples unacceptable. They cannot be Europeanized, nor should they be. Although she assumes European superiority, and while she occasionally leans on the "noble savage" stereotype, she does not suggest that this gives a right to dominance: "In our endeavours to civilise the Indians, we have not only to convince the mind and change the habits, but to overcome a certain physical organization to which labour and constraint and confinement appear to be fatal. This cannot be done in less than three generations, if at all, in the unmixed race; and meantime—they perish!" (WS, II:274).

Jameson clearly speaks as a European, but she does not condone Europeans' methods in the New World because she sees them departing so baldly from the ethical Christian approach that, she insists, they are called upon to employ. She eventually endorses the government plan of reserved lands for First Nations people, claiming that only in this way can they maintain independence from white people and ensure their own subsistence and survival. Although she thus furthers colonial aims and the strategy of Francis Bond Head, the lieutenant-governor, she nonetheless differs from other travel-narrators in that she comes to the conclusion after herself observing and meeting Native people; does not assume like so many others that the First Nations people will simply die out; interviews settlers and government agents herself; and then weighs the possibilities, all of which she feels fall short.[21] She recognizes that the Native peoples are hunters, not agriculturalists, but worries that there is no real alternative for ensuring an adequate food supply and decent living conditions. Moreover, she sees potential advantages for Native women in the change: "the first step from the hunting to the agricultural state is the first step in the emancipation of the female" (WS, III:304). To this extent, she feels—clearly viewing from a European woman's perspective—that Native people might profit from altering their way of life. Jameson fails to contemplate any alternative to the forces of modernization, any means to check the westward expansion and development and aggression of white settlers; however, she takes an independent stance, insisting that modernization is by no means to be equated with civilization. She aims to adjust Europeans' attitudes toward colonial as well as European practice.

This point is epitomized in an extended analysis of war, where Jameson contrasts Native and European approaches. Modern European styles of warfare are uncivilized, she argues, whereas Native people's modes of vengeance arise from understandable, raw, but honest emotions; they result from true harm to an individual or a tribe. Jameson decries murderousness on all sides, but the Native people's ways, focused on real feeling, can be justified in a way that modern European battles, exemplified by Napoleon's new fashion of systematized total warfare, cannot. One discerns an echo, here, to the distinction between meaningful Romantic and unmeaningful mass death discussed by Gary Kelly (chapter 3), as Jameson writes:

> I wonder if any of the recorded atrocities of Indian warfare or Indian vengeance, or all of them together, ever exceeded Massena's retreat from Portugal,—and the French call themselves civilized. A war-party of Indians, perhaps two or three hundred, (and that is a very large number,) dance their war-dance, go out and burn a village, and bring back twenty or thirty scalps. *They* are savages and heathens. We Europeans fight a battle, leave fifty thousand dead or dying by inches on the field, and a hundred thousand to mourn them, desolate; but *we* are civilized and Christians. Then only look into the motives and causes of our bloodiest European wars as revealed in the private history of courts:—the miserable, puerile, degrading intrigues which set man against man—so horridly disproportioned to the horrid result!

And then see the Indian take up his war-hatchet in vengeance for some personal injury, or from motives that rouse all the natural feelings of the natural man within him! Really I do not see that an Indian warrior, flourishing his tomahawk, and smeared with his enemy's blood, is so very much a greater savage than the pipe-clayed, padded, embroidered personage, who, without cause or motive, has sold himself to slay or be slain: one scalps his enemy, the other rips him open with a saber; one smashes his brains with a tomahawk, and the other blows him to atoms with a cannon-ball: and to me, femininely speaking, there is not a needle's point difference between the one and the other. If war be unchristian and barbarous, then war as a *science* is more absurd, unnatural, unchristian, than war as a *passion*. (WS, III:194–95)

Jameson genders brutality as masculine and peace as feminine, and, consciously asserting a feminist stance—"femininely speaking," using a sewing metaphor—she condemns scientific war as beyond the pale of civilized society. Native peoples remain on the civilized spectrum and therefore closer to the feminine side, since their conflicts arise from individual harm and the regrettable but understandable desire for individual redress. Jameson had lauded German women's ability to express their feelings, their inmost character, in daily life as "natural," and this is the quality that also makes Native warfare, although destructive, a fathomable phenomenon by contrast with modern European modes. Later, in *Sisters of Charity and the Communion of Labour*, Jameson applauds the feminine influence of Florence Nightingale and her female volunteers who traveled to Constantinople and worked to save soldiers' lives in the Crimean War; it was a means of mitigating the horrifying losses of modern warfare. In that discussion of female labor Jameson fails to address the question of the justification for the Crimean War; instead, her focus is intently on future implications for women. To her mind, nursing becomes a salient example of how the "communion of labour" between women and men can have the effect of recalibrating modernization so as to bring human charity and women's talents to bear on otherwise irrational, heartless, one-sidedly masculine endeavors. Jameson may have been criticized for seeking to relegate women to a traditional subservient role of nurse, but she saw Nightingale epitomizing a new and desirable professional training and leadership. The example demonstrates how Jameson's deeply felt theory of gender mutuality despite gender difference could appear simultaneously progressive and conventional.

Despite the tragic failure of the First Nations' banding together to oppose white men's incursions, Jameson insisted that, like women, the Native peoples should be treated not paternalistically but with respect. The Wyandots above all should be allowed to make their own choices, just as women should be allowed to bear responsibility for their own bodies and their own decisions: "No measure should be adopted, even for their supposed benefit, without their acquiescence. They are quite capable of judging for themselves in every case in which their interests are concerned. The fault of our executive is, that we acknowledge the Indians our *allies*, yet treat them [as], as well as call them, our *children*" (WS, II:328). That women should not be patronized or treated as children becomes the founding assumption in *Sisters of Charity and the Communion of Labour*. "The time is come, let us hope, when men have found out what we may truly be to them, not worshipping us as saints, or apostrophizing us as angels." She adds, "or persecuting us as witches, or crushing us as slaves," knowing that the other side of the coin of veneration, as history has shown and the experiences of the First Nations people have confirmed, is dehumanization (SCCL, 140).

That Jameson consistently viewed gender and race issues on a continuum vis-à-vis misguided or brutal government policies becomes apparent in the story of a black man who had escaped slavery by coming to Canada but was now threatened with deportation to the United States based on an accusation of horse-stealing. Jameson focuses on the nonviolent protest initiated by black women. The day the ex-slave was to be taken away there was an unarmed riot in which "2 blacks were killed, and two or three wounded." Jameson notes: "By all those passionate and persuasive arguments that a woman knows so well how to use, whatever be her colour, country, or class, they had prevailed on their husbands, brothers, and lovers, to use no arms, to do no illegal violence, but to lose their lives rather than see their comrade taken by force across the lines." Jameson sees women of all races potentially and essentially as nonviolent advocates for peace and justice, and she therefore makes sure to seek out the leader among the black women. This woman had been a slave in Virginia, and when her master died she was threatened with being sold. So she ran away. Jameson asked if she was happy in Canada, and then lets the ex-slave speak for herself: "I *was* happy here—but now—I don't know—I thought we were safe *here*—I thought nothing could touch us *here*, on your British ground, but it seems I was mistaken, and if so, I won't stay here." Jameson laments the mendacious claims of European men paternalistically to protect subalterns, only to expose and abandon them. Despite her European loyalties and occasional stereotypes, Jameson is in her travels remarkably free of racial prejudice and consistently acknowledges the cost to the vulnerable—be they Native peoples, African slaves and free blacks, women, or pensioners—of governmental policies (WS, III:340).[22] Her greatest concern is for women, but she does not think in rigid categories and recognizes how even white men, the veterans or "commuted pensioners" she finds cheated of their payments, can suffer at the hands of thoughtless and prejudicial legislators.

Indeed, Jameson was open minded and extremely interested to find out about the lives of her interlocutors. One infers from reading her books that the people she met consistently took to her; they spoke freely and treated her well, helping her at every turn. She was a good listener and must have been an astute questioner, unthreatening, pleasant, and encouraging. She appears to have relished that role and the reciprocal attraction she elicited: "Mr. Johnson tells me . . . that the Indians like me, and are gratified by my presence, and the interest I express for them, and that I am the subject of much conversation and speculation" (WS, III:134). Although occasionally complacent she was not unthinkingly patriotic; she always felt the impact of her position not only as a woman but also as a visitor and, significantly, as Irish. She frequently refers to her red hair and her "countrymen," whom she consistently seeks out and whose lively talk she enjoys even as she regrets their poverty and unkempt state. "Poor Ireland! The worst Indian wigwam is not worse than some of her dwellings; and the most miserable of these Indians would spurn the destiny of an Irish *poor-slave*—for he is at least Lord o'er himself" (WS, III:254). Later, she draws a parallel between British treatment of Ireland and men's of women: "Man's legislation for woman has hitherto been like English legislation for Ireland: it has been without sympathy; without the recognition of equality; without a comprehension of certain innate differences, physical and moral, and therefore inadequate, useless, often unjust, and not seldom cruel."[23] She recognizes the cost of colonial and sexual exploitation wherever it appears and has no trouble seeing some Europeans and people of color and women as similarly positioned, even while recognizing the differences among, and the varied troubles faced by, these groups. Ethics and Christian values were at stake and mattered more than nation or race or sex; she wished above all to reveal the moral examples to be gleaned from her interlocutors and to contrast the egregious lapses of dominant Europeans. Such exempla were to be found in what her metropolitan readers likely viewed as unexpected places.

Significantly, an argument about the false position of women reverberates in Jameson's account of her stay with the Ojibwa family she sees in Sault Ste. Marie, a visit that forms the highpoint of her Canadian narrative and clarifies for her the central concept of the "communion of labor." Given the realities of Native life, Jameson finds women to be on a par with men; that is, both sexes are constrained to work indefatigably for the sake of subsistence. "However hard the lot of woman, she is in no *false* position. The two sexes are in their natural and true position relatively to the state of society, and the means of subsistence" (WS, III:303–4). Later, in an essay on "Women's Mission and Women's Position," she puts it this way:

> The condition of the woman in savage life has been considered as peculiarly degraded. I have seen those women—lived among them. Individually, they never appeared to me so pitiable as the women of civilized life. In those communities the degradation is positive, not relative; all fare alike—the lot of one is the lot of all; and the oppressed woman is not in fact more *degraded* than the brute-man.[24]

First Nations people represent to Jameson a version of gender mutuality though work. Although European society has developed more complex economic divisions, she argues, the communal relationship of the sexes to each other should nevertheless still hold: "there must be the communion of labour in the large human family, just as there was within the narrower precincts of home" (SCCL, 13, 14). If you compare a Native woman with an upper-rank European woman, then she may appear to live the life of a drudge, but if you compare her with a European servant maid or a factory worker, "the condition of the squaw is gracious in comparison, dignified by domestic feelings, and by equality with all around her" (WS, III:305). The Native woman's hard work makes her equal to, even while she is different from, Native men. The conservative *British and Foreign Review* decried Jameson's "resolution to represent any arrangement of the position and duties of her sex whatsoever,—even that where the Squaw is the Red Man's drudge in field and wigwam . . . as more equitable and to be desired than that existing according to the present system of European civilization."[25]

However, whereas European women might look forward to improvements due to economic development, the First Nations people can only anticipate suffering for the same reason, Jameson concludes. Capitalism and imperialism can bring women's advances in Europe, but they

FIG. 8. Anna Jameson, *Wayish,ky's Lodge* (1837). Etching, Royal Ontario Museum, Toronto, Canada, 960.220.2. With permission of the Royal Ontario Museum © ROM.

are not going to aid the North American Native peoples, who are being driven from and cheated of their land and means of supporting themselves. Jameson does not offer any solutions to this profound problem, but unlike many travelers to the region she grapples with it, honestly assesses her own interests and beliefs, discards any sentimental fantasy about noble savages, and offers thought-provoking perspectives:

> God forbid that I should think to disparage the blessings of civilization! I am a woman, and to the progress of civilization alone can we women look for release from many pains and penalties and liabilities which now lie heavily upon us. Neither am I greatly in love with savage life, with all its picturesque accompaniments and lofty virtues. I see no reason why these virtues should be necessarily connected with dirt, ignorance, and barbarism. . . . But I do say, that if our advantages of intellect and refinement are not to lead on to farther moral superiority, I prefer the Indians on the score of consistency; they are what they profess to be, and we are *not* what we profess to be. They profess to be warriors and hunters, and are so; we profess to be Christians, and civilized—are we so? (WS, III:196)

Her rhetorical question is answered resoundingly in the negative with the many examples of exploitation and destruction she offers, and it rejects any naive notions of inevitable human progress.

European development in Canada is falling especially hard on Native women, and Jameson discusses this with discernment, as usual offering an economic analysis. Jameson recognizes that among Europeans the position of women is generally, if erroneously, viewed as an indicator of a society's level of development; here it allows a negative evaluation of European policy in the New World. Europeans have "injured the cause of the Indian women" through corruption and "by checking the improvement of all their own peculiar manufactures." By substituting cheap European goods for Native women's products, Europeans have artificially created a market for European products while taking away Native women's skills and the desire for their own manufactures. Europeans have "substituted for articles they could themselves procure or fabricate, those which we fabricate; we have taken the work out of their hands, and all motive to work, while we have created wants which they cannot supply. We have clothed them in blankets—we have not taught them to weave blankets. We have substituted guns for the bows and arrows—but they cannot make guns . . . we are making paupers of them" (WS, III:309–10). Jameson exposes the economy of empire for her bourgeois metropolitan audience, reading in Native women's position a *reversal* of the process of civilization.

Jameson decides that, on the one hand, the position of women is universal and that of First Nations women therefore analogous to that of European ones. Woman's "condition is decided by the share she takes in providing for her own subsistence and the well-being of society as a productive labourer." If a woman is "idle and useless by privilege of sex, a divinity and an idol," her position is "as lamentable, as false, as injurious to herself and all social progress, as where she is the drudge, slave, and possession of the man" (WS, III:312). Yet, on the other hand, economic development has meant that European women are rising out of the state of dependence just as Native women are falling further into it: "We are ourselves just emerging from a similar state, only in another form. Until of late years there was no occupation for women by which a subsistence could be gained, except servitude in some shape or other." As women's productive work goes, British and French women have the advantage over American and German ones since industrial and commercial development has been greater in those countries. But all these European women are in a better position than First Nations women, who, unlike the men, cannot hunt the furs that are the Native people's only commodity for trade, and this situation is likely to prove "fatal to any amelioration of their condition" (WS, III:311). Native women bear the brunt of the First Nations' impoverishment. Jameson offers no solution to this dilemma beyond the proposed creation of reserved lands, but she observes keenly, analyzes and publicizes what she sees, all the while managing to insert it within an eye-opening account of her time on the frontier. Native American women can thus only offer a partial model for European women's emancipation.

In North America Jameson thus expanded her notions about gender construction by tying them to issues of labor and economic development. Moreover, by viewing the parliamentary process and the workings of Canadian government firsthand, she recognized how legislation came to be adopted and could affect social conduct on a large scale. In the colonial context she witnessed explicit analogies between the sufferings of subjected peoples in general, whether based on race, ethnicity, sex, or class, but gave voice to individuals based on liberal ideas she favored over utilitarian notions of political economy. Though she harbored utopian hopes, these were not buttressed by any simplistic notion of historical progress or necessity; her Canadian travels had emphasized for her the need to revise prevalent ideas about historical development, which she saw as everywhere affected by either the unjust and destructive, or ethical and responsible, deeds, habits, legal constraints, and institutions of human actors. These insights were brought to bear on all of her later work.

4. Transnational Production and Practical Reform

Upon returning to Europe, Jameson concluded that she should renew attention to the instructive example of German women; a translation of plays by Princess Amelia of Saxony, *Social Life in Germany* (1840), would offer British readers models for social renewal. Jameson thus moved from critique via cultural comparison to advocating an alternate system. Even the title of her book suggests that, beyond the dramatic action itself, a reader will find interest in depictions of the customs, laws, and institutions that offer a different example of community life, one more likely to contribute to gender equality. Social, legal, and cultural reform was to follow from German examples that, she hoped, would motivate British readers to rethink and revise their statutes and habits.

If Jameson argues indirectly through dialogue in the introduction to *Social Life in Germany*, she clarifies her political aims unambiguously and in detail in the "Remarks" that precede each play. As she had in *Visits and Sketches*, she critiques "mistaken principles in the early education of women; the influence of the negative principle, the principle of fear, in which we are brought up, and made dissemblers on system" (SL, I:5). In the Remarks preceding *The Uncle* she devotes a long page in small type to the particulars of German divorce law, which is contrasted with restrictive English statutes:

> In the second scene of the first act of this play, an allusion occurs which seems to require a more detailed and satisfactory explanation than can well be given in a marginal note . . . The English law admits but one plea for divorce,—the infidelity of the wife. But in Saxony the legal pleas for divorce are several; viz. 1. The proved infidelity of *either* party . . . 2. Bigamy on either side. 3. Desertion of home (bed and board) by either party. 4. Quasi-desertion; that is, as I understand it, when the husband and wife have agreed to be separated for life without other cause than mutual aversion, disparity of temper or character, &c.; and coercive measures have been tried, or apparently tried, without result. 5. An attempt made by either party on the life of the other. Lastly, any disgraceful crime subjecting one party to an imprisonment of not less than four years' duration. . . . In cases of divorce on the plea of the husband's infidelity, he forfeits all claim whatever on the property of his wife. The care of the children is adjudged to the party who, upon evidence produced, appears most likely to give them a good education:—when very young, invariably to the mother, except where the guilt of infidelity rests with her. In no case can either parent be denied all access to the children. . . . [B]efore the late revolution in the Saxon government, divorce was more difficult than at present. . . . It was from consideration for the morals of the community that the law was relaxed: all which is worthy of reflection and investigation on deeper and higher grounds than mere superficial morality and expediency. (SL, I:131–32)

Such even-handed liberal divorce laws would have intrigued a British audience that had two decades earlier followed the histrionic attempts of King George IV to divorce Queen Caroline, the granddaughter of Philippine Charlotte of Brunswick-Wolfenbüttel (chapter 1), and that had recently witnessed passage of the Custody Act of 1839. More to the point, the expansive legal detail of Jameson's "remark" underscores her feminism and her hopes that readers might cull not only an attitude but also a method from the German example. (A Divorce and Matrimonial Causes Act was finally passed in 1857.)

Jameson's "Remarks" on *The Young Ward* let her indicate the advantages to women of the Germans' long and formal premarital engagement process: "a familiar and confidential intercourse, when not too long protracted, increases the chance of eventual happiness to both parties, and is on the whole, particularly favourable to the woman" (SL, II:7). She had written to Ottilie von Goethe asking specifically for clarifications on this point: "What are the ceremonies of a 'Verlobung'? In what does it differ from a marriage? Answer me this particularly."[26] It is therefore clear that she intended to expand on yet another social practice that adjusts relationships of power and control between the sexes. In addition, the lengthy commentary on *The Princely Bride* occasions a celebration of Germany's numerous lay-convents that allow women to avoid marriage altogether and still provide comfort and satisfaction: "their order confers a certain dignity, besides an elegant maintenance . . . one has at least the pleasant conviction that they will not be *obliged* to marry to secure a station in society." She describes the accommodation of a young noblewoman she met: "She had her private apartments, consisting of three rooms, where she received her own visitors; her female attendant, and six hundred florins a year for pocket-money. There was an excellent table, a complete establishment of servants, including five liveried footmen, to attend the ladies when they walked out; there was no care, and less restraint than in the domestic home" (SL, II:159–60). To Jameson's mind Germany has actually achieved the kind of female monastery that Mary Astell had so long ago proposed for England, something that could help to solve the imbalance of women to men in the mid-nineteenth-century British population. Jameson again applauds German women's freedom of movement: in the small capitals of Germany "a young lady, rich, noble, and beautiful, might put on her bonnet and walk through the streets unattended, with perfect propriety." Women's claims to space are expanded and Jameson, an Englishwoman married and therefore able to travel alone respectably, argues that this freedom should exist for unmarried British women as well.

Given that the German model is clearly meant as an example, Jameson uses the introduction to forestall objections. *Social Life in Germany* begins, as had *Characteristics of Women* and *Visits and Sketches at Home and Abroad*, with an introductory dialogue between Alda, Jameson's female stand-in, and Medon, a male interlocutor. Using a dialogue between a man and a woman allowed not only for the unforced broaching of gender issues; it also permitted Jameson to avoid alienating readers. As Clara Thomas and Judith Johnston have made clear, Jameson was well aware that her income depended on not offending her audience, but she also saw to it that they would comprehend her reformist point.

She explains why she offers German texts to her readers, why they are dramas as opposed to another genre, and why critics should find them engaging. Her goal, she says, is "to convey a more detailed and finished picture of the actual state of society in a country which I have learned to love as my own." And then she goads Medon to admit the English need for exposure to German culture: "You will allow that we know little of it, and do not understand what we know, and still less sympathise with what we understand?" In addition, she points out, translating famous works by more accomplished or renowned German authors would not serve her purpose: "they do not reflect, in one graceful and comprehensive picture, the actual state of manners, and the nicer shades of national and individual character: and these were what I required" (SL, I:ix, x). In this way Jameson differentiates her project from the kinds of translations undertaken by someone like Henry Crabb Robinson or Thomas Carlyle. German difference offers a boon for British women, though she is aware that her audience harbors prejudices; consequently she insists that she will simply offer this picture of German life and not force any view on her readers, who in turn must not pretend that the picture should conform to English expectations. Fortunately, English reviewers have matured:

> The general tone of criticism in England is much elevated and enlarged. . . . English critics . . . were long infected with the exclusive spirit which, in its excess, we thought so ridiculous in the old French school. Whatever was foreign to our own mode of existence was misunderstood; whatever was not within the circle of our experience was worthless; whatever was beyond the customary sphere of our observation and interests, trivial or even vulgar. Has not Werter's [sic] Charlotte cutting bread and butter served as a perpetual jest? But all this is passing away. This intolerant and exclusive spirit of criticism would now be contemned and disavowed by any newspaper reviewer. (SL, I:xiii–xiv)

And even to the prejudiced reader, she points out, Princess Amelia is actually like Jane Austen; her dramas "have, indeed, the same sort of

merit—that of delicate and refined portraiture, rather than striking incident or romantic passion" (SL, I:lxxii).

Jameson's translations thus mesh with her travel literature to act
as a means of critique and social enlightenment, and while she insists
that she is not telling the British how they should "behave and express
themselves" (SL, I:xv), she is nonetheless drawing meaningful contrasts
between national customs and policies with the intention of expanding
British horizons of expectation and offering specific examples and alternative methods. Medon concludes: "It is an experiment—a hazardous
one" (SL, I:xvii). The experiment did not backfire, though *Social Life
in Germany*, while commended in the reviews, proved less popular than
Jameson's other works, and the plays, though considered for performance, were not staged.

Jameson was consciously using obscure examples of German literature (dramas by an unknown woman) in a way different from the best-
known translators, Sarah Austin, Samuel Taylor Coleridge, and Thomas
Carlyle, who rendered celebrated male authors into English and thus
stoked interest in German literary productions. Judith Johnston notes
that as Jameson completed this translation she attended a series of lectures by Carlyle "On the History of Literature." He told his audience "that
we are to look to Germany for the light of intellectual truth."[27] Johnston
concludes that Jameson "was confronted, therefore, with a contrast of
two kinds of literature, that which she was working on, and lectures on a
canonized, male *oeuvre* of supposedly 'higher' literary value. . . . Carlyle
[was] always gender specific, as revealed by this and his next series of lectures in 1840 'On Heroes and Hero-worship.' The othering of women's
work must have been very apparent to Jameson."[28] Surely this is a warranted inference, given that the aim of Jameson's book, in keeping with
her earlier works, was to rectify, at every level, the false position of wom-
en vis-à-vis men. But she was also attempting something very practical.
Carlyle's emphasis on heroism and transcendence could not have been
farther from Jameson's quotidian gender concerns. Jameson, after visiting him and his wife Jane, wrote to Lady Byron in 1844: "the life [Jane]
leads, is (for her nature) neither a healthy nor a happy life—married to a
man of genius 'with the Devil in his liver' (to use his own words)! it must
be something next worse to being married to Satan himself." Jameson
as usual sympathized with the victim of masculine ferocity, and even in
her discussions with Thomas Carlyle came to the rescue of subalterns,
defending black slaves and decrying Cromwell's butchering of the Irish

in the seventeenth century—"will you believe that I had the audacity to fight him—absolutely to contradict Carlyle?"[29]

5. Jameson's Transnational Reception

Upon the publication of *Winter Studies and Summer Rambles,* Jameson's reception in Germany was uniformly positive and respectful by contrast with that in Britain, where her liberal views were criticized in conservative journals. Amalie Winter, the German translator of Jameson's book (titled *Winterstudien und Sommerstreifereien in Canada,* 1839), makes clear that the value of her work to German readers derived from its political engagement: "Through her position [as wife of the vice-chancellor of Upper Canada] she had the opportunity to get to know the Constitution and political organization of this young country, and to view its politics and party spirit more deeply than is granted other travelers. She appears to have made it her job to reveal weaknesses and abuses, and therefore there are those in her native country who have objected to and contradicted her work. In Germany, however, one will certainly know to appreciate her contribution."[30] She further points out that Jameson has consistently spoken on behalf of women wherever she sees them oppressed, in a false position, or suffering from prejudice.

Other German critics followed Winter's lead. The *Blätter zur Kunde der Literatur des Auslands* came to Jameson's defense in 1839 in an article on the "Literary Disparagements of Women in England" that spanned two issues. It was devoted to bringing to light unfair statements made anonymously by, presumably, male writers. The article treats the queen, Mrs. Norton, Lady Morgan, Mrs. Austin, as well as Anna Jameson, and the writer calls into question the British critic's refusal to engage in debate. That British critic had said that good manners did not allow him to broach the issues Jameson advocated so energetically (perhaps divorce and/or women's work), because it would require him to probe her personal reasons for doing so. Jameson's German defender insists that the fundamental principles ought to be probed and that this can be done without getting personal. "Should considerations of issues be based on the virtues of the advocate rather than on their own merits? Until now authors of sense and truth were of the opinion that people should direct their focus solely on the arguments and facts concerning an assertion."[31]

Gustav Kühne, author and editor of the *Zeitung für die Elegante Welt,* praised Jameson's travel account as "historically significant" and lauded Jameson's analysis of "the false position of the sexes to one another," something he terms a "portentous issue for our times," to be found even "among the so-called wild Indians."[32] He was particularly impressed with her explanations of the Ojibwa language, which he describes as linguistic and ethnographic work in the mode of Wilhelm von Humboldt.

The *Repertorium der gesammten Deutschen literatur* called *Winterstudien und Sommerstreifereien in Canada* "among the most interesting and enlightening works about the new world to have appeared in a long time,"[33] and the *Blätter für literarische Unterhaltung* noted that Jameson's book offered insight into the Canadian rebellions of 1837, even though these occurred after she left: "England's flawed colonial administration was responsible for the bad situation."[34]

Critics have tended to view Jameson solely in the Canadian or British context, and the upshot is that she is interpreted as a spirited but ultimately conservative writer. In Germany, however, it is clear she was viewed as liberal and was applauded by liberal commentators; indeed when she was there she moved in progressive circles with connections to the Young Germany movement. She was writing the Canada journal that became *Winter Studies and Summer Rambles* to her close friend Ottilie von Goethe, who was daughter-in-law of the renowned poet, and in their correspondence Ottilie often expressed support for revolutionary ideas, especially in the years around 1848. Although Anna Jameson did not share that support on the grounds that she preferred reform, not revolution, this difference of opinion did not diminish their friendship because on other matters, especially ideas about gender, they were of one mind.[35]

It is clear then that Jameson's liberal views participated not only in Anglo-Canadian or transatlantic dialogue but also in pan-European progressive discourses. Gustav Kühne, who reviewed Jameson's work, was a writer and editor of literary periodicals, and his texts on gender relationships and on Ireland apparently were influenced, directly or indirectly, by Jameson. He not only interpreted her Canadian book as belonging to new ethnographic studies he admired but he also flattered through imitation. He published *Weibliche und Männliche Charaktere* in 1838 (the German translation of Jameson's Shakespeare book had been titled *Frauenbilder oder Charakteristik der vorzüglichsten Frauen in Shakspeare's Dramen*, 1834) and then he composed two works about the United Irishmen and the uprising of 1798: *Die Rebellen von Irland* (1840), a novel, and a dramatic reworking, *Die Verschwörung von Dublin* (1856). Kühne was affiliated with the Young Germany movement in the 1830s and 1840s, a group of authors who sought progressive social and judicial reforms and decried the apolitical, idealist stance of Romantic writers. In 1835 the Frankfurt parliament banned the writings of the group, which included "H. Heine," throughout the German states; they accused the Young Germans of attempting, by literary means, "to attack the Christian religion in the boldest manner, to degrade the existing order, and to destroy decorum and morals in all classes of readers."[36] Anglicists who have emphasized Jameson's conservatism might be surprised to find her moving in such progressive German circles.

Indeed Kühne's two favored themes, gender and Ireland, dominate his article on "Anna Jameson."[37] The first of these themes accompanies his announcement of the arrival of this literary celebrity in Germany: he stresses Jameson's interest in German women, and then contrasts British women's upbringing as outlined in Jameson's *Visits and Sketches.*

Mistress Jameson . . . war einige Tage in Leipzig. . . . Überall leitete sie bei ihrer Theilnahme an deutscher Literatur und Geselligkeit ein ganz besonderes Interesse für die deutschen Frauen, in deren geistiger Bedeutsamkeit sie einen so wesentlichen Vorzug gegen das englische Gesellschaftsleben zu finden glaubt. Mit freudigem Erstaunen sieht sie in Deutschland eine freiere und tiefere Entfaltung der weiblichen Natur; Erscheinungen wie Rahel und Bettina fesseln ihre ganze Aufmerksamkeit, aber auch in den gewöhnlichen Kreisen der deutschen Gesellschaft hat sie ihr Wohlgefallen an dem geistig regen Verkehr der Frauen mit Männern. . . . Mistress Jameson wird ihren Landsleuten eine Charakeristik deutscher Frauen liefern. Sie gedenkt in Weimar, wo sie den Winter zubringt, ihre Arbeit auszuführen.[38]

[Mistress Jameson . . . spent several days in Leipzig. Everywhere her participation in German literary and social affairs was guided by her intense interest in German women, whose intellectual stature she believes reveals a substantial advantage when compared with English social life. She views with delighted surprise a freer and deeper development of women's nature in Germany; phenomena such as Rahel [Varnhagen] and Bettina [von Arnim] capture her full attention, but even in the common circles of German society she enjoys the energetic intellectual traffic between women and men. . . . Mistress Jameson is going to deliver to her compatriots a characterization of German women. She intends to complete her work in Weimar, where she will spend the winter.]

In Weimar Ottilie von Goethe enthusiastically received Jameson, who had been introduced by Lady Byron's nephew Robert Noel.

It would appear that Kühne's ties to Ottilie von Goethe commenced at this same period; the friendship was an intense exchange, and their correspondence lasted until Ottilie's death in 1872, when he wrote her eulogy. Both he and Ottilie dwelt on Jameson's Irishness; Kühne emphasizes how Jameson's character reflects both Irish and English traits. "Ihre feingeschnitzten Gesichtszüge verrathen eben so sehr die Tochter Englands, die sie in ihrer Bildung ist, wie die lebhaften Farben ihrer Erscheinung das Kind Irlands bekunden. Die Lebhaftigkeit ihrer Rede ist irländisch; das gehaltene Maß ihrer Bewegungen englisch."[39] (Her fine facial features betray as strongly the daughter of England, which she is in her education, as the lively colors of her appearance suggest the child of Ireland. The vivacity of her speech is Irish; the controlled measure of her movements English.) Kühne takes particular note of Jameson's volume on Shakespeare's heroines, translated into German by Adolph Wagner, the respected philologist and uncle of the composer Richard Wagner (1834). Much admired by August Wilhelm Schlegel, that book is ultimately what opened the door for her to literary society, including Kühne's notice.[40]

Kühne's *Die Rebellen von Irland* (*The Rebels of Ireland*, 1840) must to a degree have been informed by Jameson via Ottilie von Goethe. Kühne acknowledges in print that Ottilie's interest in Ireland influenced his work, and that she supplied him with the historical books he needed to complete his novel.[41] But Jameson furnished many of those books to Ottilie. So Ottilie supplied Kühne with historical information, but Jameson appears to have been a crucial conduit for such materials to Ottilie, as the extant record substantiates. In a letter of 1838, for example, Jameson regretted her inability to send Irish books; then, the next year, she succeeded in mailing novels of Samuel Lover and Lady Morgan, "Rory O'More, O'Donnel, and Florence Macarthy," as well as two other unspecified "Irish books," not to mention "the play of *the Wife*" by James Sheridan Knowles.[42] A letter from 1851 also details a big packet Ottilie received from Jameson via Robert Noel, including "1. National Education in Ireland. 2. 'Instruct, Employ, don't hand them'. (rare tract). 3. Industrial Reforms of Ireland. 4. Essay on Ireland and Irish Affairs (Sir Charles Napier). 5. The Saxon in Ireland (the latest work on Ireland of interest or authority). 6. Handbook on Irish Antiquities."[43] Jameson consistently reported to Ottilie on Irish politics in her letters; she described in detail her 1853 trip to Ireland, which she undertook to assess the suffering caused by the devastating potato famine. It would seem likely that in their frequent meetings on the Continent Jameson supplied further materials and information. In Italy in 1853, for instance, Ottilie asked Jameson "if you go once more to Ireland, you must . . . make me a present of a Broche" to match "a bracelet from irish bogg oak ornamented with irish diamonds" that she had received from the Phippses, mutual friends; moreover, "Phipps is planning to come to Florence. Now if you can find no other opportunity send me the irish books by him."[44] Ottilie's ongoing fascination with Ireland was cultural and aesthetic as well as intellectual and political, and her broad knowledge must have been a great help to Kühne's literary efforts, which involved careful research. Even after his Irish novel was published he twice wrote to Ottilie "asking her to check details in Wolfe Tone's memoirs," and he traveled to Ireland in 1862 to find out the latest. He consulted Ottilie again for his second Irish work, the drama *Die Verschwörung von Dublin* (1856),[45] on which Ottilie lavishes praise in her letters to Jameson: "As a Tragedy it is most exellent [*sic*] . . . It is a great pity, that in all probability it will not be given in many places, people are such cowards."[46] Kühne's production met with a tepid reception thanks to a growing conservatism; the text was returned to him from a producer in Berlin "mit dem Bedauern, es sei zu politisch" (with the regret, that it was too political).[47] The influence of the Young Germans dissipated after the revolutions of 1848 and tendentious political-historical works of this type lost favor.

6. Anna Jameson's Transnational Politics and Epistemology

The positive reception of Jameson's writings in Germany occurred because, not in spite of, her focus on women and gender politics, even as her liberal views were decried in Britain by conservative critics. Jameson's progressive friends on the Continent continued to applaud her writings to the end of her career and in particular appreciated her last and most articulate political works: *Sisters of Charity* (1855) and *The Communion of Labour* (1856), two lectures that were later reprinted together.[48] Here Jameson made specific suggestions about the labor, different in nature but equally weighty, that women and men should do in tandem or "communion." Rejecting Romantic idealism and utilitarian approaches, she argued for a realistic grappling with the actual obstacles faced by women in everyday life. Despite the focus on the quotidian, her impulse is cosmopolitan and utopian; it is clearly not of the detached, philosophical sort.

It sounds fine to merge distinctions of sex in general high-sounding phrases; to speak of the "claims of mankind at large"—the progress of humanity—"the destinies of the world"—the "great human brotherhood"—as is the manner of philosophers and philanthropists; but it means something more real, more vital, more heart-felt and home-felt, when we speak of "men" and of "women"—not to disunite them—not implying thereby any separation of those divine and earthly interests held in common, and through which they form in the aggregate the great social community, but to bring them before us with their *equal* but still *distinct* humanity; their *equal* but still *distinct* need of divine and earthly justice and mercy; their *equal* but still *distinct* capacities and responsibilities in the great social commonwealth.[49] (emphasis in original)

This passage underscores her central aim in the text to reframe the "woman-question" as a "human-question" (SCCL, xix, 78), to view people as inextricably linked regardless of sex, even while suggesting that there are essential differences—both biological and moral, she insists— between women and men.[50] Jameson denies the notion of the separation of spheres, even as she distinguishes between masculinity and femininity.

Jameson chiefly addresses the issue of labor for women. She sees capitalist competition, which she calls "industrial antagonism," increasing tension between the sexes, and she denounces "the fear that an influx of female labour will swamp the labour-market and diminish [men's] own gains." This fearful attitude pervades all classes and occupations; it is not limited to the working classes or to "boards of jealous poor-law guardians: it is to be found in Royal Academies of art and Royal Colleges of physicians." Since two million women in Britain must support themselves, "a material and inevitable necessity *must* bring this question to its natural solution" (SCCL, xvii, xvii–xviii). Like Mary Wollstonecraft before her, Jameson enumerates the kinds of work that women should be encouraged to do in public institutions, especially those establishments requiring care of human subjects, such as workhouses, prisons, schools, and hospitals.[51]

Significant here is how Jameson came to her conclusions. For, as I have argued, it was during her travels in America that Jameson realized the significance of the "communion of labour," that women and men must work in tandem, because the common notion of the separation of spheres was pernicious. Even though men and women might have different jobs, nonetheless there is "no more fatal, more unjust misconception" than that the sexes should be kept apart (SCCL, xx).

> I saw the effects of this kind of social separation of the sexes when I was in America. I thought it did not act well on the happiness or the manners of either. The men too often became coarse and material as clay in private life, and in public life too prone to cudgels and revolvers; and the effect of the women herding so much together was not to refine them, but the contrary; to throw them into various absurd and unfeminine exaggerations. (SCCL, xxi)

As she puts it in *Winter Studies*, "The two sexes are more than sufficiently separated by different duties and pursuits; what tends to separate them farther . . . cannot be good for either" (WS, I:232).

Jameson's utopian impulse is likewise central to her politics. On Jameson's entire trip to Canada she was preoccupied with the interdependent issues of sex roles, vocation, and the heartless, systematizing effects of modernization, and she came to some significant conclusions, expressed most explicitly in *Sisters of Charity and the Communion of Labour*: first, women have human rights, especially the right to education, to "the protection of equal laws," and to work that they choose; second, these rights will not be realized until men and women share evenly in the work of the world; and third, a truly civilized modern society characterized by this shared work, "the communion of labour," will only be achieved gradually through changes in mentality, legislation, and practice. She asks rhetorically whether her goals are utopian in the negative sense, that is, chimerical, but then emphasizes that, no,

> Whatever our practice may be, let us hold fast to our theories of possible good; let us, at least, however they outrun our present powers, keep them in sight, and then our formal lagging practice may in time overtake them. In social morals, as well as in physical truths, "The goal of yesterday" will be the starting point of to-morrow; and the things before which all England now stands in admiring wonder will become "the simple produce of the common day." Thus we hope and believe. (SCCL, 66)

The achievement of these interconnected goals was Jameson's utopian project that, following the visions of a long line of feminists beginning as early as Christine de Pizan, was characterized by gradualism, pragmatism, an emphasis on education, and a reliance on the modification of social behavior, especially relations between the sexes. And it was shaped by the combined political and sociological information she gleaned in America.[52] Ottilie circulated her copy of Jameson's lectures among her circle and was inspired to suggest a communal household including Jameson, herself and her sister, and others: "You see I intended to arrange a kind of Phalanstère" (Vienna, 9 May 1855).

Jameson carried over ideas garnered within the contact zone of North America and joined these with imported German notions gleaned from travels on the Continent, and her works were then translated and sold across Europe. Her feminism was thus gathered and expressed transnationally, and her relationship with German culture, and her desires for its influence on British society, formed part of an ongoing exchange that involved repeated visits and played itself out on a personal as well as a professional level. In that sense it can be distinguished from the aims of other British importers of German ideas, but it should not therefore be viewed as culturally less significant.

Jameson's transnationalism also ties her to earlier, less mobile bluestocking feminists such as Sarah Scott, Mary Hamilton, and Mary Wollstonecraft, who were cosmopolitan out of necessity as well as interest; gender trumped nation because feminists, alongside other progressives, felt solidarity with like-minded thinkers regardless of national origin.[53] Sophie von La Roche, for example, expressed this not only in her travels to England but also in her journal *Pomona*, as she created special issues concerning the work of foreign, especially English, women. Anna Jameson followed suit by explicating for British people the practices and values of other nations, even as translations of her work introduced British thought to continental and transatlantic readers. Hers was a hybrid epistemology; she drew on all of her travels, her reading, her knowledge of art, as well as her firsthand international experience and interviews, in order to interpret what she saw before her and to draw readers from all perspectives.

A close look at the texture of her writing reveals this transnational epistemology, her constant impulse to gather in and to translate (Latin: to "carry across").[54] Here, a passage about a seemingly trivial subject—a confrontation with swarms of mosquitoes, experienced during her travels on Lake Huron—becomes simultaneously a meditation on human universality as well as cultural difference, and it is this understanding that she wishes to reinforce for readers so that they recognize their place in an interconnected human community. Jameson encountered the swarms of mosquitoes on her bateau trip from Mackinaw to Sault Ste. Marie, a journey she undertook with Mrs. Schoolcraft, the half-Native wife of the American Indian agent, who brought along her children on this visit to introduce Jameson to her Native family. Jameson's account reveals an instinctive, automatic transnationality; translation is a constitutional drive within her even when she discusses something as mundane and local as American insects.

> The moment our boat touched the shore, we were enveloped in a cloud of mosquitoes. Fires were lighted instantly, six were burning in a circle at once; we were well nigh suffocated and smoke-dried—all in vain. At last we left the voyageurs to boil the kettle, and retreated to our boat, desiring them to make us fast to a tree by a long rope; then, each of us taking an oar—I only wish you could have seen us—we pushed off from the land, while the children were sweeping away the enemy with green boughs. This being done, we commenced supper, really half famished, and were too much engrossed to look about us. Suddenly we were again surrounded by our adversaries; they came upon us in swarms, in clouds, in myriads, entering our eyes, our noses, our mouths, stinging till the blood followed. . . . I had suffered from these plagues in Italy; you too, by this time, may probably know what they are in the southern countries of the old world; but 'tis a jest, believe me, to encountering a forest full of them in these wild regions. I had heard much, and much was I forewarned, but never could have conceived the torture they can inflict, nor the impossibility of escape, defence, or endurance. Some amiable person, who took an especial interest in our future welfare, in enumerating the torments prepared for hardened sinners, assures us that they will be stung by mosquitoes all made of brass, and as large as black beetles— he was an ignoramus and a bungler; you may credit me, the brass is quite an unnecessary improvement, and the increase of size equally superfluous. Mosquitoes, as they exist in this upper world, are as pretty and perfect a plague as the most ingenious amateur sinner- tormentor ever devised. . . . I offered an extra gratuity to the men, if they would keep to their oars without interruption, and then, fairly exhausted, lay down on my locker and blanket. But whenever I woke from uneasy, restless slumbers, *there* was Mrs. Schoolcraft, bending over her sleeping children, and waving off the mosquitoes, singing all the time a low, melancholy Indian song; while the northern lights

were streaming and dancing in the sky, and the fitful moaning of the
wind, the gathering clouds, and chilly atmosphere, foretold a change
of weather. (WS, III:166–69)

Jameson faces a New World challenge and addresses her unnamed correspondent (generally taken to be Ottilie) in order to heighten the conversational tone and the intimacy with the reader: "I only wish you could
have seen us . . . you too, may probably know." The connection strength-
ens both the differences and ties suggested by the new experience. First,
Jameson makes gender distinctions. The "voyageurs," the male boatmen,
take a draconian approach by lighting vehement fires that not only fail
to smoke out the mosquitoes but threaten to suffocate the women and
children, who then separate and retreat to the boat: a plan, however, that
also miscarries. Next, Jameson distinguishes between Europe and America. Lake Huron mosquitoes are contrasted with those of Italy, familiar
to her readers. The comparison suggests the stunning numbers of the
New World's pests and allows Jameson to contrast the present with the
past, and nature with culture. She invokes a certain humor, differentiating the vast, robust, and harsh reality of Canadian nature from the
prosaic inscriptions of a European "amateur sinner-tormentor," someone like Hieronymus Bosch from medieval or early modern religious
art, making hell appear artificial, contrived, and weak. Indeed, she links
herself, her fellow travelers, and her readers together as inhabitants of
the living, breathing "upper world" by contrast with the removed nether
world depicted in the old-master representation. Finally, she ends the
passage by referring to the indigenous and feminine response. Where
she first differentiated her observations from European experience, she
now identifies herself as a European in contrast with the obliging rowers'
and the Native woman's response. Though she has dealt with much distress on her long rough trip, our narrator cannot achieve the equanim-
ity with which Mrs. Schoolcraft copes with this plague, singing a sooth-
ing song to help her traumatized children sleep, and gently waving a
bough over them to shoo away the mosquitoes. Such a picture of mater-
nal selflessness is to Jameson both a sentimental and a universal one,
linking the values of the European reader, the frontier traveler, and the
Native mother, even as it distinguishes Jameson's agitated-metropolitan,
psychological distance from the placidity of the admirable indigenous
woman. Mrs. Schoolcraft's quiet song joins the northern lights and
moaning of the wind to define what is truly and beautifully natural; it
betokens a wet, yet plague-free tomorrow. Jameson thoroughly admires

and identifies with but also distances herself from the Native mother. She therefore, through back-and-forth commonalities and distinctions, universal values and specific differences, simultaneously invokes both a European context and an American one, both of which do, and do not, include her. She slides fluidly back and forth and takes her reader with her. Such movement in identification and understanding defines Jameson's method of translation; it is at the core of all of her writing, making her a trusted, transnational, and popular correspondent for her European audience.

Not only is Jameson's work characterized by her translational approach, it is also profitably interpreted in a transnational mode, one she seeks to foreground. In *Sisters of Charity and the Communion of Labour*, Florence Nightingale becomes Jameson's exemplar not only of how essential women can be when trained and allowed to work alongside men, but also of the productivity of British-German interchange. She notes with consternation that England has no school of nursing (SCCL, 56) and describes at length how Nightingale was trained in Germany at Kaiserswerth, a charitable hospital that had grown out of various institutions begun by the German pastor Theodor Fliedner. Nightingale's first publication on this establishment was *The Institution of Kaiserswerth on the Rhine, for the Practical Training of Deaconesses, etc.* (1851). Jameson does not fail to emphasize, however, that Pastor Fliedner conceived of his program on his own travels to England, and particularly in consultation with a Quaker Englishwoman, Mrs. Elizabeth Fry, the famous prison reformer. Jameson thus underscores the international genesis of the institution, as well as its creation by members of both sexes. Simultaneously, she berates her country-people for failing to imitate such good ideas and expresses regret that such a talented woman as Nightingale was forced to seek her training abroad (SCCL, 34). The best influences and most successful institutions, Jameson suggests, have transnational and dual-gender origins. Optimal arrangements involve linking the sexes in a "communion of labour," just as the best ideas emerge when international practices are brought together.

Jameson's conception of the grandeur of international collectivity and what she sees as true cosmopolitanism can best be seen in her effusions about the Great Exhibition at the Crystal Palace, which she visited more than twenty times: "if you could see *liberté, egalité, fraternité* of the true kind, it is seen here."[55] And indeed the Exhibition epitomizes internationalist utopianism. The audience, awed into peace by the splendor of the Exhibition, exerts its art-inspired will successfully against an authority that itself understands to react not aggressively but with restraint when the crowds cannot bear to leave on the last day.

> At 5 o'clock the bell rang for all to go out as usual, but on this occasion the people would not go. I went up into the gallery of the transept to see the effect. There was no ceremony, it was left to the spontaneous feeling of the people. The bells rang louder and louder,—no one would go. The organs played God Save the Queen, the people joined their voices, then they burst into acclamations; the voices rose, died away; rose and swelled, till the shouts were deafening, then sank and rose in another direction. The Police had orders to remain quiet. Only the bells rang loud and louder, but nobody would go. The sun set in golden splendour, pouring a flood of parting light along those immense halls and avenues. The roof, the walls, were for a short time like a flame and all the objects lighted in the most extraordinary manner. But soon the shadows fell, night came on. There was a sea of human faces around me, and below me 60,000 people dimly seen, and all talking, singing, shouting with a joyous, kindly, feeling,—but nobody would go. The bells rang louder and louder, the night came darker and darker, lamps were lighted here and there, flashing on the banners and silk draperies and Gold and Silver and glass reflected in crimson and blue and here and there, while the long lines of delicate tracery were seen in most marvellous perspective, like a fairy dream, like nothing real. At last, when two hours had thus passed and the moon had risen, the Police very gently interfered to urge the people to be reasonable and move towards the doors, but they would not hurry, and at length a troop of Engineers, quite unarmed, under the direction of the head of police, formed a line holding each other's hands and thus gradually swept the vast multitude towards the doors. There was no force, no resistance, no accident, no injury to any person, or any object. It was altogether the most sublime and picturesque spectacle I ever beheld in my life.[56]

Unlike on Vesuvius, Jameson is here able to keep her eyes fixed on the sublime object. The language of flames and troops and anthem-singing and bell-ringing and tens of thousands of participants describes not a battlefield but what to Jameson constituted a massive, awe-inspiring demonstration of a unified pacifist popular will. Ottilie von Goethe affirmed that Jameson was "not at all inclined to make a revolution";[57] Jameson decried revolution because of its potential for violence and destruction.

But Jameson was buoyed by how in this instance the masses, witnessing a display of international artistry and industry, singing, and experiencing a dream-like sunset could be inspired to utopian cooperation respected even by the disciplinary agents on hand, the police and the "troop of Engineers."

This "sublime and picturesque" moment at the Crystal Palace was a rare one for Jameson. Most of her experience led her to lament human beings' inhumane treatment of each other, and this influenced her notions about the movement of history, which, unlike those of the Whig historians of her day, were not ideas of inevitable progress. As I have indicated, Jameson refers to Scottish conjectural histories, but her focus on women suggests that such a theory is ultimately wrongheaded. In "Women's Mission and Women's Position" (1843) she laments that all books,

> prose or poetry—morals, physics, travels, history—they tell us one and all that the chief distinction between savage and civilized life, between Heathendom and Christendom, lies in the treatment and the condition of the women; that by the position of the women in the scale of society we estimate the degree of civilization of that society; that on her power to exercise her faculties and duties aright, depends the moral culture of the rising generation,—in other words, the progress of the species. . . . Such is the beautiful theory of the woman's existence, preached to her by moralists, sung to her by poets, till it has become the world's creed—and her own faith, even in the teeth of fact and experience!

Indeed, "the real state of things is utterly at variance" with this myth.[58] Consequently Jameson develops a theory of history that is, by contrast, one of severely limited and gradual improvement. Women are everywhere oppressed, everywhere in a "false position," except among the First Nations, where, however, they toil endlessly, and while she sees economic development as opening some doors for European women, as I have noted, she sees how it is closing possibilities for Native women. Change will certainly not happen inevitably or on its own.[59]

Jameson therefore advocates reform and decries British opponents of it. Those who stand in the way of progressive change are people who constitute "'that other public,'—that self-satisfied, unreasoning, cowardly, somnolent public which *we* repudiate" (SCCL, 43), people who lack mental mobility and are stuck in prejudice. As early as the *Diary of an Ennuyée* (1826) she had mocked sarcastically that particular public's

haughty view of the Other. "How I hate the discussion of politics in Italy!
. . . Let the modern Italians be what they may, what I hear them styled
six times a day at least,—a dirty, demoralized, degraded, unprincipled
race,—centuries behind our thrice blessed, prosperous, and comfort-
loving nation in civilization and morals."[60] Her satirical take on fatuous
British manners and morals has bite even at the beginning of her writing career, and her defense of the Italians takes much the same shape
that her defense not only of the Native Americans but also of women,
of blacks, of the Irish, and of commuted pensioners in Canada takes—
people with limitations, to be sure, but burdened by stereotypes, British jingoism, and a heartless system. If Jameson does not undertake
her project with firebrand polemics it is because she had to maintain
her loyal readership in order to support her family; if she often sounds
conventional to our ears she nonetheless drew vehement criticism from
reactionary periodicals like the *Monthly Review* and the *British and Foreign
Review*. Jameson's friend Mrs. Procter noted those antifeminist commentaries and, as Jameson later remembered, told her not to mind, saying
"a fig for reviewers": "The men . . . are much alarmed by certain specula-
tions about women; and . . . well they may be, for when the horse and ass
begin to think and argue, adieu to riding and driving."[61] The vehement
tone of the "other public's" reviews offers a measure of the threat Jameson was seen to pose and indicates as well the range of British criticism
circulating at this time.[62]

7. Jameson's Impact

Anna Jameson, perceived as a woman of the people, a lively middle-class
presence on the British literary scene, became also a gauge of the penetration and reception of foreign ideas in Europe in the second quarter
of the nineteenth century. At a time when nationalism, imperialism, and
militarism were preoccupying many, and while they continue to dominate scholarship, we see a cosmopolitan, transnational force emerging
from a surprising corner: a woman with the appearance of a stolid Victorian matron.

In this period of post-Napoleonic upheaval, women and subalterns
had much to fear about potential disaster and the vulnerability of their
current footing. From Olaudah Equiano's perilous travels to Dean
Mahomet's vacillating commercial enterprises to Mary Shelley's night-
marish *Frankenstein* and *The Last Man*, we see the profound concerns of

subalterns, slaves, people of color, and women about survival, betrayal, privation, and disaster. People who, given their social positions, might be expected to espouse radical points of view express surprisingly conservative opinions and devise end-of-the-world scenarios. Subalterns had a lot to lose, and many sought stability over upheaval. In February 1849, pondering the revolutions occurring on the Continent, Jameson wrote to Ottilie von Goethe: "England is tranquil, and we are fully resolved to have no revolutions, which like a storm or a fever fit may do some good, but not without doing harm. The beautiful part of our social policy is, that our government has *within* itself a principle of development which enables it to reform itself without any violent pressure from adverse and external causes; in this consists our safety while all Europe is convulsed. We shall have here alterations and reforms, but all spontaneously and quietly. The very *noise* and *agitation* of which you read in our newspapers are the proof of our safety. As long as people can talk and speak freely and make a great noise, they don't make conspiracies and revolutions."[63] Jameson's timidity about revolutionary activity is matched by the intensity of her written arguments; at midcentury she has faith that the pen can actually serve to bring about social reform.

As Clara Thomas and Judith Johnston have pointed out, Jameson articulated arguments that became commonplace among later feminists. She called Adelaide Anne Procter, Barbara Leigh Smith Bodichon, Bessie Rayner Parkes, and Anna Mary Howitt her "adopted nieces";[64] gave advice concerning the *Waverley Journal* and later the *English Woman's Journal*, edited by Parkes; and in general became a guiding light for the Langham Place Circle. She attended the British and Foreign Anti-Slavery Society's convention in June 1840. She participated on the Married Women's Property Committee, and the petition presented to Parliament in March 1856 went out under her name and Mary Howitt's; she herself delivered and published the two influential lectures I have discussed, *Sisters of Charity* and *The Communion of Labour*, the culmination of her thinking on gender and labor; and she attended the meetings of the newly created National Association for the Promotion of Social Science (1857), which aimed to achieve social reform—including women's rights and education—and which from the start included women in the organization and among its speakers.

Consequently it may well be Jameson's quotidian and critical transnationalism that has kept her from becoming a canonized author. Her method and her message made her an unsuitable candidate to promote the glory of English studies; she has only in the last decades been taken up by scholars who appreciate that her writings offer a telling counter-narrative. She excelled in nonfiction prose, criticism, travel accounts, and translations rather than novels or poetry; she wrote first and fore-most to make money through popular publications, and her consequent choice of subjects and genres relegated her to what is often considered hackwork by the academy. She spent much time out of England, traveled frequently and criticized British ways. Moreover her very productivity and prodigiousness might have worked against her. Like Daniel Defoe, she wrote so copiously and cleverly in so many fields that she was viewed as a dilettante or simply taken for granted. The choice of a representa-tive Jamesonian text becomes difficult when one is faced with volumes upon volumes of histories, biographies, travel guides, travel accounts, criticism, art history, and memoirs. How does one pin down the identity of this author? What, in a nutshell, can she be said to stand for? It is fortunate that a writer with transnational and translational proclivities need no longer be ignored, and that, indeed, current interest in global-ization and cosmopolitanism corresponds with the ways Jameson viewed her world, allowing a new access to her varied oeuvre.

Afterword

Les Terrains Plus Vastes

In this book about British-German cultural transfer I have followed the recent "spatial turn" in historiography and concerned myself with *terrains vastes*. I began with the University of Göttingen and its English ties, expanded through Lower Saxony to Weimar and back across the Channel, toured to Naples and then moved beyond the Atlantic to Canada and returned to Europe. Actors expanded along with the geography: not only significant figures played a part, from professors to tourists to gymnasts to settlers and indigenous Americans, but also material, geographical, and infrastructural elements that brought the various actors to crucial places at telling moments. Publications such as books, textbooks, and periodicals; personal communications in the form of letters and journals; artistic representations, contracts, records; libraries, collections, shelves of books, and souvenirs; modes of discourse; systems of rank, transport, law, and war; mosquitoes and an erupting volcano: all have contributed to this story of British-German ties during the Personal Union.

As my account appeared to expand ever outward and become more inclusive, it worked its way into a figure of associations in the manner of Bruno Latour's actor networks. The very different protagonists displayed distinct styles of transfer and mediation in interconnected ongoing systems, rotating around various geographical and institutional "centers of calculation." I will take up one more such center as a concluding emblem of the type of British-German transfer I have been describing:

The "Garden Kingdom of Dessau-Wörlitz," created by Prince Leopold Friedrich Franz of Anhalt-Dessau in the last decades of the eighteenth century, offers both a conclusion to my book and initiates a discussion of questions for further study.

Prince Franz (1740–1817), often called "Father Franz" by his manifestly fond subjects, took over rule of the small principality of Anhalt-Dessau, sandwiched between Weimar and Prussia, in 1758. An Anglophile, he modeled the park at Wörlitz on English gardens that he visited on four different trips to Britain, and the development of the Garden Kingdom demonstrates how creating space for human, material, and intellectual connection could further progressive aims. Indeed, Prince Franz was motivated not merely by novelty, aesthetics, or the desire for outdoor diversion; he recognized the sociopolitical significance of his estate and wished it to convey Enlightenment ideas to the general public.[1] For one thing, the estate was fully accessible to the people at all times, every day of the year, as it had no walls nor gates nor even sunken fences. The palace, and its collections and library, were open to the public as well. He advocated religious tolerance and conveyed this by building a synagogue in proximity to a Christian church and a representation of natural religion, so that visitors walking through the landscape would see these, juxtaposed within one fan view, thereby rendered equivalent and in harmonious relationship; he constructed a nonsectarian cemetery as well. Freedom of the press meant the possibility for publication of the Jewish newspaper *Sulamith*. Prince Franz established housing for the poor that included not only shelter but also education; he built a hospital, instituted a scheme of social security, and improved the roads.

On his four trips to England he witnessed not only new-style English gardens that he wished to imitate but also agricultural reforms and manufactures; he created a smaller replica of the iron Coalbrookdale Bridge. He also admired the Dissenting academies and came home to engage Johann Bernhard Basedow in the establishment of his Rousseauian school, the Philanthropin, at Dessau in 1774. To demonstrate that the glory of ancient times could be resuscitated, Prince Franz yearly imitated the Olympic Games in competitions at Drehberg from 1776 to 1799; he sponsored a pentathlon, and visitors attended from far and wide.[2] Prince Franz also constructed a "Forster Pavilion" between 1781 and 1784 to honor Georg and his father, Johann Reinhold, and to house geographic and ethnological exhibits. He had received forty-four Tahitian and Tongan artifacts and a map from the Forsters in London in the summer of 1775, just after they had returned from the second Cook voyage; it was necessary to construct a fitting site for display of these precious objects. (The Wörlitz collection is the third largest one devoted to Forster materials; it follows those of the Pitt Rivers Museum and the collection at the University of Göttingen.) Georg Forster himself visited Dessau-Wörlitz three times, in 1779, 1785, and 1788. He was taken with the prince's reforms and made friends with the prince's liberal companions Friedrich Wilhelm von Erdmannsdorf, Basedow, and Joachim Heinrich Campe, with whom he continued to correspond.[3]

Friedrich Franz moreover traveled to Italy in 1765–66 and from 1788 to 1794 he and his colleague Erdmannsdorf, fellow traveler on the Grand Tour and resident architect, constructed a model of Vesuvius in his Wörlitz park, and on special occasions this mountain was filled with fireworks launched at night to mimic volcanic eruptions. John Claudius Loudon, a Scottish horticulturalist who traveled through this part of Germany in 1814, described the phenomenon:

> In the representation of eruptions, the hollow which surrounds the crater, and out of which it seems to rise, overflows with water, which is thrown up by a machine within the mountain, and which, like a magnificent cascade, rushes down, foaming and roaring, over the rocky ridge into the lake. A stone bridge, which is thrown over this hollow, leads to the great caldron, where the fireworks, projected through the mouth of the crater, are prepared, and in which, when the volcano is working, all kinds of inflammable materials are burned; when an immense smoke issues from the numerous apertures, and covers the top of the mountain with heavy black clouds. At the same time millions of sparks, rising from the gulf, form columns of fire, and streams of melted lava appear to flow down the sides of the mountain.[4]

On one side of the volcano Prince Franz built the "Villa Hamilton," a copy of William Hamilton's dwelling at Posillipo, in which Franz displayed Wedgwood copies of ancient vases—especially the famous Portland vase collected by Hamilton—as well as samples of lava and other geological specimens.[5] On the other side of the volcano was an outdoor theater inspired by those at Pompeii and Herculaneum. The volcano, according to Simon Werrett, "was taken to represent enlightenment itself, as a constructive force shaping the environment for the benefit of mankind"[6] and, it should be added, for the enhancement of its builder's status, his reputation among visitors, and their moral and cultural instruction.

Prince Franz clearly succeeded in his political and didactic aims to

FIG. 9. Karl Kuntz, *Der Stein zu Wörlitz* (1797). Reconstruction of Vesuvius in the English garden of Prince Leopold Friedrich Franz. Copyright and courtesy of Kulturstiftung Dessau Wörlitz, Germany, photograph by Heinz Frässdorf.

create an evocative landscape that would impress and enlighten visitors. When Goethe toured Wörlitz in May 1778, he wrote to Charlotte von Stein: "It is endlessly beautiful here. As we wandered among the lakes, canals and forests yesterday evening, I was moved by the way in which the gods had allowed the Prince to create a dream all around him. When one walks through it, it is like the telling of a fairy tale; it has the character of the Elysian Fields."[7] Goethe then sought to imitate Wörlitz park with Duke Carl August in Weimar. Commentators have noted the mystical Masonic elements of the park and likened the effects of Wörlitz to the enchantments in Mozart's *Magic Flute*, an opera that was first performed there on 11 August 1794.[8]

The idyll was not destroyed by revolution or the Napoleonic wars.

GutsMuths in 1793 used Dessau's yearly Olympic festival as an example of how a sovereign can maintain the affection and unity of the community: "How important, and how much to be recommended, in an age of revolutions!"[9] When Napoleon descended upon Dessau after victory at the Battle of Jena in October of 1806, Prince Franz further demonstrated political acumen in protecting his lands. His encounter with Napoleon is vividly described by the Oxford professor F. Max Müller, who grew up in Dessau and frames his 1897 account as a childhood memory of his mother, who was a granddaughter of the educator Basedow. In Müller's rendering the two men embody a confrontation of Enlightenment cosmopolitanism with a new imperial politics.

> The old Prince had to receive him bareheaded at the foot of the staircase of his castle. My mother, then a child of six, remembered seeing her own grand and beautiful prince standing erect before the small and pale Corsican. The Prince, however, in his meeting with the Emperor, was not afraid to wear the Prussian order of the Black Eagle on his breast, and when he was asked by Napoleon whether he too had sent a contingent to the Prussian army, he said, "No, sir." "Why not?" asked the Emperor. "Because I have not been asked," was the answer. "But if you had been asked?" continued the Emperor. "Then I should certainly have sent my soldiers," the Prince replied; and he added, "Your majesty knows the right of the stronger." This was a not very prudent remark to make, but the Emperor seems to have liked the outspoken old man. He invited him to inspect with him the bridge over the Elbe which had been burnt by the Prussians to cover their retreat. He demanded that it should be rebuilt at once, and on that condition he promised to grant neutrality to the duchy. Nay, before leaving Dessau, in the morning he went so far as to ask his host whether he could do anything for him. "For myself," the Prince replied, "I want nothing. I only ask for mercy for my people, for they are all to me like my children."[10]

This account may well be embroidered through family lore; however, the tone of the description accords with the general record of liberal Prince Franz, who was indeed able to achieve neutrality for the duchy and did impress Napoleon to the extent that he received an invitation, which was apparently declined, to visit France.[11] Motivated by Enlightenment ideals, delighted by English ways, all the while following patriarchal and absolutist traditions, Prince Franz pursued his manifold endeavors in

Anhalt-Dessau. He thereby demonstrated the profound extent to which travel could inspire plans for reform, the long-standing influence and depth of the English model in German life despite or because of French intellectual and military incursions, and the way in which an Anglophile's plucky retort to a French emperor finds its way back to a British audience through a well-placed local mediator.

Prince Franz's garden at Wörlitz thus epitomizes the ongoing European transfer of ideas, goods, people, and methods for progressive enlightenment ends into the nineteenth century. Were I writing a more traditional history, I might have chosen the figure of Prince Franz—or Georg Forster or Joseph Johnson—and composed a full chapter explaining the academic or intellectual or cultural prominence he achieved. But much of what I have described was not completed by these figures; what they began was continued, furthered, and changed—"translated" in Latour's terms—by other mediators, especially bluestockings in my account, who helped make visible the social effects that mattered for this historical narrative. So I am less concerned about the men's eminence or the egocentric network surrounding them and more interested in their function as dynamic conduits, mediators themselves, as well as in the mediators they rouse or enable. This approach has consequently facilitated the writing of feminist and gender history, since the intellectual women with whom these figures worked have not been subordinated to a narrative about them but to a story of the issues and goals that impelled eventual reform efforts.

Hence the study has been organized around geographical and institutional "centers of calculation"—Göttingen, Weimar, Naples, Canada, or Dessau—and has then "followed the actors" who functioned in and emerged from them, drawing attention to what they cared about and to the language in which they themselves articulated those concerns. As Latour has argued, "We have to resist the idea that there exists somewhere a dictionary where all the variegated words of the actors can be translated into the few words of the social vocabulary. . . . We have to resist pretending that actors have only a language while the analyst possesses the *meta*-language in which the first is 'embedded.'"[12] Latour is critiquing traditional sociology, but historians too can profit from considering what is lost when scant attention is paid to the precise and reverberating meanings of actors in context before their words or movements are contained by a preconceived notion or category of thought. Anna Jameson, who has received much attention and might be described as a hero of my account, is, however, first and foremost a dynamic mediator and translator: a vehicle who, through the resonant language of her popular and trusted voice, via travel and correspondence and literary endeavors, proceeds to gather, alter, and propagate notions and books and material goods so that they influence and eventually issue in an enacted politics. That is, by various means, using different tools, she hoped to shape political discourses until public opinion, legislation, and the enforcement of legislation might serve to bring about social change in Britain and Germany—a process that for the most part, however, she did not live to see, and that was substantially promoted and carried out by other actors.

Viewing the creation of history by way of dynamic actor-networks therefore allows for a decentered reading that navigates *terrains vastes* to come to broad, if provisional, conclusions. Questions necessarily remain. For example, how exactly did the materials gathered by the Forsters in the Pacific, published in England and Germany, acquired by Prince Franz of Anhalt-Dessau and displayed to the general public at Wörlitz, affect the process of enlightenment in Dessau and beyond? What did inhabitants of the region and visitors to the park take away from this intriguingly populated and evocative landscape? I have quoted Goethe and suggested that, inspired, he returned to Weimar to design Wörlitz-like gardens there; I have explained how Salzmann, having worked with Basedow at Prince Franz's famous Philanthropic school, started his own institution, hired GutsMuths, and published significant pedagogical works with transnational consequences. But there are further repercussions that might be pursued. How did Goethe's Wörlitz experience shape not only the Weimar landscape but also his own work as a civil servant or his literary endeavors? What can be said about the other mediators and products that emerged from the stimulating environment of Wörlitz? And how did Wörlitz, as a mediator itself, alter the European story that the English gardens on which it was modeled were telling about the meaning of social spaces, the function of parks? The tale of competition between English and French styles can be enhanced by consideration of German examples and transnational movements.

How did Georg Forster respond to Wörlitz and the Forster Pavilion? How did Forster's South Sea experiences affect not only his German reception but indeed his later radical agitation, writings, and English-German translations? The biographical accounts have surprisingly little to say of the impact of what must have been the central formative experience of Forster's life; his early travels are oddly divorced from his later politics. And again, what of the material goods that came from the Pacific and the people on whom he bestowed them? We have record of various South Sea items he presented to friends, but we have no knowledge, for example, of what happened to the cloth that he gave Caroline Michaelis, part of which was turned into an exotic ball gown, and that perhaps decorated pillows and windows in the Böhmer and Schlegel and Schelling households for years, likely stimulating observations, providing topics of conversation, creating hybrid cultural experiences and spaces. Mary Louise Pratt has suggested that we need to discover how Europe "construct[ed] itself from the outside in, out of materials infiltrated, donated, absorbed, appropriated, and imposed from contact zones all over the planet."[13] Though it may seem a trivial example, what cultural work was accomplished by Caroline's prized bolt of cloth?

More generally, how was Georg Forster the voyager influenced by the academic approach to travel cultivated at the University of Göttingen? And how did that approach affect Alexander von Humboldt the explorer? Johann David Michaelis, the professor of Near Eastern studies and translator of *Clarissa* (chapter 2), modeled the academic approach to travel in his conception and direction of the Yemen expedition supported by King Frederick V of Denmark and completed by Carsten Niebuhr from 1761 to 1767: Michaelis created a list of questions to be answered by the explorers, nearly four hundred pages long, that was published in German and French and Dutch and became widespread in Europe, shaping other scientific journeys.[14] We know that Georg Forster carried that book with him on Cook's voyage.[15] To what extent did Michaelis set Forster's agenda? To what extent did Michaelis condition Humboldt the explorer?

Indeed, Humboldt was educated at Göttingen along with his brother Wilhelm; after traveling through Europe with Georg Forster he then conducted his celebrated scientific work in South America from 1799 to 1804. Pratt has characterized the travel accounts emerging from this style of journey as "anti-conquest," a "strategy of innocence" veiling an attempt to exercise power over the visited territory.[16] But whose power and whose strategy is under scrutiny? Humboldt likely imbibed at Göttingen long-standing ideas about what an expedition should entail; his method points to a network of earlier actors who may or may not have molded Humboldt's findings, fame, and legacy.

And it was not only Michaelis's influence that mattered; Michaelis had himself instructed the historian and political theorist August Schlözer, who then taught at Göttingen, initiated a popular lecture course on travel, and made the subject into an academic discipline. Schlözer completed editions of travel texts, including some for children, and developed a collection of travel literature that remains a notable part of the Göttingen Library holdings. The intellectual advantages of journeys had to be maximized, according to Schlözer, who, as I outlined in chapter 2, was at the time conducting an educational experiment on his daughter Dorothea and was even then taking her along on an extended trip to Italy; with a similar penchant for application he did sociological and historical work that bridged tourism and academic research expeditions. His well-attended lectures were offered from 1772 to 1795, sometimes to more than two hundred students. It is not known whether Alexander von Humboldt attended his course, but in the lecture notes of Ernst Friedrich Haupt, who attended in the winter term of 1795, one cannot miss Schlözer's pragmatic emphasis: the advantages and disadvantages of different ways and means of travel, costs, lodgings, and even the virtues and vices of different companions. Traveling with women "is either unbearable or heavenly sweet. There is no medium"; traveling with servants "is expensive, often useless or even burdensome." Since servants sometimes accompanied their masters to lectures, Schlözer in discussing them switched into Latin, which servants would not have understood. He explained how they should be treated en route: they should pay for their own meals out of an allowance, since innkeepers will otherwise take advantage; a servant who has traveled a lot will have an inflated sense of self-worth, which is insufferable; a new servant should never be hired along the way.[17] Did such instruction help to form Humboldt's nimble and successful travel style? If so, how might the impact on his outcomes be determined?

A danger of historiography in a Latourian mode, of course, is that of infinite regression, of pursuing six degrees of separation for every actor and ending up with confusing and undifferentiated reams of information. The goal, however, is not to reach a point of chaos but one of saturation. At a certain moment the network of associations takes a shape that is meaningful, and at that instant the historian should bring to bear on the material the kind of judgment and conclusions that the associations suggest and warrant, informed, naturally, by the historian's goals and knowledge. The difference and the benefit is that a network-oriented historiography emphasizes the performative and the inclusive and thereby demonstrates not which protagonist wields power and can control the actions and fates of others, but how authority is created, assumed, and distributed, how resources move, how actors work as a collective to shape what was and what might have been.

The story of cultural transfer I have offered here is unquestionably partial. I have not addressed the manifold cultural repercussions of business ties, for instance; I have not spelled out the role of agents like the Remnants in Hamburg or the Bests in London, who were active cultural mediators; I have not discussed trends following upon flows of immigration and emigration. This book represents one part of a new historiographical focus—promoted by scholars such as Jeremy Black, Hermann Wellenreuther, Brendan Simms, and others—on British-German links that were accelerated by the Personal Union. My aim has been to decenter historiography with a lens that zooms in to account for the movements of individuals and then opens up to see the *terrains vastes*, consistently taking account of women as the significant actors they were. In the process, such Swiftian changes in perspective have, I hope, allowed for fresh ways of seeing and querying the past, for holding asymmetrical ideas in the mind at once, as David Blackbourn has advised. As I have argued elsewhere, feminist historiography depends on this kind of mental agility, on recognizing simultaneously the micronarratives of individual striving and the grand narrative of women's long-standing oppression. The same holds geographically, with individual provincial existences gradually being associated in networks of the *terrains vastes*, and politically, with each instance or event accumulating in a slow collective process of broad sociocultural change.[18] It is a version of what Latour terms a "compositionist" approach, challenging familiar models of revolutionary substitution and incommensurable paradigm shifts.[19] Even though much of the story of British-German cultural transfer remains to be told, then, my project might itself be viewed in Latourian terms: the study forms only part of a system of associations, and it remains for future studies to take up the arguments, translate and modify them, and expand the terrain.

Notes

Introduction

1. Stefanie Stockhorst, ed., *Cultural Transfer through Translation: The Circulation of Enlightened Thought in Europe by Means of Translation* (Amsterdam: Rodopi, 2010), 19–20.

2. Mary Louise Pratt, *Imperial Eyes: Travel Writing and Transculturation* (London: Routledge, 1992), 5–6. The pervasive influence of Pratt's book likely accounts for the dominance of this expression, first coined by Cuban sociologist Fernando Ortiz, among U.S. scholars.

3. For a helpful summary of exchange terms, see Peter Burke, *Cultural Hybridity* (London: Polity, 2009).

4. Michel Espagne, *Les transferts culturels franco-allemands* (Paris: Presses Universitaires de France, 1999); Hans-Jürgen Lüsebrink and Rolf Reichardt, eds., *Kulturtransfer im Epochenumbruch Frankreich-Deutschland 1770 bis 1815*, 2 vols. (Leipzig: Leipziger Universitätsverlag, 1997); Hans-Jürgen Lüsebrink, *Interkulturelle Kommunikation: Interaktion, Fremdwahrnehmung, Kulturtransfer*, 2nd ed. (Stuttgart: J. B. Metzler, 2008); Barbara Schmidt-Haberkamp, Uwe Steiner, and Brunhilde Wehinger, eds., *Europäischer Kulturtransfer im 18. Jahrhundert: Literaturen in Europa—Europäische Literatur?* (Berlin: Berliner Wissenschaftsverlag, 2003); Agnieszka Pufelska and Iwan Michelangelo D'Aprile, eds., *Aufklärung und Kulturtransfer in Mittel- und Osteuropa* (Saarbrücken: Wehrhahn Verlag, 2009); also Stockhorst, *Cultural Transfer through Translation*.

5. Nick Harding, *Hanover and the British Empire 1700–1837* (Woodbridge: Boydell Press, 2007), 8; Hermann Wellenreuther, "Von der Interessenharmonie zur Dissoziation: Kurhannover und England zur Zeit der Personalunion," *Niedersächsisches Jahrbuch für Landesgeschichte* 67 (1995): 36.

6. Prior to that the texts relied upon included J. H. Plumb's *The First Four Georges* (London: Batsford, 1956) and Ragnhild Hatton's *George I* (London: Thames and Hudson, 1978). See also *Britain and Germany Compared: Nationality, Society and Nobility in the Eighteenth Century*, ed. Joseph Canning and Hermann Wellenreuther (Göttingen: Wallstein Verlag, 2001), for essays more focused on comparison than on transfer and Rosemary Ashton, *The German Idea* (Cambridge: Cambridge University Press, 1980).

7. See, e.g., Pheng Cheah and Bruce Robbins, eds., *Cosmopolitics: Thinking and Feeling beyond the Nation* (Minneapolis: University of Minnesota Press, 1998); Steven

Vertovec and Robin Cohen, eds., *Conceiving Cosmopolitanism: Theory, Context, and Practice* (Oxford: Oxford University Press, 2002).

8. Pauline Kleingeld, "Six Varieties of Cosmopolitanism in Late Eighteenth-Century Germany," *Journal of the History of Ideas* 60.3 (1999): 505–24; Adriana Craciun, *British Women Writers and the French Revolution: Citizens of the World* (Palgrave Macmillan, 2005)

9. Seyla Benhabib, *Situating the Self* (Cambridge: Polity Press, 1992); Keith Baker and Peter Hanns Reill, *What's Left of Enlightenment? A Postmodern Question* (Stanford: Stanford University Press, 2001); and Daniel Gordon, "On the Supposed Obsolescence of the French Enlightenment," in Gordon, *Postmodernism and the Enlightenment* (New York: Routledge, 2001).

10. Johannes Paulmann, "Interkultureller Transfer zwischen Deutschland und Grossbritannien: Einführung in ein Forschungskonzept," in *Aneignung und Abwehr: Interkultureller Transfer zwischen Deutschland und Großbritannien im 19. Jahrhundert*, ed. Rudolf Muhs, Johannes Paulmann, and Willibald Steinmetz (Bodenheim: Philo, 1998), 21–43, esp. 35.

11. The desirability of integrating women's history into mainstream historiography has been debated by feminist scholars. See Judith M. Bennett, *History Matters: Patriarchy and the Challenge of Feminism* (Philadelphia: University of Pennsylvania Press, 2006); Bonnie G. Smith, *The Gender of History: Men, Women, and Historical Practice* (Cambridge: Harvard University Press, 1998); Judith P. Zinsser, *History and Feminism: A Glass Half Full* (New York: Twayne, 1993); Karen Offen, *European Feminisms 1700–1950: A Political History* (Stanford: Stanford University Press, 2000).

12. Benedict Anderson, *Imagined Communities: Reflections on the Origin and Spread of Nationalism* (London: Verso, 1994 [1983]).

13. Bernhard Fabian, "English Books and Their Eighteenth-Century German Readers," in *The Widening Circle: Essays on the Circulation of Literature in Eighteenth-Century Europe*, ed. Paul J. Korshin (Philadelphia: University of Pennsylvania Press, 1976) ; Kwame Anthony Appiah, "Cosmopolitan Patriots," *Critical Inquiry* 23 (Spring 1997): 617–39, reprinted in Cheah and Robbins, *Cosmopolitics,* 91–114.

14. James Raven, "An Antidote to the French? English Novels in German Translation and German Novels in English Translation," *Eighteenth Century Fiction,* 14.3–4 (2002): 715–34; also James Raven, Peter Garside, and Rainer Schöwerling, *The English Novel 1770–1829: A Bibliographical Survey of Prose Fiction Published in the British Isles* (Oxford: Oxford University Press, 2000); Mary Helen McMurran, *The Spread of Novels: Translation and Prose Fiction in the Eighteenth Century* (Princeton: Princeton University Press, 2009); and Mirella Agorni, *Translating Italy for the Eighteenth Century: Women, Translation and Travel Writing 1739–1797* (Manchester: St Jerome, 2002).

15. Sarah Annes Brown, "Women Translators," in *The Oxford History of Literary Translation in English: Volume 3 1660–1790,* ed. Stuart Gillespie and David Hopkins (Oxford: Oxford University Press, 2005), 111–20; Susanne Stark, "Women," in *The Oxford History of Literary Translation in English: Volume 4 1790–1900,* ed. Peter France and Kenneth Haynes (Oxford: Oxford University Press, 2006). See also Stark, *"Behind Inverted Commas": Translation and Anglo-German Cultural Relations in the Nineteenth Century* (Clevedon: Multilingual Matters, 1999).

16. Paulmann, 31.

17. Bruno Latour, *Reassembling the Social: An Introduction to Actor-Network-Theory* (Oxford: Oxford University Press, 2005); Michel Callon and John Law, "After the

Individual in Society: Lessons on Collectivity from Science, Technology and Society,"
Canadian Journal of Sociology 22.2 (Spring 1997): 165–82.
  18. Clifford Geertz, *The Interpretation of Culture* (New York: Basic Books, 1973), 27.
  19. L. Deložel, "Narratives of Counterfactual History," in *Essays on Fiction and Perspective,* ed. G. Rossholm (Bern: Peter Lang, 2004), 109–28, 117.
  20. Sylvia Harcstark Myers, *The Bluestocking Circle: Women, Friendship, and the Life of the Mind in Eighteenth-Century England* (Oxford: Clarendon Press, 1990); Gary Kelly, "General Introduction" to *Bluestocking Feminism: Writings of the Bluestocking Circle, 1738–1785*, 6 vols. (London: Pickering and Chatto, 1999), I:ix–liv; Nicole Pohl and Betty Schellenberg, eds., *Reconsidering the Bluestockings* (San Marino, Calif.: Huntington Library, 2003); Elizabeth Eger and Lucy Peltz, eds., *Brilliant Women: Eighteenth-Century Bluestockings* (London: National Portrait Gallery, 2008). Kelly specifies Englishwomen who were connected at various distances to the original Bluestocking circle because of their religious views or politics (xlix–l)—Anna Seward, Clara Reeve, Amelia Opie, and Mary Wollstonecraft herself, for example; for my purposes and to my mind all of these women absorbed and embody bluestocking (note that I consistently employ the lowercase) aspirations.
  21. Elizabeth Eger, *Bluestockings: Women of Reason from Enlightenment to Romanticism* (Basingstoke: Palgrave Macmillan, 2010); Karen O'Brien, *Women and Enlightenment in Eighteenth-Century Britain* (Cambridge: Cambridge University Press, 2009); Harriet Guest, *Small Change: Women, Learning, Patriotism, 1750–1810* (Chicago: University of Chicago Press, 2000); Rebecca D'Monte and Nicole Pohl, eds., *Female Communities 1600–1800: Literary Visions and Cultural Realities* (London: St. Martin's, 2000); Ruth P. Dawson, *The Contested Quill: Literature by Women in Germany, 1770–1800* (Cranbury, N.J.: Associated University Presses, 2002); Ulrike Gleixner and Marion W. Gray, eds., *Gender in Transition: Discourse and Practice in German-Speaking Europe, 1750–1830* (Ann Arbor: University of Michigan Press, 2006); see also Jennie Batchelor and Cora Kaplan, eds., *Women and Material Culture, 1660–1830* (Basingstoke: Palgrave Macmillan, 2007).
  22. Eger, 21, 209.
  23. Kelly, "General Introduction," xlvii.
  24. Anke Gilleir and Alicia C. Montoya, introduction to *Women Writing Back/Writing Women Back: Transnational Perspectives from the Late Middle Ages to the Dawn of the Modern Era,* ed. Anke Gilleir, Alicia Montoya, and Suzan van Dijk (Leiden: Brill, 2010), 18–19. See also Annamaria Lamarra and Eleonara Federici, eds., *Nations, Traditions and Cross-Cultural Identities: Women's Writing in English in a European Context* (Oxford: Peter Lang, 2010).
  25. Latour, *Reassembling the Social*; John Law, "Notes on the Theory of the Actor-Network: Ordering, Strategy, and Heterogeneity," *Systems Practice* 5 (August 1992): 379–93; Bruno Latour, trans. Monique Girard Stark, "Factures/Fractures: From the Concept of Network to the Concept of Attachment," *RES: Anthropology and Aesthetics* 36 (Autumn 1999): 20–31; Callon and Law, "After the Individual in Society"; John Law, *After Method: Mess in Social Science Research* (London: Routledge, 2004); Anders Blok and Torben Elgaard Jensen, *Bruno Latour: Hybrid Thoughts in a Hybrid World* (London: Routledge, 2011).
  26. Latour, *Reassembling the Social,* 12.
  27. Donna Haraway, "A Game of Cat's Cradle: Science Studies, Feminist Theory, Cultural Studies," *Configurations* 2.1 (1994): 59–71, 65. Some feminists have ques-

tioned the extent to which the network comes to revolve around the fact finder; see Susan Leigh Star, "Power, Technologies and the Phenomenology of Conventions: On Being Allergic to Onions," in *A Sociology of Monsters? Essays on Power, Technology and Domination*, ed. J. Law (London: Routledge, 1991), 26–56; Vicky Singleton, "Feminism, Sociology of Scientific Knowledge and Postmodernism," *Social Studies of Science* 26 (1996): 445–68.

28. Ann Thomson, Simon Burrows, and Edmond Dziembowski, introduction to *Cultural Transfers: France and Britain in the Long Eighteenth Century* (Oxford: Voltaire Foundation, 2010), 8–9.

29. David Blackbourn, "'The Horologe of Time': Periodization in History," *PMLA* 127.2 (March 2012): 301–7, quotation 305–6.

30. Blackbourn, 305.

Chapter 1

1. I would like to thank the Herzog August Bibliothek for a fellowship that allowed me to complete the research for this chapter, and the publisher Vandenhoeck und Ruprecht for generous access to its archive.

2. Vormärz is the period in the German states after the defeat of Napoleon and before the March revolution of 1848; decrees restricting political activity and invoking censorship were passed in order to inhibit the spread of liberal and democratic ideas, especially those of writers associated with the "Young Germany" movement. That movement involved a group of authors who sought progressive social and judicial reforms and decried the apolitical, idealist stance of Romantic writers.

3. German women's literacy, reading, and writing have been used to date and define the "eighteenth century"; see Barbara Becker-Cantarino, ed., *German Literature of the Eighteenth Century: The Enlightenment and Sensibility*, vol. 5 of the Camden House History of German Literature (Rochester, N.Y.: Camden House, 2005); also Bethany Wiggin, "Dating the Eighteenth Century in German Literary History," *Eighteenth-Century Studies* 40.1 (2006): 126–32; British women's vigorous and influential literary activities have been analyzed in many critical volumes, including a full literary history by Susan Staves, *A Literary History of Women's Writing in Britain, 1660–1800* (Cambridge: Cambridge University Press, 2006), and an analysis of women's professionalization by Betty Schellenberg, *The Professionalization of Women Writers in Eighteenth-Century Britain* (Cambridge: Cambridge University Press, 2005); on French women as *salonnières* and authors, see Dena Goodman, *The Republic of Letters: A Cultural History of the French Enlightenment* (Ithaca: Cornell University Press, 1996), and Carla Hesse, *The Other Enlightenment: How French Women Became Modern* (Princeton: Princeton University Press, 2001).

4. See Barbara Becker-Cantarino, "Introduction: German Literature in the Era of Enlightenment and Sensibility," in her edited volume, *German Literature of the Eighteenth Century*, 4–5.

5. Götz von Selle, ed., *Die Matrikel der Georg-August-Universität zu Göttingen 1734–1837* (Hildesheim: August Lax, 1937), 184–255.

6. Michael Maurer, *Aufklärung und Anglophilie in Deutschland* (Göttingen: Vandenhoeck & Ruprecht, 1987), 47–50.

7. Maurer, 39.

8. B. Q. Morgan and A. R. Hohlfeld, *German Literature in British Magazines 1750–1860* (Madison: University of Wisconsin Press, 1949), 128, 130, 131; V. Stockley,

German Literature as Known in England 1750–1830 (Port Washington, N.Y.: Kennikat Press, 1929; facsimile 1969), 34–36.

9. *Gentleman's Magazine* 19 (1749): 245–46, 345–49; see Theoder Wolpers, "Literaturvermittlung zwischen Göttingen und England im 18. Jahrhundert," in *"Eine Welt Allein ist Nicht Genug": Grossbritannien, Hannover und Göttingen 1714–1837*, ed. Elmar Mittler (Göttingen: Niedersächsische Staats- und Universitätsbibliothek, 2005), 401–35, esp. 411–14. For an informative account of how British scholars benefited from multifarious contact with Göttingen professors, see Thomas Biskup, "The University of Göttingen and the Personal Union, 1737–1837," in *The Hanoverian Dimension in British History, 1714–1837*, ed. Brendan Simms and Torsten Riotte (Cambridge: Cambridge University Press, 2007), 128–60; also Hermann Wellenreuther, "Göttingen und England im 18. Jahrhundert," in *250 Jahre Vorlesungen an der Georgia Augusta 1734–1984* (Göttingen: Vandenhoeck & Ruprecht, 1985), 30–63.

10. Maurer, 64–66.

11. Clarissa Campbell Orr, "Charlotte of Mecklenburg-Strelitz, Queen of Great Britain and Electress of Hanover: Northern Dynasties and the Northern Republic of Letters," in *Queenship in Europe 1660–1815: The Role of the Consort*, ed. Clarissa Campbell Orr (Cambridge: Cambridge University Press, 2004).

12. Georg Forster is often called "George" Forster because for a time he grew up in England and with his father accompanied James Cook on his second voyage. See chapter 2.

13. Maurer, 291.

14. Bernhard Fabian, "English Books and their Eighteenth-Century German Readers," in *The Widening Circle: Essays on the Circulation of Literature in Eighteenth-Century Europe*, ed. Paul J. Korshin (Philadelphia: University of Pennsylvania Press, 1976), 140, 164–65.

15. Fabian, 165.

16. Maurer, 48.

17. See, e.g., Abraham Vandenhoeck, *Bibliopolium Vandenhoeckianum: or, a catalogue of books in most faculties and languages. Collected in Italy, France, Germany, England and Holland, by Abram. Vandenh To be sold (the Price being mark'd [at the beginning] of each Book) Monday the 14th [of Decem]ber 1730, at his Shop, at the Sign of Virgil's Head opposite the New Church in the Strand* (London, 1730).

18. A catalog of bookseller John Wilcox from 1735 announces that his sale will be held "at Virgil's Head, opposite the New Church in the Strand, the shop which was Mr. Abraham Vandenhoeck's who is gone to live at Hamburgh"; John Wilcox, *A catalogue of books, being The Libraries of A Right Reverend Prelate. Thomas Wickham, M. D. and J. Shaw, Attorney, deceas'd. Consisting Of many thousand Valuable Books in almost all Languages and Faculties* (London, 1735).

19. Wilhelm Ruprecht, *Väter und Söhne: Zwei Jahrhunderte Buchhändler in einer deutschen Universitätsstadt* (Göttingen: Vandenhoeck & Ruprecht, 1935), 57.

20. Ruprecht, 54. Barbara Lösel, *Die Frau als Persönlichkeit im Buchwesen: Dargestellt am Beispiel der Göttinger Verlegerin Anna Vandenhoeck (1709–1787)* (Wiesbaden: Otto Harrassowitz, 1991), 17–18. This thesis contains a bibliography of books published by Vandenhoeck from 1750 to 1787.

21. Lösel, 39, 28.

22. Lösel, 29–40. Lösel has summarized her findings about Anna Vandenhoeck in article form in the anthology *"Des Kennenlernens Werth": Bedeutende Frauen Göttingens*, ed. Traudel Weber-Reich (Göttingen: Wallstein Verlag, 1993), 13–26.

23. Quoted in Ruprecht, 55.

24. Ruprecht, 62–71, Lösel, 21–27.

25. See Fabian, 163, and Maurer, 41–44.

26. D. Bertoloni Meli, "Caroline, Leibniz, and Clarke," *Journal of the History of Ideas* 60 (1999): 469–86, quote at 471.

27. Bertoloni Meli, 473.

28. See also John Van der Kiste, *The Georgian Princesses* (Stroud: Sutton Publishing, 2000), 36.

29. Bertoloni Meli, 472.

30. Joachim Berger, *Anna Amalia von Sachsen-Weimar-Eisenach (1739–1807): Denk- und Handlungsräume einer 'aufgeklärten' Herzogin* (Heidelberg: Winter, 2003).

31. Jacqueline Pearson, *Women's Reading in Britain 1750–1835: A Dangerous Recreation* (Cambridge: Cambridge University Press, 1999), 153.

32. Bärbel Raschke, "Die Bibliothek der Herzogin Anna Amalia," in *Herzogin Anna Amalia Bibliothek: Kulturgeschichte einer Sammlung* (Munich: Hanser Verlag, 1999), 83–86, quotation at 83–84.

33. Ingrid Münch, "Testament und Begräbnis der Herzogin Philippine Charlotte v. Braunschweig-Lüneburg (1716–1801)," *Braunschweigisches Jahrbuch* 68 (1987): 51–82, 70. This essay offers the fullest biographical sketch of Philippine Charlotte, and there is a short bibliography.

34. See Sabine Heißler, "Christine Charlotte von Ostfriesland (1645–1699) und Ihre Bücher, oder, Lesen Frauen Anderes?" *Daphnis: Zeitschrift für Mittlere Deutsche Literatur* 27 (1998): 335–418; also Marc Serge Rivière and Annett Volmer, eds., *The Library of an Enlightened Prussian Princess: Catalogue of the Non-music Sections of the Amalien-Bibliothek* (Berlin: Verlag Arno Spitz, 2002).

35. Other examples are Caroline of Hesse, see Herrmann Braeunig-Oktavio, "Die Bibliothek der grossen Landgräfin Caroline von Hessen," *Archiv für Geschichte des Buchwesens* 6 (1966): 682–875; Viktor Amadeus and Elise von Hessen-Rotenburg, see *The Corvey Library and Anglo-German Cultural Exchanges, 1770–1837* (Munich: Wilhelm Fink, 2004); Luise of Sachsen-Gotha, see Jenny von der Osten, *Luise Dorothee Herzogin von Sachsen-Gotha 1732–1767* (Leipzig: Breitkopf und Härtel, 1893). Of Philippine Charlotte's daughter Anna Amalia, Bärbel Raschke observes that "Der Katalog verzeichnet überraschend viel Literatur von Frauen, über Frauen und für Frauen": women's biographies, collections of letters, travel literature, women's history, sentimental novels by and about female protagonists, as well as feminist polemics; Raschke, 85.

36. Rivière and Volmer, 66, 71.

37. Hans Droysen, ed., *Aus den Briefen der Herzogin Philippine Charlotte von Braunschweig 1732–1801,* vol. 1, 1732–1768 (Wolfenbüttel: Zwissler, 1916). The intended volume 2 never appeared.

38. Droysen 83–86.

39. For the view of dynastic ties from the British side, see Clarissa Campbell Orr, "Dynastic Perspectives," in *The Hanoverian Dimension in British History, 1714–1837,* ed. Brendan Simms and Torsten Riotte (Cambridge: Cambridge University Press, 2007), 213–51.

40. Droysen 30, 32.

41. See a full bibliography of his work in *Johann Joachim Eschenburg und die Künste und Wissenschaften zwischen Aufklärung und Romantik,* ed. Cord-Friedrich Berghahn and Till Kinzel (Heidelberg: Winter, 2013).

42. "In Ansehung des Standes wird . . . kein Unterschied gemacht; die Auffüh-

NOTES TO PAGES 33–40 · 177

rung macht diesen ganz allein"; Johann Friedrich Wilhelm Jerusalem, "Absicht und erste Einrichtung des Collegii Carolini," in *Nachgelassene Schriften*, 2 vols. (Braunschweig: n.p., 1793) 93; quoted in Maurer, 54.

43. Maurer, 56.

44. This title does not appear on Lösel's list.

45. See Horst Steinmetz, ed. and afterword, *Friedrich II., König von Preussen, und die deutsche Literatur des 18. Jahrhunderts: Texte und Dokumente* (Stuttgart: Reclam, 1985).

46. Johann Friedrich Wilhelm Jerusalem, *Ueber die Teutsche Sprache und Litteratur. An Ihro Koenigliche Hoheit die verwittwete Frau Herzogin von Braunschweig und Lueneburg* (Berlin: n.p., 1781). See also *Ueber die deutsche Litteratur: Koenig Friderich, Jerusalem, Tralles* (Munich: Joh. Baptist Strobl, 1781).

47. Jerusalem, 10.

48. *Monthly Review* 65 (1781): 504–8.

49. Morgan and Hohlfeld, esp. 128–74. Translations published around the turn of the century in the magazines and by Joseph Johnson will be discussed in the next chapter.

50. Benedict Anderson, *Imagined Communities: Reflections on the Origin and Spread of Nationalism*, Revised Edition (London and New York: Verso, 1991), esp. 37–46.

51. Fabian, 147.

52. *Vollständiges Verzeichniss der Bücher, welche um beygesezte Preise zu haben sind bey sel. Abraham Vandenhöcks Witwe, Universitätsbuchhändlerin zu Göttingen.* 2 vols. (Göttingen: Vandenhoeck, 1785).

53. Mechthild Raabe, *Leser und Lektüre im 18. Jahrhundert: Die Ausleihbücher der Herzog August Bibliothek Wolfenbüttel 1714–1799* (Munich: K. G. Saur, 1989).

54. Pauline Kleingeld, "Six Varieties of Cosmopolitanism in Late Eighteenth-Century Germany," *Journal of the History of Ideas* 60 (1999): 505–24.

55. "6 Pfund Silber und 1000 Taler" for the church, and "3000 Taler" for the widows' fund (Lösel, 41).

56. Philippine Charlotte was careful with her money, which she managed herself. Her husband died with substantial debts, but Philippine Charlotte amassed a fortune of 730,000 Reichstaler. Her will shows that she distributed her money according to personal preference for her children. Anna Amalia and the divorced Elisabeth, with whom Philippine Charlotte never reconciled, got the least and contested the will (Münch, 55).

57. Kwame Anthony Appiah, "Cosmopolitan Patriots," in Pheng Cheah and Bruce Robbins, eds., *Cosmopolitics: Thinking and Feeling beyond the Nation* (Minneapolis: University of Minnesota Press, 1998), 91–114.

Chapter 2

1. Thomas Biskup, "The University of Göttingen and the Personal Union, 1737–1837," in Brendan Simms and Torsten Riotte, eds., *The Hanoverian Dimension in British History, 1714–1837* (Cambridge: Cambridge University Press, 2007), 128–60, esp. 144–48.

2. Joseph Johnson published Thomas Henry's *Memoirs of Albert de Haller* in 1783 with a frontispiece portrait of Haller by William Blake.

3. For the publication history of Richardson's novel in Germany, see Astrid Krake, "'Translating to the Moment'—Marketing and Anglomania: The First German Translation of Richardson's *Clarissa*," in *Cultural Transfer through Translation*, ed.

Stefanie Stockhorst (Amsterdam: Rodopi, 2010), 103–19; for the European afterlife of Richardson's *Clarissa*, see Christine Lehmann's structuralist treatment, *Das Modell Clarissa: Liebe, Verführung, Sexualität und Tod der Romanheldinnen des 18. und 19. Jahrhunderts* (Stuttgart: Metzler, 1991).

4. Bruno Latour, *Reassembling the Social: An Introduction to Actor-Network-Theory* (Oxford: Oxford University Press, 2005); Michel Espagne, *Les transferts culturels franco-allemands* (Paris: 1999); Hans-Jürgen Lüsebrink and Rolf Reichardt, *Kulturtransfer im Epochenumbruch: Frankreich-Deutschland 1770 bis 1815* (Leipzig: 1997); Michael Werner and Bénédicte Zimmermann, "Vergleich, Transfer, Verflechtung: Der Ansatz der 'histoire croisée' und die Herausforderung des Transnationalen," *Geschichte und Gesellschaft* 28.4 (2002): 607–36; Stefanie Stockhorst, ed., *Cultural Transfer through Translation: The Circulation of Enlightened Thought in Europe by Means of Translation* (Amsterdam: Rodopi, 2010).

5. See Peter Burke, *Cultural Hybridity* (London: Polity, 2009), for a discussion of cultures that are "open" versus those that are more "closed" to others' influences.

6. Johann David Michaelis, *Allerunterthänigste Bittschrift an Seine Königliche Majestät in Preussen, um Anlegung einer Universität für das schöne Geschlecht* (Göttingen, 1747), 5.

7. Johann David Michaelis, "Vorrede: Von dem Geschmack der Morgenlaendischen Dichtkunst," preface to Johann Friedrich Loewens, *Poetische Nebenstunden in Hamburg* (Leipzig: Johann Wendler, 1752), ix–xlvii, quotation at xlvi.

8. *Clarissa, Die Geschichte eines vornehmen Frauenzimmers*, trans. Johann David Michaelis (Göttingen: Verlegts Abram Vandenhoeck, 1748–53), ii–iv.

9. Elizabeth Carter, in addition to being an acclaimed poet, was also a noted translator; she rendered into English Francesco Algarotti's *Il Newtonianismo per le dame* (first published in Italian 1737, English 1739), as well as *All the Works of Epictetus* (1758) from the Greek.

10. Given Michaelis's protofeminism it would seem odd to read the preface against the grain and to suggest that anxiety about the feminine lay behind Michaelis's failure to translate Carter's "Ode to Wisdom," yet this is what the only critic to analyze the translation at length has done. Thomas O. Beebee argues that Michaelis undertakes a "weak" translation, attempting to remain close to the text, and he is so unassertive that when he encounters Elizabeth Carter's "Ode"—the words of an actual woman—he is debilitated: "women's writing can appear only as an absolute difference, as the product of another race expressed in an alien language incapable of translation" (141). As I suggest, nothing we know of Michaelis's biography, oeuvre, intentions, or translation practice can support such a conclusion. Beebee, Clarissa *on the Continent: Translation and Seduction* (University Park: Pennsylvania State University Press, 1990).

11. Sherry Simon, *Gender in Translation: Cultural Identity and the Politics of Transmission* (London: Routledge, 1996), 10–11.

12. Simon, 12, 13.

13. Some feminist commentators endorse such an approach on the grounds that issues of gender inequality can be highlighted by such foreignizing methods; see Luise von Flotow, *Translation and Gender* (Manchester: St Jerome, 1997), esp. 8–9.

14. Stuart Gillespie and Robin Sowerby, "Translation and Literary Innovation," in *The Oxford History of Literary Translation in English, Volume 3: 1660–1790*, ed. Stuart Gillespie and David Hopkins (Oxford: Oxford University Press, 2005), 21–37, quotation at 22. Frederick Burwick, writing on "Romantic Theories of Translation," also urges a

consideration of both the occasion and purpose of early nineteenth-century translations: *Wordsworth Circle* 39.3 (Summer 2008): 68–74.

15. Márta Minier, "'The Translatress in Her Own Person Speaks': A Few Marginal Notes on Feminist Translation in Practice, in Creative Writing and in Criticism," in *Identity and Cultural Translation: Writing across the Borders of Englishness*, ed. Ana Gabriela Macedo and Margarida Esteves Pereira (Oxford: Peter Lang, 2006), 39–54, esp. 43, 52.

16. He writes in the preface: "Er hat gesucht die verschiedene Schreib-Art, die die Briefe der verschiedenen Personen unterscheidet, nachzuahmen . . . Eine wörtliche Uebersetzung ist bey Büchern unangenehm, die vergnügen sollen: er hat daher die Freyheit gebraucht, die Worte im deutschen so zu setzen, wie sie seiner Meinung nach in dieser Sprache am besten lauteten" (a4–a5).

17. Georg Christoph Lichtenberg, ed., *Goettinger Taschen Calender vom Jahr 1781*, facsimile edition with an afterword by Wolfgang Promies (Mainz: Dieterich, 1989).

18. Bärbel Kern and Horst Kern, *Madame Doctorin Schlözer: Ein Frauenleben in den Widersprüchen der Aufklärung* (Munich: Verlag C. H. Beck, 1990), 52. Further citations to this study will appear parenthetically in the text.

19. See Eckart Klessmann, *Universitätsmamsellen: Fünf aufgeklärte Frauen zwischen Rokoko, Revolution und Romantik* (Frankfurt: Eichborn Verlag, 2008); *"Des Kennenlernens Werth": Bedeutende Frauen Göttingens*, ed. Traudel Weber-Reich (Göttingen: Wallstein Verlag, 2002 [1993]).

20. Caroline Schlegel-Schelling, *Die Kunst zu Leben*, ed. and intro. Sigrid Damm (Frankfurt: Insel Verlag, 1997), 91–95.

21. Monika Siegel, "'Ich hatte einen Hang zur Schwärmerey': Das Leben der Schriftstellerin und Übersetzerin Meta Forkel-Liebeskind im Spiegel ihrer Zeit" (PhD diss., University of Darmstadt, 2001), 99. Biographical information offered about Meta Forkel Liebeskind comes from this work, available online at http://tuprints.ulb.tu-darmstadt.de/222/1/Meta.pdf (accessed 20 February 2013).

22. Schlegel-Schelling, 172.

23. Madame de Staël-Holstein, *Germany*, 2 vols. (New York: H. W. Derby, 1861) I:44; see also Sylvia Möhle, *Ehekonflikte und sozialer Wandel: Göttingen 1740–1840* (Frankfurt: Campus Verlag, 1997), 20.

24. Möhle, 84.

25. For debates surrounding divorce in Britain even in the nineteenth century, see Anna Jameson's attempts at reform (chapter 4); for an overview, see Lawrence Stone, *The Road to Divorce* (Oxford: Oxford University Press, 1990); Roderick Phillips, *Untying the Knot: A Short History of Divorce* (Cambridge: Cambridge University Press, 1991).

26. Möhle, 149. Meta Forkel wrote to the university court because this was the juridical body authorized to handle cases involving professors.

27. Ruth Stummann-Bowert, "Philippine Engelhard," in *Des Kennenlernens Werth: Bedeutende Frauen Göttingens*, ed. Traudel Weber-Reich (Göttingen: Wallstein Verlag, 2002), 27–52, quotations at 31, 32: "für ein Frauenzimmer hat sie zu viel Muth, denkt und redt zu frey"; "sie sagt alles heraus."

28. Ruth Dawson, "Philippine Gatterer Engelhard," in *Bitter Healing: German Women Writers from 1700 to 1830*, ed. Jeannine Blackwell and Susanne Zantop (Lincoln: University of Nebraska Press, 1990), 190–193.

29. Translated by Walter Arndt; reprinted in Blackwell and Zantop, 194–99.

30. Christine Haug, "'Diese Arbeit unterhält mich, ohne mich zu ermüden':

Georg Forsters Übersetzungsmanufaktur in Mainz in den 1790er Jahren," *Georg-Forster-Studien* 13 (2008): 99–128.

31. Joan DeJean, "Transnationalism and the Origins of the (French?) Novel," in *The Literary Channel: The Inter-National Invention of the Novel,* ed. Margaret Cohen and Carolyn Dever (Princeton: Princeton University Press, 2002), 37–49, quotation at 38–39. Other pathbreaking studies of intra-European translation include Gillian E. Dow, ed., *Translators, Interpreters, Mediators: Women Writers 1700–1900* (Oxford: Peter Lang, 2007); Werner Huber, ed., *The Corvey Library and Anglo-German Cultural Exchanges, 1770–1837* (Munich: Wilhelm Fink Verlag, 2004); Wilhelm Graeber and Geneviève Roche, *Englische Literatur des 17. und 18. Jahrhunderts in französischer Übersetzung und deutscher Weiterübersetzung* (Tübingen: Max Niemeyer Verlag, 1988); Hilary Brown, *Benedikte Naubert (1756–1819) and Her Relations to English Culture* (Leeds: Maney Publishing; and London: MHRA and Institute of Germanic Studies, 2005); Ana Gabriela Macedo and Margarida Esteves Pereira, eds., *Identity and Cultural Translation: Writing across the Borders of Englishness* (Bern: Peter Lang, 2006); Mirella Agorni, *Translating Italy for the Eighteenth Century: Women, Translation and Travel Writing 1739–1797* (Manchester: St Jerome, 2002).

32. Mary Helen McMurran, "National or Transnational? The Eighteenth-Century Novel," in Cohen and Dever, *Literary Channel,* 50–72, quotations at 53, 51; also McMurran, *The Spread of Novels: Translation and Prose Fiction in the Eighteenth Century* (Princeton: Princeton University Press, 2010).

33. See also Mirella Agorni, "The Voice of the 'Translatress': From Aphra Behn to Elizabeth Carter," *Yearbook of English Studies* 28 (1998): 181–95. Parts of this discussion appear in her later monograph *Translating Italy for the Eighteenth Century* (note 31).

34. Sherry Simon has documented how many female translators over the centuries "combined their interest in translation with progressive social causes." Her group does not include Forkel or Wollstonecraft, but she argues that this focus is not coincidental, since these women all "understood that the transmission of significant literary texts was an essential, not an accessory, cultural task"; Simon, *Gender in Translation,* chap. 2, quotation at 40.

35. Biographical information about Meta Forkel Liebeskind comes from Monika Siegel, "'Ich hatte einen Hang zur Schwärmerey': Das Leben der Schriftstellerin und Übersetzerin Meta Forkel-Liebeskind im Spiegel ihrer Zeit" (PhD diss., Technische Universität Darmstadt, 2001). After composing my own chapter I came across Marie-Luise Spieckermann's "Dorothea Margareta Liebeskind (1765–1853): Übersetzerin zwischen wissenschaftlicher Literatur und Unterhaltungsromanen englischer Autorinnen," in *Übersetzungskultur im 18. Jahrhundert: Übersetzerinnen in Deutschland, Frankreich und der Schweiz,* ed. Brunhilde Wehinger and Hilary Brown (Saarbrücken: Wehrhahn Verlag, 2008), 141–64; Spieckermann's work, like my own, relies and expands on Siegel's pathbreaking biography.

36. Alexander von Humboldt, *Kosmos II* (1847): 72. Quoted in Marita Gilli, "George Forsters Modernität: Ein Porträt," in *Weltbürger-Europäer-Deutscher-Franke: Georg Forster zum 200. Todestag,* ed. Rolf Reichardt and Geneviève Roche (Mainz: Universitätsbibliothek, 1994), 3–14, quotation at 13.

37. Forster's efforts were even noted later in the British periodical *German Museum* 2 (1800): 453: "Other nations do, indeed, translate into their own language accounts of voyages and travels; but there is not one that has produced a collection so complete and judiciously selected, as the *Magazine of Voyages,* commenced by the late celebrated Forster, and still continued with critical care."

38. Haug (see note 30). Cf. Roche, who says that Forster received from Voß up to fifteen Taler a sheet and that Forkel received up to five ("'Völlig nach Fabrikenart,'" in Reichardt and Roche (see note 36), 101–36, quotation 107–8).

39. Mary Bell Price and Lawrence Marsden Price, *The Publication in the Eighteenth Century of English Literature in Germany* (Berkeley: University of California Press, 1934).

40. See Georg Forster, *Briefe 1790 bis 1791*, ed. Brigitte Leuschner and Siegfried Scheibe, vol. 16 (1980) of *Georg Forsters Werke*, Akademie der Wissenschaften der DDR (Berlin: Akademie-Verlag), 298–99, 4 June 1791.

41. Siegel, 100. Forster, *Werke*, 16:564, 17 September 1791.

42. Commentators focus on one paragraph from one letter of Forster to Voß (21 November 1791) in which Forster apologizes for errors in the Paine translation, and this is expanded upon and repeatedly invoked by critics (Georg Forster, *Georg Forsters Briefe an Christian Friedrich Voß*, ed. Paul Zincke [Dortmund: Verlag Ruhfus, 1915], 103–4). But Voß was evidently seeking ways of avoiding trouble with the publication of a text that had been banned abroad, and carping about the translation offered a way of hiding his lack of courage to Forster, the left-leaning star whom he needed on his publishing list. Marie-Luise Spieckerman suggests this is "ein bloßer Vorwand" on the part of Voß (see "Dorothea Margareta Liebeskind," 150). Nonetheless scholars from the 1950s to today have read the letter straight. Hans Arnold fails to evaluate Forkel's work but says only that she was not up to the translation of Paine though he admits that she had also translated Ramsay and Volney for Forster, without explaining why the Paine would have been commissioned had her work been unacceptable: "Mit der Übersetzung Paines wurde dann aber doch Dorothea Margarethe Forkel, die spätere Frau Liebeskind, betraut, die für Forster auch Ramsays *History of the American Revolution* und Volneys *Ruines* übersetzte, sonst aber in englischen Romanen zu Hause war. Auch sie war 'von dem Paine ganz bezaubert,' nur leider—wie Forster, der wegen Arbeitsüberlastung nicht zu der beabsichtigten Revision kam, erst von Voss erfahren mußte—der Übersetzungsaufgabe nicht eben gewachsen" (Hans Arnold, "Die Aufnahme von Thomas Paines Schriften in Deutschland," *PMLA* 74.4 [1959]: 365–86, quotation at 371). Forkel is mentioned at least five times in Forster's correspondence with Voß, and this is the only instance in which any negative evaluation is made about her work; no other translator is scrutinized by scholars in this way. Other letters to Forster about the works translated by Forkel suggest that friends and correspondents appreciated them (see *Briefe 1790 bis 1791*). Ludwig Uhlig says that Forster only commissioned the translation of Piozzi's *Observations* from Forkel because she was his wife's childhood friend and she needed money, and of course he had to do a thoroughgoing revision ("Freilich mußte er diese Übersetzung gründlich revidieren") (Ludwig Uhlig, *Georg Forster: Lebensabenteuer eines gelehrten Weltbürgers* [Göttingen: Vandenhoeck & Ruprecht, 2004], 242).

43. Theo Stemmler, "Einleitung," in Thomas Paine, *Die Rechte des Menschen* (Frankfurt: Suhrkamp Verlag, 1973), 26. I thank Gesa Dane for alerting me to and lending me her copy of this modern edition.

44. Helpful surveys of the astonishing breadth and depth of Enlightenment translation include André Lefevere, ed., *Translation / History / Culture* (London: Routledge, 1992); Stuart Gillespie and David Hopkins, eds., *The Oxford History of Literary Translation in English: Volume 3, 1660–1790* (Oxford: Oxford University Press, 2005); T. R. Steiner, *English Translation Theory 1650–1800* (Amsterdam: Van Gorcum, 1975). For twentieth-century theorizations, see Lawrence Venuti, ed., *The Translation Studies Reader* (London: Routledge, 2000). For Johnson, see Stuart Gillespie, "Translation and Canon-Formation," in *The Oxford History of Literary Translation in English. Volume*

3: 1660–1790, ed. Stuart Gillespie and David Hopkins (Oxford: Oxford University Press, 2005), 7–20, esp. 13.

45. Thomas Carlyle, "The State of German Literature" (1827) in *Critical and Miscellaneous Essays*, vol. 1 (New York: AMS Press, 1969). Quoted in Lefevere, 58.

46. Simon, 62–65.

47. See also Avi Lifschitz, "Translation in Theory and Practice: The Case of Johann David Michaelis's Prize Essay on Language and Opinions (1759)," in Stockhorst, *Cultural Transfer through Translation*, 29–43.

48. Women sought to combat these forces; I argue in chapter 3 that reactions to Vesuvius demonstrate how later women sought to amend a typical Romantic view of transformation by advocating process-oriented approaches instead.

49. There were six London editions printed for Joseph Johnson (1790, 1791, 1793, 1795, 1799, and 1805), a Dublin edition 1798, and American editions from Providence 1795, Wilmington 1796, Philadelphia 1796, and Baltimore 1811. The following discussion of Wollstonecraft's translation draws on an unpublished chapter of my dissertation, "Gender and Utopia in Eighteenth-Century England" (UC Berkeley, 1994): "'Panting after Perfection': The Ideal Mother and the Limits of Utopia in Mary Wollstonecraft," 223–302.

50. This is the same Duke who sponsored yearly Olympic-style games at Drehberg and undertook modernizing efforts on his estate at Wörlitz, described in the afterword.

51. J. C. F. GutsMuths, *Gymnastik für die Jugend: Enthaltend eine praktische Anweisung zu Leibesübungen* (Schnepfenthal: Verlag der Erziehungsanstalt, 1793); the second edition is available in a modern reprint (Frankfurt: Wilhelm-Limbert Verlag, 1970). This was translated into English and published by Joseph Johnson in 1800; there were other editions in 1802 and 1803.

52. Christian Carl André, *Bildung der Töchter in Schnepfenthal* (Göttingen: J. D. Dieterich, 1789); *Kleine Wandrungen auch größere Reisen der weiblichen Zöglinge zu Schnepfenthal, um Natur, Kunst und den Menschen immer besser kennen zu lernen* (Leipzig: Crusius, 1788). The first book was written in 1786, but published after the second.

53. Henry Crabb Robinson, *Diary, Reminiscences, and Correspondence*, ed. Thomas Sadler, 2 vols. (Boston: James R. Osgood and Co, 1871), I:133–34.

54. Barbara Taylor, *Mary Wollstonecraft and the Feminist Imagination* (Cambridge: Cambridge University Press, 2003), 2, 4.

55. Janet Todd, *Mary Wollstonecraft: A Revolutionary Life* (London: Weidenfeld & Nicolson, 2000), 135–36; Taylor, *Mary Wollstonecraft*, 304. According to Thomas Laqueur, Salzmann may not only have convinced Wollstonecraft of the need to be candid with children about sexuality; his book *Über die heimlichen Sünden der Jugend* (*On the Secret Sins of Youth*, Frankfurt 1786) may have convinced her also that masturbation would induce physical and moral weakness; see Thomas W. Laqueur, *Solitary Sex: A Cultural History of Masturbation* (New York: Zone Books, 2003), 54.

56. Ralph Wardle, *Mary Wollstonecraft* (Lawrence: University Press of Kansas, 1951), 124–25. Since Wollstonecraft maintains Salzmann's vivid story with the moral "Wie gut ist es, daß es reiche Leute in der Welt gibt!" (How happy it is that there are rich people in the world!), I would argue that Wollstonecraft's attack on class distinctions in this work is weak at best. The alterations involving the mother figure are more substantial and revealing. Gary Kelly briefly discusses Wollstonecraft's translation as "hack-work," but he bases his treatment on Wardle's comparison; *Revolutionary Feminism: The Mind and Career of Mary Wollstonecraft* (London: Macmillan, 1992), 77–78.

57. Ingrid-Charlotte Wolter, *Mary Wollstonecraft und Erziehung: Eine Erziehungskonzeption zur Entkulturation* (Trier: Wissenschaftlicher Verlag, 2008), 170. Wolter argues that in the *Elements of Morality*, as opposed to Wollstonecraft's earlier writings, the family as a whole becomes the main character; by contrast I argue that Wollstonecraft's emphasis on the mother-instructor figure suggests a continuity with her earlier educational stories and their sometimes severe female mentor figures.

58. Salzmann, *Elements of Morality*, trans. Mary Wollstonecraft, 3 vols., 3rd ed. (London: J. Johnson, 1792), I. ii–iii. Further citations to this translation will be made parenthetically in the text, with page numbers preceded by the volume number in roman numerals.

59. Wollstonecraft, trans., *Elements of Morality* I. iii.

60. This process happened in the other direction as well; see Wilhelm Graeber and Geneviève Roche, *Englische Literatur des 17. und 18. Jahrhunderts in französischer Übersetzung und deutscher Weiterübersetzung: Eine kommentierte Bibliographie* (Tübingen: Max Niemeyer Verlag, 1988).

61. See Todd, 135.

62. *Livre Élémentaire de Morale. Avec une introduction pour s'en servir utilement; ouvrage traduit de l'allemand de M. Salzmann, Professeur & Prédicateur à l'Institut de Dessau* (Leipzig: chez Siegfried Lebrecht Crusius, 1785), xi: "The characters in this book are for the most part German, because the author wrote principally for her nation. I have left them this way, not changing any of their customs, their way of thinking, or of their style. This will give pleasure to those readers who, free of national prejudices, like to acquaint themselves with people and habits different from those of their own country."

63. Christian Gotthilf Salzmann, *Moralisches Elementarbuch, nebst einer Anleitung zum nützlichen Gebrauch desselben*, Neue verbesserte Auflage (Leipzig: Siegfried Lebrecht Crusius, 1785), reprinted with an afterword by Hubert Göbels (Dortmund: Harenberg, 1980), 156. Translations in parentheses are my own throughout; further citations will appear parenthetically in the text.

64. For Wollstonecraft, gluttony ranks among the worst sins. In the *Original Stories*, Mrs. Mason, the mother figure, lectures young Caroline on it (IV:399–401), and in the *Vindication of the Rights of Men*, Wollstonecraft decries "drunken riot and beastly gluttony" (V:36).

65. The crime's manifesting itself in the face of the servant suggests Wollstonecraft's continued interest in reading physiognomy; see, for example, her translation of Johann Kasper Lavater, the Swiss pastor, poet, and physiognomist, and the *Cave of Fancy*. Moira Ferguson and Janet Todd discuss the connection in *Mary Wollstonecraft* (Boston: Twayne, 1984), 39. English interest in Lavater's theories was long-standing; translations were consistently excerpted in British periodicals from 1775 to 1857; see Morgan and Hohlfeld, 139–323.

66. Thomas Holcroft, for example, in his translation of Madame de Genlis's *Tales of the Castle* (1785), says in the "Advertisement" that to avoid offending British sensibilities "the incident of Doralice sucking the eyes of Eglantine . . . is omitted" since it would have "offended, even violently, the delicacy of an English reader." Madame La Comtesse de Genlis, *Tales of the Castle: or, Stories of Instruction and Delight*, trans. Thomas Holcroft (London: G. Robinson, 1785), A4.

67. Salzmann's version simply reads "greift die Arbeit frisch an, so werdet ihr immer vergnügt seyn, und gute Ärndten werden euren Fleiß belohnen!" (135) (go to your work with vigor; in this way you will always be happy, and good harvests will repay your industry).

68. See, in particular, the work of Mitzi Myers: "Reform or Ruin: 'A Revolution in Female Manners'," *SECC* 11 (1982): 199–216; "Impeccable Governesses, Rational Dames, and Moral Mothers: Mary Wollstonecraft and the Female Tradition in Georgian Children's Books," *Children's Literature* 14 (1986): 31–59; "Pedagogy as Self-Expression in Mary Wollstonecraft," in *The Private Self*, ed. Shari Benstock (Chapel Hill: University of North Carolina Press, 1988), 192–210.

69. Mary Wollstonecraft, *A Vindication of the Rights of Woman*, ed. Deidre Shauna Lynch, 3rd ed. (New York: Norton, 2009), chap. 9, 151.

70. Wollstonecraft, *Vindication of the Rights of Woman*, 154.

71. Mary Wollstonecraft, *Letters Written During a Short Residence in Sweden, Norway, and Denmark*, ed. Carol Poston (Lincoln: University of Nebraska Press), 161.

72. In Salzmann's version the father similarly points out that Luise has brought the punishment on herself, but he expresses compassion and emphasizes how much he wished to make his daughter happy: "Armes unglückliches Mädchen! sagte der Vater, bringst du dich nicht selbst um die grosse Freude, die ich dir itzo machen wollte?" (Poor unhappy girl! said the father, are you not denying yourself the great pleasure that I wanted to grant you?) So Wollstonecraft increases the pressure on the girl: the mother manipulates Mary emotionally, proffers a less substantial reason for doing so, and gives little indication of compassion for the girl—no sense that it is difficult for her to deny her daughter a pleasure to which the girl had so looked forward.

73. Mary Wollstonecraft, *Thoughts on the Education of Daughters* (1787), in *The Works of Mary Wollstonecraft*, ed. Janet Todd and Marilyn Butler, 5 vols (London: William Pickering, 1989), V.15.

74. *The Collected Letters of Mary Wollstonecraft*, ed. Janet Todd (London: Allen Lane/Penguin, 2003), 164. Janet Todd suggests in a footnote that the "German book" must be Salzmann's, "which Wollstonecraft was translating and which took many months to appear in instalments" (n. 380, p. 164).

75. Elisabeth Gibbels, *Mary Wollstonecraft zwischen Feminismus und Opportunismus: Die discursiven Strategien in deutschen Übersetzungen von A Vindication of the Rights of Woman* (Tübingen: Gunter Narr Verlag, 2004), 80–97.

76. The Weissenborn essay appears in J. C. F. GutsMuths, ed., *Bibliothek der pädagogischen Literatur* (Gotha: Perdes, 1800), 208. Quoted in Gibbels, 87.

77. For a description of their three-month incarceration, see Johann Heinrich Liebeskind's *Rückerinnerungen von einer Reise durch einen Teil von Deutschland, Preußen, Kurland und Livland—während des Aufenthaltes der Franzosen in Mainz und der Unruhen in Polen* (Strasburg and Königsberg, 1795); also Klessmann, *Universitätsmamsellen*.

78. *The Monthly Register and Encyclopedian Magazine* came out in three volumes during the years 1802–03; Crabb Robinson contributed three famous "Letters on the Philosophy of Kant from an undergraduate at the University of Jena."

79. Richard Littlejohns, "Early Romanticism," in *The Literature of German Romanticism*, ed. Dennis F. Mahoney, vol. 8 of the Camden House History of German Literature (Rochester: Camden House, 2004), 61–78. For Caroline as translator herself, see Ursula El-Akramy, "Caroline Schlegel-Schelling als Salonniere und Shakespeare Übersetzerin," in *Mittlerin zwischen den Kulturen—Mittlerin zwischen den Geschlechtern? Studie zur Theorie und Praxis feministischer Übersetzung*, ed. Sabine Messner and Michaela Wolf (Graz: Institut für Theoretische und Angewandte Translationswissenschaft, 2000). For an analysis of Caroline's impact on Hegel, who lived in the same house in Jena for two years, see Seyla Benhabib, "On Hegel, Women and Irony," in her *Situating the Self: Gender, Community and Postmodernism in Contemporary Ethics* (Cam-

bridge: Polity, 1992), 242–59. Gerda Lerner discusses the progressive notions of the Jena circle in *The Creation of Feminist Consciousness* (Oxford: Oxford University Press, 1993), esp. 235–37.

80. J. C. F. GutsMuths, *Gymnastik für die Jugend. Enthaltend eine praktische Anweisung zu Leibesübungen. Ein Beitrag zur nöthigsten Verbesserung der körperlichen Erziehung. Von GutsMuths, Erzieher zu Schnepfenthal.* (Schnepfenthal: Im Verlage der Buchhandlung der Erziehungsanstalt, 1793); *Gymnastics for youth: or a practical guide to healthful and amusing exercises for the use of schools. An essay toward the necessary improvement of Education, Chiefly as it relates to the Body; freely translated from the German of C. G. Salzmann, Master of the Academy at Schnepfenthal, and Author of Elements of Morality. Illustrated with copper plates* (London: J. Johnson, 1800); note that in the English edition the work is misattributed to Salzmann—in a footnote the translator admits that the name Guts-Muths appears on the title page, but he assumes that this is a pseudonym (89).

81. Gerald P. Tyson, *Joseph Johnson: A Liberal Publisher* (Iowa City: University of Iowa Press, 1979), 62; Helen Braithwaite, *Romanticism, Publishing and Dissent: Joseph Johnson and the Cause of Liberty* (Basingstoke: Palgrave Macmillan, 2003).

82. Tyson, 140; Braithwaite, 162.

83. See Elisabeth Gibbels, *Mary Wollstonecraft zwischen Feminismus und Opportunismus: Die discursiven Strategien in deutschen Übersetzungen von* A Vindication of the Rights of Woman (Tübingen: Gunter Narr Verlag, 2004), 80–97.

84. Michael Sosulski, *Theater and Nation in Eighteenth-Century Germany* (Aldershot: Ashgate, 2007), 95.

85. Kai Reinhart and Michael Krüger, "Funktionen des Sports im modernen Staat und in der modernen Diktatur," *Historical Social Research* 32.1 (2007): 43–77.

86. See, for example, Willi Schröder, *Johann Christoph Friedrich GutsMuths: Leben und Wirken des Schnepfenthaler Pädagogen* (Sankt Augustin: Academia, 1996); Roland Naul, *Olympic Education* (Maidenhead: Meyer and Meyer, 2008).

87. Henry Crabb Robinson, *Diary, Reminiscences, and Correspondence*, ed. Thomas Sadler, 2 vols. (Boston: James R. Osgood and Co, 1871), I:133–34.

88. Josef Ulfkotte, "'Dem Wakkern fügte sich die glückliche Stunde': Zur wechselseitigen Wahrnehmung von Johann Christoph Friedrich GutsMuths und Friedrich Ludwig Jahn," in *Johann Christoph Friedrich GutsMuths (1759–1839) und die philanthropische Bewegung in Deutschland*, ed. Michael Krüger (Hamburg: Feldhaus, 2010), 15–30.

89. Heikki Lempa, *Beyond the Gymnasium: Educating the Middle-Class Bodies in Classical Germany* (Lanham, Md.: Lexington, 2007).

90. Teresa Sanislo, "Protecting Manliness in the Age of Enlightenment: The New Physical Education and Gymnastics in Germany, 1770–1800," in *Gender in Transition: Discourse and Practice in German-Speaking Europe, 1750–1830*, ed. Ulrike Gleixner and Marion W. Gray (Ann Arbor: University of Michigan Press, 2006), 265–81, quotation at 277–78.

91. Lempa, 84.

92. Erich Geldbach, "The Beginning of German Gymnastics in America," *Journal of Sport History* 3.3 (1976): 236–72.

93. Lempa, 76; Fred E. Leonard, *Pioneers of Modern Physical Training* (New York: Association, 1915), 21; Ulfkotte, 17.

94. For an overview, see Leonard, on whom I have drawn in the outline below.

95. Phokion Clias, *An Elementary Course of Gymnastics Exercises*, 4th ed., xii.

96. GutsMuths's predecessor at the Schnepfenthal school, Christian Carl André,

published in the 1780s *Education of Daughters in Schnepfenthal* (*Bildung der Töchter in Schnepfenthal* [Göttingen: J. D. Dieterich, 1789]); and *Small Hikes as well as longer trips of the female pupils at Schnepfenthal, for the purpose of increasing their knowledge of Nature, Art, and Human Beings* (*Kleine Wandrungen auch größere Reisen der weiblichen Zöglinge zu Schnepfenthal, um Natur, Kunst und den Menschen immer besser kennen zu lernen* [Leipzig: Crusius, 1788]).

97. Johann Adolph Ludwig Werner published *Gymnastics for female Youth, or feminine physical development for Health, Strength, and Grace* (*Gymnastik für die weibliche Jugend, oder weibliche Körperbildung für Gesundheit, Kraft, und Anmuth* [1834]); Antoine Martin Bureaud-Riofrey, *Treatise on Physical Education, specially adapted to Young Ladies*, 2d ed (London: Longman, 1838).

98. Jan Todd, *Physical Culture and the Body Beautiful* (Macon, Ga.: Mercer University Press, 1998), 51, 54.

99. Christiane Eisenberg, for one, has argued that German gymnastics failed to enter British physical culture because of a British *Sonderweg*—an earlier industrialization and emphasis on the privatized individual—which, she suggests, forestalled the absorption of German influence. Oddly enough she comes to this conclusion after detailing the various inroads into British physical culture made by Clias, Carl Voelcker, and others, as well as the substantial impact of the German Gymnastics Club in London. Although I take issue with Eisenberg's claim about a British *Sonderweg* in this context, there is no reason to contest her larger claim that Germany absorbed British-style sport to a greater extent than Britain absorbed German gymnastics; Christiane Eisenberg, "'German Gymnastics' in Britain, or the Failure of Cultural Transfer," in *Migration and Transfer from Germany to Britain 1660–1914*, ed. Stefan Manz, Margrit Schulte Beerbühl, and John R. Davis (Munich: Saur, 2007, 131–46). See also Eisenberg, *'English Sports' und deutsche Bürger: Eine Gesellschaftsgeschichte 1800–1939* (Paderborn: Schöningh, 1999). On the Sonderweg Eisenberg cites, see Bernd Weisbrod, "Der englische 'Sonderweg' in der neueren Geschichte," *GG* 16 (1990): 233–52; Hermann Wellenreuther, "England und Europa: Überlegungen zum Problem des englischen Sonderwegs in der europäischen Geschichte," in *Liberalitas*, ed. Norbert Finzsch and Hermann Wellenreuther (Stuttgart: Steiner, 1992), 89–123; Perry Anderson, "Components of the National Culture," *New Left Review* 50 (1968): 3–20.

100. This book, in tune with GutsMuths's increasingly politicized commitment to liberty, is dedicated to the free cities of "Hamburg, Lübeck, Bremen, und ihren weisen, väterlichgesinnten Senaten aus Gefühle patriotischer Hochschätzung."

101. Tyson, 182–83; Braithwaite, 148, 152.

Chapter 3

1. William C. Somerville, *Letters from Paris* (Baltimore: Edward Coale, 1822), 10; [Samuel Wilkeson], "Historical Writing of Judge Samuel Wilkeson," *Publications of the Buffalo Historical Society* 5 (1902): 176; Johann Jakob Leuthy, *Geschichte des Cantons Zürich von 1831–1840* (Zürich: Leuthy's Verlags-Bureau, 1845), 397; Viscomte de Beaumont-Vassy, *Histoire de mon temps*, 2nd ed. (Paris: Amyot, 1864), II:338.

2. One antecedent of such a view was a liberal Enlightenment notion of historical progress, which posited that conflict or rebellion was required for new growth. Thomas Jefferson, writing from Paris to William Smith in 1787, mused: "what signify a few lives lost in a century or two? The tree of liberty must be refreshed from time

to time with the blood of patriots & tyrants. It is its natural manure" (13 November 1787). See also Helen Maria Williams, *Letters Written in France, in the summer of 1790 to a friend in England* (London: T. Cadell, 1790), Letter X, 81–82, and Wilhelm von Humboldt, *Ideen zu einem Versuch, die Grenzen der Wirksamkeit des Staats zu bestimmen* (Breslau: Trewendt, 1851), 48: "der Krieg [ist] eine der heilsamsten Erscheinungen zur Bildung des Menschengeschlechts. . . . Es ist das freilich furchtbare Extrem, wodurch jeder thätige Muth gegen Gefahr, Arbeit und Mühsehligkeit geprüft und gestählt wird."

3. Georg Forster, letters to Therese Heyne Forster, 24.10. 1793, 2.12. 1793: "Die Lava der Revolution fließt majestätisch und schont nichts mehr"; "Ihr seht, daß der Vulkan noch nicht schweigt; noch bebt die Erde unter unsern Füßen."

4. Quoted in Mary Louise Pratt, *Imperial Eyes: Travel Writing and Transculturation* (London: Routledge, 1992, 2003), 141.

5. *The Catholic World: Monthly Magazine of General Literature and Science* 50 (Oct. 1889–Mar. 1890): 8.

6. William Howitt, *The Rural and Domestic Life of Germany: Characteristic Sketches of its Cities and Scenery, Collected . . . in the Years 1840, 41, and 42* (London: Longman, Brown, Green and Longmans, 1842), 513.

7. An interesting and perhaps unique antecedent is Martin Opitz, who had used Vesuvius to comment upon the Thirty Years' War following the eruption of 1632 in his didactic poem "Vesuvius" (1633); see Barbara Becker-Cantarino, *Martin Opitz: Studien zu Werk und Person* (Amsterdam: Rodopi, 1982), esp. 65–82.

8. See David A. Bell, *The First Total War: Napoleon's Europe and the Birth of Warfare as We Know It* (Boston: Houghton Mifflin, 2007), 270–74; John A. Davis, *Naples and Napoleon: Southern Italy and the European Revolutions (1780–1860)* (Oxford: Oxford University Press, 2006), 107–231.

9. Vincenzo Gioberti, *Opere. Del Primato Morale e Civile degli Italiani*, vol. 3 (Losanna: Bonamici e Compagnia, 1846), 3:393: "le più terribili rivolte degl'Italiani contro il dominio straniero, succedettero in quelle torride regioni, dove pare che gl'impeti e i tumulti crudeli degli uomini gareggino coi fuochi sotterranei e coi tremiti rovinosi della terra e del mare." See also Nelson Moe, *The View from Vesuvius: Italian Culture and the Southern Question* (Berkeley: University of California Press, 2002), 116. Lady Blessington, in Marguerite Blessington and Edith Clay, *Lady Blessington at Naples* (London: H. Hamilton, 1979), 27; she visited Naples in 1823.

10. Sontag's representation has its basis in fact, as many travelers to Naples described their invitations to the Hamiltons' in such terms. Duchess Anna Amalia equated the vases and Emma, calling Hamilton's wife and his Etruscan cabinet "zwey seltene Gegenstände" that made his abode the more appealing. Emma does the "Attitudes" as if by magic: "sie bewirck dieses Zauber Werck durch das einfache Mittel ihres *Shawls* u ihres schönen Haares"; Anna Amalia, *Briefe über Italien* (St. Ingbert: Röhrig Universitätsverlag, 1999), 50. The Comtesse de Boigne emphasized that no one could possibly imitate Emma: "pour égaler son succès, il faut commencer par être parfaitement belle de la tête aux pieds"; *Mémoires de la Comtesse de Boigne*, ed. M. Charles Nicoullaud, 14th ed., 3 vols. (Paris: Plon, 1907), 1:115. Elisabeth Vigée Lebrun, who painted Emma, wrote: "Nothing, indeed, was more remarkable than the ease Lady Hamilton acquired in spontaneously giving her features an expression of sorrow or of joy, and of posing marvelously to represent different people. Her eyes a-kindle, her hair flying, she showed you a bewitching bacchante; then, all of a sudden, her face expressed grief, and you saw a magnificent repentant Magdalen";

Memoirs of Elisabeth Louise Vigée Le Brun, trans. Lionel Strachey (New York: Doubleday, 1903), 67.

11. Germaine de Staël, *Corinne, or Italy*, trans. Sylvia Raphael, intro. John Isbell (Oxford: Oxford University Press, 1998). Bad omens accompany their "perilous" approach through the "pestilential" Pontine Marshes to the city, where the aloe plant inspires "fear" and the ocean "terror," where Oswald is "on fire" even before he climbs Vesuvius, and a cloud covers the moon, a "fatal" portent that returns as Corinne dies at the end of the story (187–91, 404). The environment around Vesuvius "reminds one of hell," and the mountain holds "an independent force" that threatens or protects human beings "according to unfathomable laws" (193–94).

12. Staël, *Corinne*, 225.

13. Angelica Goodden, *Madame de Staël: The Dangerous Exile* (Oxford: Oxford University Press, 2008), 1, 19.

14. Bell, 160.

15. Bell, 49, 25; see also 30, 48–49.

16. Goodden, 7.

17. Barbara Korte, *English Travel Writing from Pilgrimages to Postcolonial Explorations*, trans. from the German by Catherine Matthias (London: Macmillan; and New York: St. Martin's, 2000), 126. Already in 1724 Mary Astell had commended Mary Wortley Montagu's *Turkish Letters* for demonstrating "to how much better purpose the Ladys Travel than their Lords"; see Ruth Perry, *The Celebrated Mary Astell: An Early English Feminist* (Chicago: University of Chicago Press, 1986), 275–77.

18. Brian Dolan, *Ladies of the Grand Tour* (London: Flamingo, 2001), 11, 9, 272.

19. Chloe Chard, *Pleasure and Guilt on the Grand Tour: Travel Writing and Imaginative Geography 1600–1830* (Manchester: Manchester University Press, 1999), 128–29.

20. Elizabeth Bohls, *Women Travel Writers and the Language of Aesthetics, 1716–1818* (Cambridge: Cambridge University Press, 1995), 17.

21. Mirella Agorni, *Translating Italy for the Eighteenth Century: British Women, Translation and Travel Writing (1739–1797)* (Manchester: St. Jerome, 2002), 110.

22. Gary Kelly, "Death and the Matron: Felicia Hemans, Romantic Death, and the Founding of the Modern Liberal State," in *Felicia Hemans: Reimagining Poetry in the Nineteenth Century*, ed. Nanora Sweet and Julie Melnyk (Basingstoke: Palgrave, 2001), pp. 196–211; also Kelly, "Introduction: Felicia Hemans, the Reading Public, and the Political Nation," in *Felicia Hemans: Selected Poems, Prose, and Letters*, ed. Gary Kelly (Peterborough, Ontario: Broadview Press, 2002), 15–85.

23. Susan J. Wolfson, introduction to *Felicia Hemans: Selected Poems, Letters, Reception Materials*, ed. Susan J. Wolfson (Princeton: Princeton University Press, 2000), xiii–xxix, quotation at xxv.

24. Grant F. Scott, "The Fragile Image: Felicia Hemans and Romantic Ekphrasis," in Sweet and Melnyk, *Felicia Hemans*, 36–54, quotation at 50. That hint of skepticism, as well as the role of the artist, serve to distinguish this poem from Percy Shelley's "Ozymandias," which also emphasizes the return of a monument to dust and questions the potency of the despot. Shelley depends on the role of the artist in creating the image that gives the face and gives the poem its meaning—the irony would be lost without the sneering visage fallen to the sands—whereas in Hemans the implication is that the woman, anonymous and representative of all mothers, transformed into a monument by chance, creates meaning that would exist even unobserved, not monumentalized by the power of the volcano or the poet. See Isobel Armstrong, "Natural and National Monuments—Felicia Hemans's 'The Image in Lava': A Note," in Sweet and Melnyk, *Felicia Hemans*, 212–30.

25. The ending of the novel is ambiguous and scholars disagree on the extent to which Shelley intends to convey human annihilation.

26. Gary Kelly, "Death and the Matron," 197.

27. Kelly, "Introduction," 28.

28. See E. P. Thompson, *The Making of the English Working Class* (New York: Vintage Books, 1966), esp. 221–33.

29. Hester Lynch Piozzi, *Observations and Reflections made in the Course of a Journey through France, Italy, and Germany*, 2 vols. (London: Strahan and Cadell, 1789), 2:4.

30. Maximilien Misson, *Nouveau Voyage D'Italie*, 4th ed., 3 vols. (La Haye: Henry van Bulderen, 1702), 2:58: "font des mines, pour avoir le plaisir de faire sauter de plus grands rochers."

31. John Moore, *A View of Society and Manners in Italy: with Anecdotes relating to some Eminent Characters*, 2 vols., 3rd ed. (London: W. Strahan and T. Cadell, 1783), 2: 215.

32. Johann Wolfgang von Goethe, *Sämtliche Werke*, ed. Christoph Michel und Hans-Georg Dewitz, 40 vols. (Frankfurt: Deutscher Klassiker Verlag, 1993), vol. 15/pt. I:209; "[dass] eine gegenwärtige Gefahr etwas reizendes hat und den Widerspruchsgeist im Menschen auffordert ihr zu trotzen."

33. Edmund Burke, *A Philosophical Enquiry into the Origin of our Ideas of the Sublime and the Beautiful and other Pre-Revolutionary Writings,* ed. David Womersley (London: Penguin, 1998), 96.

34. Burke, see esp. 146–51, 86–89, 107–27.

35. See the helpful summary of Kari Lokke in "Schiller's *Maria Stuart*: The Historical Sublime and the Aesthetics of Gender," *Germanisch-Romanische Monatshefte* 82 (1990): 123–41, esp. 123.

36. Goethe, vol. 15/pt. I:209–10. Men who were not able to experience the crater and eruptions deeply regretted it. Robert Gray pined, "What a sublime sight must they afford!"; Robert Gray, *Letters During the Course of a Tour through Germany, Switzerland and Italy, in the Years 1791 and 1792 with Reflections on the Manners, Literature, and Religion of those Countries* (London: F. and C. Rivington, 1794), 419. Lady Anne Miller's husband managed "with great fatigue and difficulty, [to gain] the mouth of the *crater*; but the wind setting in his face, he was obliged to descend without being able to look down into it"; Lady Anne "prevailed with him not to attempt it a second time, though he alleged he had not seen it to his liking"; Lady Anne Riggs Miller, *Letters from Italy, Describing the Manners, Customs, Antiquities, Paintings, &c. of that Country, In the Years 1770 and 1771 to a Friend residing in France. By an English Woman*, 2nd ed., rev. and corrected, 2 vols. (London: Edward and Charles Dilly, 1777), 1:2, 2:145.

37. Mary Shelley, *Letters of Mary Wollstonecraft Shelley*, ed. Betty T. Bennett, 3 vols. (Baltimore: Johns Hopkins University Press, 1980), 1:85; see also *The Journals of Mary Shelley 1814–1844*, ed. Paula Feldman and Diana Scott-Kilvert, 2 vols. (Oxford: Clarendon, 1987), 1:241–49. Percy Bysshe Shelley, *Letters* in *Complete Works of Percy Bysshe Shelley*, ed. Roger Ingpen and Walter E. Peck, 10 vols. (New York: Gordian Press; and London: Ernst Benn, 1965), 10:17–19. For Percy's interest in volcano imagery, see P. M. S. Dawson, *The Unacknowledged Legislator: Shelley and Politics* (Oxford: Clarendon, 1980), 44–45, 70, 171, 255.

38. Marlon B. Ross, "Romantic Quest and Conquest: Troping Masculine Power in the Crisis of Poetic Identity," in *Romanticism and Feminism,* ed. Anne Mellor (Bloomington: Indiana University Press, 1988), 26–51, 44.

39. Meena Alexander, *Women in Romanticism: Mary Wollstonecraft, Dorothy Wordsworth, and Mary Shelley* (London: Macmillan, 1989), 181–83.

40. I thank John Brewer for alerting me to the account of Sir William Drummond.

See Richard Hamblyn, "Private Cabinets and Popular Geology: The British Audiences for Volcanoes in the Eighteenth Century," in *Transports: Travel, Pleasure, and Imaginative Geography, 1600–1830,* ed. Chloe Chard and Helen Langdon (New Haven: Yale University Press, 1996), 179–205. Hamblyn helpfully explains the shifting notions of scientific professionalism in this period of gentlemen virtuosi, geology buffs, and eventually specialized naturalists. He also elucidates the debate between Neptunists and Vulcanists, a significant discussion I unfortunately do not have the space to treat here.

41. Ross, "Romantic Quest," 32.

42. Cf. Noah Heringman, "The Style of Natural Catastrophes," *Huntington Library Quarterly* 66 (2003): 97–133, who argues that English scientists (Hamilton and Humphry Davy), like Piozzi, recognized their incapacity to fathom nature, a claim of which I am unconvinced. Their realization, according to Heringman, can be read in their recourse to aesthetic discourses to describe disasters: "The style of natural catastrophes derives its aesthetic character from the recognition that these phenomena mark a limit to the domestication of nature." Though Heringman notes that the poet he finds most influential on these scientists uses feminine metaphors—womb and birth—to describe the earth and disaster, Heringman does not analyze gender, nor does he take account of travel literature.

43. Elisa von der Recke, *Tagebuch einer Reise durch einen Theil Deutschlands und durch Italien, in den Jahren 1804 bis 1806,* ed. Hofrath Boettiger, 4 vols. (Berlin: Nicolai, 1815), 3:304, 276–77.

44. Mariana Starke, *Letters from Italy, between the years 1792 and 1798, Containing a View of the Revolutions in that Country,* 2 vols. (London: R. Phillips, 1800), 2:131. Starke's complete account reads: "At Resina we got upon mules, who carried us to the Cross, from whence we walked to the Crater, aided by our Guides. (A stout stick and a pair of boots are likewise necessary appendages to this excursion.) After having examined the Crater, and then refreshed ourselves at the Hermitage upon Vesuvius, we descended to Resina."

45. Lady Morgan, *Italy. A New Edition,* 3 vols. (London: Henry Colburn, 1821), 3:167. Lady Morgan was a writer well versed in the language of landscape aesthetics and its gendered character, especially evident in her biography of the artist Salvator Rosa, whose destructive sublime landscapes she contrasts with the representations of Claude and Poussin. See Mellor, *Romanticism and Gender,* 98.

46. Friederike Brun, *Prosaische Schriften* (Zurich: Orell, Fuessli und Compagnie, 1800), 4:350–51: "edle Gedanken der Unsterblichkeit," "der Unzertrennbarkeit moralischer Wesen," "Rührend ist das schüchtern aufkeimende, junge Leben der Vegetazion in den alten Lava massen." Only one woman's account I have seen could be said to convey true enthusiasm about viewing the crater. See Catherine Wilmot, who nonetheless nearly "fainted with fright" and is at pains to underscore how extraordinary her ascent is for a woman; *An Irish Peer on the Continent (1801–1803),* ed. Thomas U. Sadleir (London: Willimans and Norgate, 1920), 150–52. Mary Berry demonstrates some interest by measuring the crater, but focuses on the picnic she enjoyed at the edge of it; Mary Berry, *Extracts of the Journals and Correspondence of Miss Berry from the Year 1783 to 1852,* ed. Lady Theresa Lewis, 3 vols. (London: Longmans, Green, and Co., 1865), 1:91.

47. Staël, *Corinne, or Italy,* 226–227.

48. Staël, *Corinne, or Italy,* 225.

49. Chard, 184.

50. Marshall Brown, "Romanticism and Enlightenment," in *The Cambridge Companion to British Romanticism*, ed. Stuart Curran (Cambridge: Cambridge University Press, 1993), 25–47, quotations at 30–31.

51. Friedrich Johann Lorenz Meyer, *Darstellungen aus Italien* (Berlin: Vossische Buchhandlung, 1792), 361, 373: "Des Vulkans rauchender Gipfel hatte mir gewinkt; der Wunsch mich ihm zu nähern, besiegte die Ermüdung nach einer langsamen und unbequemen Reise von Rom her."

52. Moore, *A View of Society and Manners in Italy*, 2:210–11.

53. Johann Gottfried Seume, *Spaziergang nach Syrakus im Jahre 1802*, ed. Jörg Drews (Frankfurt: Insel Verlag, 2001), 279–83: "Was vorherzusehen war, geschah: die Dame konnte, als wir absteigen mußten, zu Fuße nicht weit fort und blieb zurück; und ich war so ungallant, mich nicht darum zu bekümmern"; "So durstig ich auch war, war mir doch das Mädchen fast willkommener als das Wasser: und wenn ich länger hier bliebe, ich glaube fast ich würde den Vulkan gerade auf diese Wege vielleicht ohne Führer noch oft besuchen"; "Aber das Wasser war mir oben lieber als hier die köstlichen Tränen [Lacrimae Christi], und die Hebe des ersten wohl auch etwas lieber als die Hebe der zweiten"; "machte siedend rund umher / Das Land zum größten Grab der Erde"; "Unter diesen Phantasien schlief ich ruhig ein."

54. Anonymous review [Georg Forster], *Göttingische Anzeigen von gelehrten Sachen* 23 (7 February 1789): 226–29, quote at 226.

55. This had occurred in 1785; see Dupaty's *Mémoire justificatif pour trois hommes condamnés à la roue* (Paris: Philippe-Denys Pierres, 1786).

56. Charles Jean-Baptiste Mercier Dupaty, *Briefe über Italien vom Jahr 1785. Aus dem Französischen von Georg Forster*, 2 vols. (Mainz: Universitätsbuchhandlung, 1789), translator's preface vii–xii, quotes at vii, viii.

57. Thomas P. Saine, *Georg Forster* (New York: Twayne Publishers 1972), 102. Forster died before the last volume, concerning the trip to England and France, was composed and published.

58. Georg Forster, *Ansichten vom Niederrhein* (Berlin: Voss, 1791), 121–22: "und meines Erachtens erreicht man besser seinen Endzweck, indem man wieder erzählt, was man bei einem Kunstwerke empfand und dachte, also, wie und was es *bewirkte*, als wenn man es ausführlich *beschreibt*. . . . Durch diese Fortpflanzung der Empfindungen ahnden wir dann,—nicht wie das Kunstwerk wirklich gestaltet war,—aber gleichwohl, wie reich oder arm es seyn musste, um diese oder jene Kräfte zu äussern" (emphasis in original).

59. *Göttingische Anzeigen von gelehrten Sachen* 23 (7 February 1789): 228.

60. For Forster's pictorial approach to discourses of revolution, see Rolf Reichardt, "Die visualisierte Revolution: Die Geburt des Revolutionärs Georg Forster aus der politischen Bildlichkeit," *Forster-Studien* 5 (2000): 163–227; also Ludwig Uhlig, who argues that the volcano was more than a metaphor to Forster the scientist, for whom the natural-historical analogy indicated how contending powers play themselves out; *Georg Forster: Lebensabenteuer eines gelehrten Weltbürgers* (Göttingen: Vandenhoeck & Ruprecht, 2004), 296.

61. Charles Marguerite Jean Baptiste Mercier Dupaty, *Sentimental Letters on Italy; Written in French by President Dupaty, in 1785. Published at Rome in 1788, and translated the same year by J. Povoleri, at Paris*, 2 vols. (London: J. Bew, 1789), 2:147. Further citations will appear parenthetically in the text.

62. Shelley's *Frankenstein* is itself a travel account composed of Walton's letters to his sister.

63. Anna Jameson, *Diary of an Ennuyée* (1826), in *Visits and Sketches at Home and Abroad with Tales and Miscellanies* (London: Saunders and Otley, 1834), IV:149. Further citations will appear parenthetically in the text. Jameson's text, her first work, is like Staël's *Corinne* a combination of fiction and nonfiction, of which, Judith Johnston writes, "the strongest, most vital elements . . . are the predominating non-fictional passages"; *Anna Jameson: Victorian, Feminist, Woman of Letters* (Aldershot: Scolar Press, 1997), 1, see also 23, 101–3. Jameson herself said that "the intention was not to create an illusion, by giving to fiction the appearance of truth, but, in fact, to give to truth the air of fiction" (from *Loves of the Poets*, xi, quoted in Johnston, 57, 102). Whether Jameson might have fictionalized some of the account of the ascent—which may be true of Dupaty and many other writers of the period—interests me less than how she finally represented the experience.

64. William Gilpin, *Observations, Relative Chiefly to Picturesque Beauty, Made in the Year 1772, On several Parts of England* (London: R. Blamire, 1786; facsimile edition, Poole, England: Woodstock Books, 1996), 2:45.

65. Gilpin, 2:45–46. Gilpin's quotation comes from Virgil's *Aeneid*, IX.229–30. My thanks to Michael Seidel for locating the reference.

66. Olwen Hufton, *The Prospect Before Her: A History of Women in Western Europe, Volume One 1500–1800* (London: Fontana Press, 1997), 19: "a deep chasm opened up between the culture of the rich and comfortable (mannered society) and the rest, between the informed and the ignorant, between high and popular culture, and these differences were as conspicuous as the disparities in their material lives." See also Jeremy Black, *Eighteenth-Century Europe*, 2nd ed. (New York: St. Martin's Press, 1999), esp. 112–17. Cf. Robert B. Shoemaker, who does not even see in class a foolproof distinction; for England "class is . . . not the best principle along which to organise a study of gender" since "gender roles also cross social divides"; Robert B. Shoemaker, *Gender in English Society 1650–1850: The Emergence of Separate Spheres?* (London: Longman, 1998), 12.

67. The collecting of lava seems to be particularly characteristic of male travelers' accounts and absent from women's. Keyßler alludes to the stones in his pocket, "Steine, welche ich in der Tasche bey mir führte"; in Johann Georg Keyßler, der Königlichen Grossbrittanischen Societät der Wissenschaften Mitglied, *Reisen durch Deutschland, Boehmen, Ungarn, die Schweiz, Italien, und Lothringen*, 2 vols. (Hannover: In der Helwingschen Hof-Buchhandlung, 1776); two volumes with continuous pagination, 2:752. John Evelyn was a collector of "pumice"; *The Diary of John Evelyn*, ed. E. S. de Beer, 6 vols. (Oxford: Clarendon, 1955), 2:178. Joseph Jérôme le Français de Lalande devotes an entire chapter to Vesuvian lava, in his *Voyage d'un François en Italie, fait dans les Années 1765 & 1766*, 8 vols. (text), 1 vol. (maps and illustrations) (Venice & Paris: Desaint, 1769), 7: 189–206. Goethe gives much time and space to reporting examinations of the lava flows and the retrieval of specimens. See esp. his "Geologische Notizen," in *Sämtliche Werke*, ed. Christoph Michel und Hans-Georg Dewitz, 40 vols. (Frankfurt: Deutscher Klassiker Verlag, 1993), vol. 15/pt. I: 803–4. Only one woman I have encountered in the literature appears to have gathered lava with the intent of putting together a collection: Lady Bessborough, who ascended the mountain with her mother in 1793 (Dolan, *Ladies*, 109).

68. Laura Strumingher, "The Vésuviennes: Images of Women Warriors in 1848 and Their Significance for French History," *History of European Ideas* 8 (1987): 451–88, quotation at 485; the best-known cartoons were produced by Edouard de Beaumont in *Le Charivari*. A few working-class women sought to rehabilitate the image

for feminist ends; they even wrote a manifesto and feminized the volcano: "The lava contained for so long a period of time, and which must eventually spread out round us, is not at all incendiary; it is completely regenerative" (454). Also Claire Goldberg Moses, *French Feminism in the 19th Century* (Albany: SUNY Press, 1984), chap. 6; Karen Offen, *European Feminisms 1700–1950: A Political History* (Stanford: Stanford University Press, 2000), chap. 5.

69. Ronit Lentin, "Introduction: (En)gendering Genocides," in *Gender and Catastrophe*, ed. Ronit Lentin (London: Zed Books, 1997), 2–17, quotation at 7–8.

70. Margaret Kelleher, "Woman as Famine Victim: The Figure of Woman in Irish Famine Narratives," in Lentin, *Gender and Catastrophe*, 241–54, quotation at 251.

71. Princesse de Gonzague, *Lettres de Madame la Princesse de Gonzague sur L'Italie, La France, L'Allemagne et les Beaux-Arts. Nouvelle Édition corrigée et augmentée*, 2 vols. (Hamburg: Fauche, 1797), 2:26: "un terrible exemple de l'instabilité des choses humaines"; "Que deviendroient leur caquet philosophique, en voyant la terre trembler, les villes disparoître!"

72. Hester Lynch Piozzi, *Observations and Reflections*, ed. Herbert Barrows (Ann Arbor: University of Michigan Press, 1967), 248–49.

73. Meyer, 439–40: "Bedarf diese schönste Lobrede auf den weiblichen Charakter eines Kommentars?—"

74. Roger Cohen, "Iran's Second Sex," *New York Times* (27 June 2009), A19.

75. David Marshall, "The Problem of the Picturesque," *Eighteenth-Century Studies* 35.3 (2002): 413–37, quotation at 430.

76. Anne Mellor argues that for women writers the masculine sublime is brought indoors in the form of male predatoriness and tyranny. Women writers who grew up in the sublime landscapes of Scotland, Wales, and Ireland felt at home there and represented the landscape as a "*female* friend, a sister, with whom they share their most intimate experiences and with whom they cooperate in the daily business of life, to the mutual advantage of each" (*Romanticism and Gender*, 85–106). See also Barbara Freeman, *The Feminine Sublime: Gender and Excess in Women's Fiction* (Berkeley: University of California Press, 1995). Vesuvius, however, is not a friend or a nurturing feminine presence, but rather an obstruction that unequivocally presents sublime horror. While, as Elizabeth Bohls has argued, women writers cherished the sublime as an aesthetic category (15) and the Vesuvius accounts affirm this, female travel-narrators nonetheless posited an alternative to the masculine sublime, rejecting the solitary confrontation with the obstacle and embracing a social and rational response.

77. For an account of Bluestocking interest in the sublime, see Samuel Monk, *The Sublime: A Study of Critical Theories in 18th-Century England* (New York: Modern Language Association of America, 1935), 212–21. Monk speculates that women's different approach, which he actually sees as more thoroughly "romantic" and especially to be discerned in the gothic, can be traced to their lack of classical education: "They were therefore, by virtue of their sex, somewhat outside the tradition" (216).

78. As far as I have been able to determine, female artists chose not to represent Vesuvius erupting. To be sure, there are standard views of Naples with Vesuvius in the background, as, for example, in typical souvenir vistas of the city, or portraits that locate the sitter by offering a view of the volcano through a window. But I have as yet found no formal works by women that concentrate on the volcano alone erupting. There is one informal exception: a student's attempt to copy the work of Hackert. I am referring to a watercolor of Eliza Gore, *Eruption of Vesuvius* (1775). She and her sister Emily, both talented artists, accompanied their father to Italy; it is not clear

whether they joined him on his trip with Philipp Hackert and Richard Payne Knight to Sicily. Charles Gore was so interested in the German artist that, when invited to move to Weimar in 1791, he did so. Eliza's work was displayed and admired there. The Gores were active members in the cultural community and lived in the Jäger-haus. Eliza Gore died in Weimar in 1802; Charles Gore died there in 1807, and the family's estate came to the Weimar library in 1811. (Rolf Bothe and Ulrich Hauss-mann, *Goethes "Bildergalerie": Die Anfänge der Kunstsammlungen zu Weimar* [Berlin: G + H Verlag, 2002], 108–9, 265–67. Eliza Gore's picture of Vesuvius is reproduced but mislabeled on page 265; it apparently should have appeared under number 44 on page 266.)

Otherwise I have sought in vain for women's representations of Vesuvius erupt-ing, even though many female artists from northern Europe lived and studied in Italy. As in the portraits of Vigée Lebrun, to which I have alluded, the smoking vol-cano generally forms part of a backdrop for a different subject. Duchess Wilhelmine of Bayreuth may have made a sketch in 1755, but this is contested and in any case it served as an amateur's journal entry, not a work of art to be sold and displayed. See Helke Kammerer-Grothaus, "'Voyage d'Italie' (1755): Markgräfin Wilhelmine von Bayreuth im Königreich Neapel," in *Wilhelmine und Friedrich II. und die Antik-en, by* Helke Kammerer-Grothaus and Detlev Kreikenbom (Stendal: Winckelmann-Gesellschaft, 1998), 7–41, see 14–15. Cornelia Knight undertook landscape drawings and watercolors when she lived in Naples, but the only pictures she published were of the Roman countryside in *Latium*. Though it feels premature to conclude definitively, my sense is that women did not draw the erupting mountain because they felt no interest in staying at the edge of the crater long enough to do so.

79. Barbara Maria Stafford notes that these representations should be distin-guished from the "studies produced by professional or amateur volcanologists" because "their purpose is ostentatious display of artistic effects rather than probing scrutiny"; *Voyage into Substance: Art, Science, Nature, and the Illustrated Travel Account, 1760–1840* (Cambridge: MIT Press, 1984), 249.

80. It has been suggested that J. M. W. Turner's revolutionary use of lighting effects was itself prompted by volcanic ash: the eruption of the Indonesian volca-no Tambora in 1815 threw ash into the atmosphere, and the resulting hazy sunsets inspired Turner's atmospheric representations. I thank my colleague Ken Verosub for alerting me to this theory; see Clive Oppenheimer, "Climatic, Environmental and Human Consequences of the Largest Known Historic Eruption: Tambora Volcano (Indonesia) 1815," *Progress in Physical Geography* 27.2 (2003): 230–59, 244.

81. Wendy Wassyng Roworth, "Kauffman and the Art of Painting in England," in *Angelica Kauffman: A Continental Artist in Georgian England,* ed. Wendy Wassyng Row-orth (London: Reaktion Books, 1992), 11–95, quotation at 21–22.

82. Victoria C. Gardner Coates, "Making History: Pliny's Letters to Tacitus and Angelica Kauffmann's *Pliny the Younger and His Mother at Misenum*," in *Pompeii in the Public Imagination,* ed. Shelley Hales and Joanna Paul (Oxford: Oxford University Press, 2011), 48–61. Gardner Coates suggests that Kauffmann "was not particular-ly accomplished at landscape painting" and would therefore not have depicted an erupting volcano (58, n23), but since Kauffmann has chosen to depict it in the back-ground I think it more likely that she consciously wishes to demote the eruption in favor of a focus on human ties and the ways historiography, written or painted, facili-tates human connections through time.

83. Kauffmann's art has sometimes been explained as woman-centered because

she often painted for female patrons, but in this instance the picture was done for George Bowles, so the patron's sex is unlikely to have followed that pattern. Another picture from the group of three to which this painting belongs represents Cornelia as an ideal mother.

84. Percy Shelley, *Works*, 10:26; Johann Joachim Winckelmann, *Critical Account of the Situation and Destruction by the First Eruptions of Mount Vesuvius, of Herculaneum, Pompeii, and Stabia* (London: T. Carnan and F. Newbery, 1771), 28–32; Goethe, *Sämtliche Werke*, vol. 15/pt. I:220: "Es ist viel Unheil in der Welt geschehen, aber wenig das den Nachkommen so viel Freude gemacht hätte. Ich weiß nicht leicht etwas Interessanteres."

85. Meyer, 415: "aufbewahrt für die Wiederentdeckung eines Jahrhunderts, das aus diesem wichtigen Fund Vortheile zu ziehen wußte, welche die Jahrhunderte der Unwissenheit würden verschmähet haben. Einen zehnfachen Ersatz erhielt so die Welt für jene Verwüstung eines kleinen Strich Landes durch die Feuerfluthen des Vesuvs."

86. Lalande, 7:210: "cette lave du Vésuve a été un préservatif heureux contre l'injure des temps & le pillage des Barbares." I thank John Brewer for informing me that the Vesuvius account in Lalande's volumes was actually written by the geologist Dolomieu.

87. Piozzi, 2:34–35. Göran Blix associates this type of view with a Romantic French archeological understanding of history and a new perception of lost worlds, but since the writings of an earlier English woman anticipate such an outlook, it seems desirable to probe this perspective in a broader European context with attention to gender; see Blix, *From Paris to Pompeii: French Romanticism and the Cultural Politics of Archaeology* (Philadelphia: University of Pennsylvania Press, 2009), esp. 158–74.

88. See also Thomas Watkins, who, standing on the same spot as Piozzi, could only imagine future tourists viewing, not his demise, but that of other nearby cities; *Travels through Swisserland, Italy, Sicily, the Greek Island, to Constantinople. in the Years 1787, 1788, 1789*, 2 vols. (London: T. Cadell, 1792), 1:419.

Chapter 4

1. I would like to thank Barbara Schaff for the opportunity to present an early version of this chapter at the University of Göttingen, and Frank Kelleter for discussions that inspired my undertaking the topic in the first place.

2. Ali Behdad, "The Politics of Adventure: Theories of Travel, Discourses of Power," in *Travel Writing, Form, and Empire: The Poetics and Politics of Mobility*, ed. Julia Kuehn and Paul Smethurst (New York: Routledge, 2009), 86.

3. Steve Clark, introduction to *Travel Writing and Empire: Postcolonial Theory in Transit*, ed. Steve Clark (London: Zen Books, 1999), 3.

4. James J. Sheehan, *German History 1770–1866* (Oxford: Clarendon, 1989), 261.

5. Sheehan, *German History*, 392, 449–50, 483–84.

6. Alexis de Tocqueville, *De la démocratie en Amerique*, 2 vols. (Paris: Pagnerre, vol. 1, 1835, vol. 2, 1840); Harriet Martineau, *Society in America* (New York and London: Saunders and Otley, 1837), v. Owen founded New Harmony and Wright Nashoba; Lee founded the Shakers, Rapp the Harmonists, and Metz the Amana community.

7. Mary Louise Pratt, *Imperial Eyes: Travel Writing and Transculturation* (London: Routledge, 1992), 152, 155.

8. Pratt, *Imperial Eyes*, 168; Doris Beck and Paul Beck, eds., *Flora Tristan: Utopian Feminist* (Bloomington: Indiana University Press, 1993).

9. Editions appeared in 1838 (England), 1839 (North America), 1839 (Germany), 1852 (popular abridgment titled *Sketches in Canada and Rambles Among the Redmen*), then reissued at least a dozen times in the twentieth century and twice in the twenty-first (2002, 2008).

10. Though scholars have begun to show an appreciation for Anna Jameson's lucid travel writings, critics focusing exclusively on her Canadian sojourn, despite making significant insights about North America, have overemphasized the colonial purport of her travels and thereby skewed the interpretation of her full and consistently reform-oriented career. See esp. Jennifer Henderson, *Settler Feminism and Race Making in Canada* (Toronto: University of Toronto Press, 2003), and Wendy Roy, *Maps of Difference: Canada, Women, and Travel* (Montreal: McGill-Queen's University Press, 2005).

11. In a letter to Ottilie von Goethe of 20 April 1839, written from Dresden, Jameson talks about "the Irish rebels—or louses which is a better & a truer word"; quoted by permission of the Goethe and Schiller Archive, Weimar, Germany, GSA 40/VIII, 5. This is an unpublished part of the letter Needler excerpts as #70 in his edition: G. H. Needler, ed., *Letters of Anna Jameson to Ottilie von Goethe* (London: Oxford University Press, 1939). Suggesting Denis Brownell Murphy's participation among the United Irishmen is Adele Ernstrom: "They made the first of several moves when they left Ireland for Whitehaven in 1798, fleeing suppression of the United Irishmen to which Denis Murphy had belonged. Murphy's Irish Jacobinism, and his nationalism, very likely influenced the outlook of his eldest daughter whose precocious gifts he encouraged"; "The Afterlife of Mary Wollstonecraft and Anna Jameson's *Winter Studies and Summer Rambles in Canada,*" *Women's Writing* 4.2 (1997): 277–96, 284. An unsubstantiated claim is also made in the introduction of G. H. Needler's edition of the *Letters*.

12. Clara Thomas, *Love and Work Enough: The Life of Anna Jameson* (Toronto: University of Toronto Press, 1967); Judith Johnston, *Anna Jameson: Victorian, Feminist, Woman of Letters* (Aldershot: Scolar Press, 1997); Gerardine Macpherson, *Memoirs of the Life of Anna Jameson* (London: Longmans, Green, and Co., 1878); Anna Jameson, *Letters and Friendships (1812–1860)*, ed. Mrs. Steuart Erskine (New York: E. P. Dutton & Company, 1915); G. H. Needler, ed., *Letters of Anna Jameson to Ottilie von Goethe* (London: Oxford University Press, 1939).

13. Thomas, *Love and Work Enough*, 112–14.

14. Anna Jameson, *Visits and Sketches at Home and Abroad with Tales and Miscellanies Now First Collected and a New Edition of the Diary of an Ennuyée*, 4 vols. (London: Saunders and Otley, 1834), I:160. Further citations will be made parenthetically in the text, with volume and page numbers preceded by VS.

15. See Karen O'Brien, *Women and Enlightenment in Eighteenth-Century Britain* (Cambridge: Cambridge University Press, 2009), who shows how, in terms of women's "political and civil rights, the period from the late eighteenth century to the early nineteenth century was one of no progress; indeed, there is evidence that the property rights of widows and married women actually declined during this period" (9). See also O'Brien's explanation of women's place in "conjectural history" (68–109), which, as I argue, Jameson seeks to refute.

16. Christa Zeller Thomas, "'I shall take to translating': Transformation, Translation and Transgression in Anna Jameson's *Winter Studies and Summer Rambles in Cana-*

da," in *Translators, Interpreters, Mediators: Women Writers 1700–1900,* ed. Gillian E. Dow (Bern: Peter Lang, 2007), 175–90, esp. 187.

17. Clara Thomas, *Love and Work Enough,* 90–91.

18. Jameson, *Winter Studies and Summer Rambles in Canada,* 3 vols. (London: Saunders and Otley, 1838), 30–36, quotation at 33. Further citations will appear parenthetically in the text, with the page number preceded by WS.

19. Erskine, *Letters and Friendships,* 150.

20. Letter to Ottilie von Goethe, 1 June 1837, in *Letters,* ed. Needler, 93; also Letter to Dennis Brownell Murphy, 21 June 1837, quoted in *Letters and Friendships,* ed. Erskine, 154. Both letters were written from Niagara Falls.

21. Contemporaneous travel narratives taking greater racialist and imperialist stances are those by Catharine Parr Traill, *The Backwoods of Canada* (London: Charles Knight, 1836) and Frederick Marryat, *A Diary in America,* 6 vols. (London: Longmans, 1839). Johnston distinguishes Jameson's account from theirs in *Anna Jameson,* 111–23.

22. For an extended discussion of Jameson's shifting tone toward the First Nations people, from being uninformed and stereotypical to being more nuanced and informed by her own experience, see Wendy Roy, *Maps of Difference: Canada, Women, and Travel* (Montreal: McGill-Queen's University Press, 2005), 39–46. Jennifer Henderson has a less positive reading, relying on a Foucauldian approach, and argues that Jameson furthered "governmental strategies" (12, 15), inscribing "the subtle technologies designed to cultivate forms of selfhood and habits of conduct suitable to a liberal political order" (10). She argues that Jameson, interested in theater, does this by seeing Canada as an empty stage on which female selfhood can act itself out. Canada, the "arctic zone," becomes a Foucaultian heterotopia, "a training-ground for the self-governing woman" (84). Although she helpfully inserts Jameson's Canadian sojourn into the context of Canadian politics, she then limits the effects of Jameson's work to its impact on Canada. Moreover, Henderson never defines more specifically what the "governmental strategies" she repeatedly invokes actually are. Such a concentration obscures the extent to which the "heterotopia" becomes, not just a template for Canada, but a means of critiquing British international policy, something that in turn calls into question the formidable nets of Foucauldian discipline to which Henderson clings so tenaciously.

23. Jameson, *Memoirs and Essays,* 214–15.

24. Anna Jameson, *Memoirs and Essays* (1846), 239. This essay, "Women's Mission and Women's Position," first appeared in *Athenaeum* in 1843 in response to the *Report of the Royal Commission on the Employment of Women and Young People in Mines* (1842).

25. *British and Foreign Review* 8 (1839): 137; quoted in Thomas, *Love and Work Enough,* 140.

26. Needler, *Letters,* 114.

27. Needler, *Letters,* 104.

28. Johnston, *Anna Jameson,* 143.

29. Jameson letter to Lady Byron, 26 January 1844; quoted in Thomas, *Love and Work Enough,* 160. Carlyle, notoriously anti-Irish and racist, published *Oliver Cromwell's Letters and Speeches* in 1845 and *Occasional Discourse on the Nigger Question* in 1853.

30. Anna Jameson, *Winterstudien und Sommerstreifereien in Canada. Ein Tagebuch von Mrs. Jameson. Aus dem Englischen uebersetzt von A. W.,* 3 vols. (Braunschweig: Vieweg und Sohn, 1839), ii. For my identification of the correct translator of Jameson's work, see

"Anna Jameson in Germany: 'A.W.' and Women's Translation," *Translation and Literature* 19 (2010): 190–95.

31. *Blätter zur Kunde der Literatur des Auslands* 4 (1839). Nr. 129 (21 November 1839): 513–14, and continued in nr. 130 (24 November 1839): 517–19. (Stuttgart und Augsburg: J. G. Cotta, 1839), 518, 519: "Aber eines davon bekennt sich zu einem Grundsatz, über den wir einige Worte sagen müssen, damit nicht, wenn wir ihn ungerügt lassen, der Autor sich zu Schulden kommen lasse, darnach zu handeln. Er sagt: 'Mrs. Jameson hat es so jedem, der ihr in ihrer Eigenschaft als Advocatin antworten will, unmöglich gemacht, sich nicht auch nach ihrem persönlichen Antheil an der von ihr mit solcher Wärme verfochtenen Sache zu erkundigen. Die Regeln der Höflichkeit verbieten uns dieß zu tun.'

"Ist es denn aber unmöglich, auf die Gründe zu antworten, die ein Schriftsteller für eine gegebene Meinung anführt, ohne [519] die besondere, davon ganz verschiedene Frage in Anregung zu bringen, welches persönliche Interesse denn der Schriftsteller bei der fraglichen Sache habe? sollen denn Streitfragen nach den Verdiensten ihrer Advocaten statt nach ihren eignen Verdiensten untersucht werden? Bis jetzt waren Schriftsteller von Logik und Wahrheitsliebe der Meinung, daß sie für eine Behauptung angeführten Gründe und Thatsachen das Einzige seyen, worauf die darüber Verhandelnden ihr Augenmerk zu richten hätten."

32. Ferdinand Gustav Kühne, *Portraits und Silhouetten* (Hannover: Kius Verlag, 1843), 176–77.

33. *Repertorium der gesammten deutschen Literatur,* herausgegeben E. G. Gersdorf, vol. 21, Jahrgang 1839 (Leipzig: Brockhaus, 1839), 358–59: "Dass sie vorzugsweise auf die Stellung sowohl der canadischen als indianischen Frauen Rücksicht nimmt und ihre Lage häufig schildert, liess sich erwarten, da Mrs. J. eine eifrige, doch höchst besonnene Vertheidigerin der Emanzipation ihres Geschlechtes ist, und wenn hiebei hin und wider eine irrige Ansicht oder einseitige Auffassung der Lebensverhältnisse mit unterläuft, so soll uns diess nicht ungerecht machen gegen die sonstige Vortrefflichkeit ihrer Gesinnungen."

34. *Blätter für literarische Unterhaltung* I, nr. 149 (Mittwoch, 29 May 1839): 602–4; "doch trägt sie kein Bedenken, die Erklärung hinzuzufügen, daß im Ganzen Englands fehlerhafte Colonialregierung an der übeln Lage Schuld sei, in welcher diese schönen Provinzen sich befinden . . . Mangel an echter Theilnahme, Mangel an richtiger Beurtheilung der Verhältnisse und Mangel an tieferer Einsicht in die Bedürfnisse des Landes haben bewirkt, daß es trotz seiner natürlichen Entwickelungsfähigkeit doch bis jetzt dürftig bevölkert und arm geblieben ist und seine Kräfte nicht auf eine ihnen entsprechende Weise entfaltet hat."

35. Jameson to Ottilie: "we dislike revolutions & sudden innovations." GSA XXI/1169 (17 July 1856).

36. *Beschluss der Bundes-Versammlung vom 10. Dezember 1835.*

37. This is a compilation of short reports that first appeared 1835–37 in the *Zeitung für die elegante Welt,* later reprinted in *Portraits und Silhouetten* (Hannover: Kius, 1843).

38. *Zeitung für die elegante Welt* 35, Nr. 206 (19 October 1835): 824; *Portraits und Silhouetten,* 174. Vol. 35 (1835) of the *Elegante Welt* also contains a lengthy excerpt from Jameson's *Visits and Sketches at Home and Abroad,* "Errinerungen an Dresden," translated by D. Vogel, published over several issues (numbers 61–68), which demonstrates the interest of Germans in a foreigner's views of their country.

39. Kühne, *Portraits und Silhouetten,* 174–75.

40. The translation of Jameson's Shakespeare book enjoyed enthusiastic reviews

in German journals; the *Blätter für literarische Unterhaltung* lauded the efficient explication and substantial content of Jameson's slim octavo volume ("es ist in diesem mäßigen Octavbande gewiß eben so viel Kern als in manchem fünfbändigen Commentar zu Shakspeare" [there is certainly as much substance in this modest octavo volume as in some five-volume criticisms of Shakespeare]), applauded Jameson's emphasis on Imogen in *Cymbeline*, and found Jameson's interpretation of Lady Macbeth superior to August Wilhelm Schlegel's ("[es] urtheilt die Verf. weit richtiger als A. W. Schlegel" [the author judges far more correctly than A. W. Schlegel]). By the mid-nineteenth century there were three different translations of Jameson's book. Thomas Lowndes, in the *Bibliographer's Manual of English Literature*, felt compelled to annotate his list with the comment *"these three rival translations of Mrs. Jameson's Characteristics of the Women of Shakespeare are evidence of the great popularity of the work in Germany"* (italics in original).

41. Kühne, *Lebensbild und Briefwechsel*, 166: he thanks Ottilie for the "Vorrath von gedruckten Schätzen, den Sie um mich gehäuft haben." See also H. H. Houben's "Introduction" to Ottilie von Goethe, *Erlebnisse und Geständnisse 1832–1857*, xvi: "die Stoffe zu seinem 1840 erschienenen Roman 'Die Rebellen von Irland' und zu dem sich daran anschließenden Drama 'Die Verschwörung von Dublin' verdankte er der noch immer 'irländischen Seele' Ottiliens, sie verschaffte ihm die gedruckten Quellenwerke für seine historischen Studien."

42. Needler, ed., *Letters*, 108, 113, 118. Ottilie gave Kühne a binder, complete with lock and key, for notes about Ireland which, however, he ultimately used to collect love poems to his wife; Kühne, *Lebensbild und Briefwechsel*, 149–50.

43. Needler, *Letters*, 180; Jameson sent another account of the "State of Ireland" on 22 December 1856 (214).

44. Ottilie von Goethe to Anna Jameson, 15 November 1853, GSA XXI/1169. All citation from this source are quoted by permission of the Goethe- and Schiller Archive, Weimar.

45. Patrick O'Neill, *Ireland and Germany: A Study in Literary Relations* (New York: Peter Lang, 1985), 177–78.

46. Ottilie von Goethe to Anna Jameson, Venice, 18 February 1856. GSA XXI/1169.

47. Kühne, *Lebensbild und Briefwechsel*, 179.

48. See, e.g., Ottilie von Goethe to Anna Jameson, Vienna 9 May 1855, GSA XXI/1169. "I received your Sisters of Charity . . . what is irish in you, comes more out in this. Pereira wishes very much to read it, but I could not give it to her, as I had given it to the Duchess of Acesenza to read." Also 29 May 1855 (Pereira has read *Sisters*) and 29 December 1855 (Ottilie's son Wolf has taken the *Sisters* to Rome so that Jameson's niece Gerardine can read it).

49. Jameson SCCL, x–xi.

50. See also her *Commonplace Book* in which she writes, "I firmly believe that as the influences of religion are extended, and as civilization advances, those qualities which are now admired as essentially *feminine* will be considered as essentially *human*" (85). In the meantime she notes her difference from Harriet Martineau: "she insists that there is no sexual distinction in mind—I think there is—is mind altogether independent of organization?" (letter of Jameson to Lady Byron, 24 September 1843; quoted in Thomas, *Love and Work Enough*, 157).

51. Although Jameson does not name Mary Wollstonecraft as her inspiration, there is debate whether she is the figure mentioned by Jameson as a martyr who "has not died without lifting up a voice of eloquent and solemn warning." Johnston doubts

this (*Anna Jameson*, 198–99); however, Adele M. Ernstrom argues that, because Wollstonecraft's reputation so suffered from William Godwin's *Memoirs of the Author of a Vindication of the Rights of Woman*, feminists in the first half of the nineteenth century, including Jameson, did not mention her directly but nonetheless were deeply influenced by her work; "The Afterlife of Mary Wollstonecraft and Anna Jameson's *Winter Studies and Summer Rambles in Canada*," *Women's Writing* 4.2 (1997): 277–97.

52. I trace a utopian feminist tradition beginning as early as Christine de Pizan in my article "Feminism and Utopianism," in *The Cambridge Companion to Utopian Literature*, ed. Gregory Claeys (Cambridge: Cambridge University Press, 2010), 174–99. Adele Ernstrom has argued that Jameson's utopianism may have been influenced by utopian socialism; I agree that it was likely fueled by it, but that the unmistakable echoes of earlier feminists, seen in the specific areas of concern and the manner of her arguments, links her to a longer feminist tradition; Ernstrom, "Afterlife of Mary Wollstonecraft," 289.

53. For a discussion of the cosmopolitanism of Enlightenment women writers, see my *Women's Utopias of the Eighteenth Century*, esp. 131–55.

54. Thomas Gerry sees this impulse in Jameson's artistic representations of her Canadian travels in "'I am translated': Anna Jameson's Sketches and *Winter Studies and Summer Rambles in Canada*," *Journal of Canadian Studies* 25.4 (1990–91): 34–49. Reproductions and discussions of her sketches and watercolors can also be found in Wendy Roy, *Maps of Difference*, 64–82.

55. Needler, *Letters*, 176–77.

56. Needler, *Letters*, 182–83.

57. 6 January 1854, GSA XXI/1:169.

58. Jameson, *Memoirs and Essays*, 216–18.

59. Adele N. Ernstrom, in "The Afterlife of Mary Wollstonecraft and Anna Jameson's *Winter Studies and Summer Rambles in Canada*," argues that in this Jameson is operating within a Rousseauian discourse of the noble savage and the corrupting influence of civilization, in the manner of Mary Wollstonecraft, who ascribed the "corruption within civilization as a result of courtly culture and the influence of commerce" (288). However, while I agree that Jameson reveres Mary Wollstonecraft, Jameson carefully differentiates between aspects of "savage" life she finds noble and aspects she does not, and she does not decry commerce. In fact, she praises U.S. cities (e.g., Buffalo and Detroit) for their vitality and trade as opposed to Canadian cities, which she often describes as listless and underdeveloped (II:78–80, II:313–15). Hence I have emphasized Jameson's distinction between civilization, an ideal—informed by ethics and Christian virtues—and modernization, a reality based on exploitation and heartless system that she critiques vehemently.

60. *Diary* 310, quoted in Thomas, *Love and Work Enough*, 35.

61. Macpherson, *Memoirs of the Life of Anna Jameson*, 150.

62. For an analysis of the range of the reviews, see Thomas, *Love and Work Enough*, 139–43.

63. Needler, *Letters*, 163–64; emphasis in original.

64. Thomas, *Love and Work Enough*, 209.

Afterword

1. See Maiken Umbach, "Visual Culture, Scientific Images and German Small-State Politics in the Late Enlightenment," *Past & Present* 158 (February 1998): 110–

45; see also Umbach, *Federalism and Enlightenment in Germany, 1740–1806* (London: Hambledon Press, 2000). Umbach's work informs the following discussion.

2. J. C. F. GutsMuths, *Gymnastik für die Jugend* (Schnepfenthal: Erziehungsanstalt, 1793), 61–63.

3. Burkhard Gäbler, "Die kunsttheoretischen und erziehungstheoretischen Anschauungen Georg Forsters und seine Beziehungen zur Dessau-Wörlitzer Aufklärung," in *Georg Forster: Leben, Werk, Wirkung*, Wissenschaftliches Kolloquium 30. Juni 1984 anlässlich der Eröffnung der Forster-Stätte in Wörlitz (Wörlitz: Staatliche Schlösser und Gärten, 1985), 39–52.

4. John Claudius Loudon et al., *An Encyclopaedia of Gardening* (London: Longman, Rees, Orme, Brown, Green and Longman, 1835; first shorter edition published 1822), 194. See also August von Rode, *Beschreibung des Fürstlichen Anhalt-Dessauischen Landhauses und Englischen Gartens zu Wörlitz* (Dessau: Heinrich Tänzer, 1814; facsimile, Wörlitz: Kettmann Verlag, 1996).

5. The park at Wörlitz has been named a UNESCO site; the volcano was restored in 2005 and reignited with much festivity, including performances of Lady Emma Hamilton's *Attitudes* in the Villa Hamilton. These can be viewed online. See Friedrich Wilhelm von Erdmannsdorf, *Kunsthistorisches Journal einer fürstlichen Bildungsreise nach Italien 1765/66*, trans. from the French and ed. Ralf-Torsten Speler (Munich: Deutscher Kunstverlag, 2001).

6. Simon Werrett, *Fireworks: Pyrotechnic Arts and Sciences in European History* (Chicago: University of Chicago Press, 2010), 218.

7. Quoted in Jost Hermand, "Rousseau, Goethe, Humboldt: Their Influence on Later Advocates of the Nature Garden," in *Nature and Ideology*, ed. Joachim Wolschke-Buhlmahn, Dumbarton Oaks Colloquium on the History of Landscape Architecture vol. 18 (Washington D.C.: Harvard University, 1997), 35–58, quotation at 38–39.

8. See James Stevens Curl, *The Art and Architecture of Freemasonry* (London: B. T. Batsford, 1991), esp. 177–81, 193; Christopher McIntosh, *Gardens of the Gods: Myth, Magic, and Meaning in Horticulture* (London: I. B. Tauris, 2005), 96–102; *Belehren und nützlich seyn: Franz von Anhalt-Dessau, Fürst der Aufklärung 1740–1817* (Wörlitz: Staatliche Schlösser und Gärten, 1990), 85–86.

9. GutsMuths, 63.

10. F. Max Müller, "Royalties," in *Cosmopolis* 7 (July 1897): 16–38, quotation at 24–25.

11. Hartmut Ross, Erdmute Alex, Reinhard Alex, Doris Hempel, Sebastian Pawlak, Ingo Pfeifer, Uwe Quilitzsch, and Ludwig Trauzettel, *Belehren und nützlich seyn: Franz von Anhalt-Dessau, Fürst der Aufklärung 1740–1817* (Wörlitz: Staatliche Schlösser und Gärten, 1990), 42.

12. Bruno Latour, *Reassembling the Social: An Introduction to Actor-Network-Theory* (Oxford: Oxford University Press, 2005), 48.

13. Mary Louise Pratt, *Imperial Eyes: Travel Writing and Transculturation* (London: Routledge, 1992), 137.

14. Thomas Biskup, "The University of Göttingen and the Personal Union 1737–1837," in *The Hanoverian Dimension in British History 1714–1837*, ed. Brendan Simms and Torsten Riotte (Cambridge: Cambridge University Press, 2007), 128–60, esp. 147. Ali Behdad has helpfully historicized European travel narratives by distinguishing late eighteenth-century travel reports about the Middle East as concerned with "the science of adventure," whereas the late seventeenth century probed "the exotics of adventure," and the mid-nineteenth century "the commerce of adventure"; Ali

Behdad, "The Politics of Adventure: Theories of Travel, Discourses of Power," in *Travel Writing, Form, and Empire: The Poetics and Politics of Mobility*, ed. Julia Kuehn and Paul Smethurst (New York: Routledge, 2009), 80–94. For an argument about the role of the Yemen project in furthering anti-Semitism, see Jonathan M. Hess, "Johann David Michaelis and the Colonial Imaginary: Orientalism and the Emergence of Racial Antisemitism in Eighteenth-Century Germany," *Jewish Social Studies* 6.2 (2000): 56–101, esp. 75–82.

15. Biskup, 147.

16. Pratt, 7.

17. August Ludwig Schlözer, *Entwurf zu einem Reise-Collegio* (Göttingen: Vandenhoeck, 1777); August Ludwig Schlözer, *Vorlesungen über Land- und Seereisen, nach dem Kollegheft des stud. Jur. E. F. Haupt*, ed. Wilhelm Ebel (Göttingen: Musterschmidt-verlag, 1962), 5, 54, 49–50. For an extended discussion of Schlözer in the context of the University of Göttingen and his role in the development of ethnography, see Justin Stagl, *A History of Curiosity: The Theory of Travel 1550–1800* (Chur, Switzerland: Harwood Academic Publishers, 1995), esp. 233–68.

18. Alessa Johns, "Feminism and Utopianism," in *The Cambridge Companion to Utopian Literature*, ed. Gregory Claeys (Cambridge: Cambridge University Press, 2010), 174–99, esp. 186–89; Alessa Johns, *Women's Utopias of the Eighteenth Century* (Urbana: University of Illinois Press, 2003), 100–102.

19. Bruno Latour, "An Attempt at a 'Compositionist' Manifesto," *New Literary History* 41.3 (Summer 2010): 471–90. See also Donald Wesling, "Michel Serres, Bruno Latour, and the Edges of Historical Periods," *Clio* 26.2 (Winter 1997): 189–204.

Works Cited

Primary Sources

Algarotti, Francesco. *Il Newtonianismo per le dame* (1737). Translated by Elizabeth Carter as *Sir Isaac Newton's philosophy explain'd for the use of the ladies. In six dialogues on light and colours.* London: E. Cave, 1739.

André, Christian Carl. *Bildung der Töchter in Schnepfenthal.* Göttingen: J. D. Dieterich, 1789.

André, Christian Carl. *Kleine Wandrungen auch größere Reisen der weiblichen Zöglinge zu Schnepfenthal, um Natur, Kunst und den Menschen immer besser kennen zu lernen.* Leipzig: Crusius, 1788.

Anonymous. *Beschluss der Bundes-Versammlung vom 10. Dezember 1835.* Reports 1835–37.

Anonymous review. *Blätter für literarische Unterhaltung.* 1, nr. 149. (Mittwoch, 29 May 1839): 602–4.

Anonymous review. *Blätter zur Kunde der Literatur des Auslands.* 4 (1839). Nr. 129 (21 November 1839): 513–14, and nr. 130 (24 November 1839): 517–19; Stuttgart: J. G. Cotta, 1839.

Anonymous review. *British and Foreign Review* 8 (1839): 137.

Anonymous review. *The Catholic World: Monthly Magazine of General Literature and Science* 50 (Oct. 1889–Mar. 1890).

Anonymous review. *Gentleman's Magazine* 19 (1749): 245–46, 345–49.

Anonymous review. *Göttingische Anzeigen von gelehrten Sachen* 23 (7 February 1789).

Anonymous review. *Monthly Review* 65 (1781): 504–8.

Anonymous review. *Repertorium der gesammten deutschen Literatur.* Edited by E. G. Gersdorf. Vol. 21. Leipzig: Brockhaus, 1839.

Beaumont-Vassy, Viscomte de. *Histoire de mon temps.* 2nd ed. Paris: Amytot, 1864.

Beecher, Catharine E. *Physiology and Calisthenics: For Schools and Families.* New York: Harper, 1856.

Berry, Mary. *Extracts of the Journals and Correspondence of Miss Berry from the Year 1783 to 1852.* Edited by Lady Theresa Lewis. 3 vols. London: Longmans, Green, and Co., 1865.

Blessington, [Lady] Marguerite, and Edith Clay. *Lady Blessington at Naples.* London: H. Hamilton, 1979.

Boccage, Madame du. *Lettres Contenant Ses Voyages en France, en Angleterre, en Hollande, et en Italie, faits pendant les Années 1750, 1757 & 1758.* Dresden: George Conrad Walther, 1771.

Boigne, Comtesse de. *Mémoires de la Comtesse de Boigne.* Edited by M. Charles Nicoullaud, 14th ed., vol. 1, 3 vols. Paris: Plon, 1907.

Brun, Friederike. *Prosaische Schriften.* Zurich: Orell, Fuessli und Compagnie, 1800.

Bureaud-Riofrey, Antoine Martin. *Treatise on Physical Education, specially adapted to Young Ladies.* 2nd ed. London: Longman, 1838.

Burke, Edmund. *A Philosophical Enquiry into the Origin of our Ideas of the Sublime and the Beautiful and Other Pre-Revolutionary Writings.* Edited by David Womersley. London: Penguin, 1998.

Carlyle, Thomas. *Occasional Discourse on the Nigger Question.* London: Chapman and Hall, 1853.

Carlyle, Thomas. *Oliver Cromwell's Letters and Speeches* (1845). 4 vols. London: Chapman and Hall, 1897.

Carlyle, Thomas. "The State of German Literature" (1827). In *Critical and Miscellaneous Essays.* Vol. 1. New York: AMS Press, 1969.

Clias, Phokion. *An Elementary Course of Gymnastics Exercises.* 4th ed. London: Sherwood, Gilbert, and Piper, 1825.

Crabb Robinson, Henry. *Diary, Reminiscences, and Correspondence.* Edited by Thomas Sadler. 2 vols. Boston: James R. Osgood and Co., 1871.

Dupaty, Charles Marguerite Jean Baptiste Mercier. *Mémoire justificatif pour trois hommes condamnés à la roue.* Paris: Philippe-Denys Pierres, 1786.

Dupaty, Charles Marguerite Jean Baptiste Mercier. *Sentimental Letters on Italy; Written in French by President Dupaty, in 1785. Published at Rome in 1788, and translated the same year by J. Povoleri, at Paris.* 2 vols. London: J. Bew, 1789.

Epictetus. *All the Works of Epictetus, which are now extant.* Translated by Elizabeth Carter with introduction and notes. London: S. Richardson, 1758.

Ferber, John James. *Travels through Italy in the Years 1771 and 1772. Described in a Series of Letters to Baron Born, on the Natural History, particularly the Mountains and Volcanos of that Country. Translated from the German by R. E. Raspe.* London: L. Davis, 1776.

Forster, Georg. *Briefe 1790 bis 1791.* Edited by Brigitte Leuschner and Siegfried Scheibe, vol. 16. *Georg Forsters Werke.* Akademie der Wissenschaften der DDR. Berlin: Akademie-Verlag, 1980.

Forster, Georg. *Georg Forsters Briefe an Christian Friedrich Voß.* Edited by Paul Zincke. Dortmund: Verlag Ruhfus, 1915.

Genlis, Madame La Comtesse de. *Tales of the Castle: or, Stories of Instruction and Delight.* Translated by Thomas Holcroft. London: G. Robinson, 1785.

Gilpin, William. *Observations, Relative Chiefly to Picturesque Beauty, Made in the Year 1772, On Several Parts of England.* London: R. Blamire, 1786; facsimile, Poole, England: Woodstock Books, 1996.

Godwin, William. *Memoirs of the Author of a Vindication of the Rights of Woman.* London: J. Johnson, 1798.

Goethe, Johann Wolfgang von. "Geologische Notizen." In *Sämtliche Werke*, edited by Christoph Michel and Hans-Georg Dewitz, 40 vols. Vol. 15, part I: 803–4. Frankfurt: Deutscher Klassiker Verlag, 1993.

Goethe, Johann Wolfgang von. *Sämtliche Werke.* Edited by Christoph Michel und Hans-Georg Dewitz. 40 vols. Frankfurt: Deutscher Klassiker Verlag, 1993.

Gonzague, Princesse de. *Lettres de Madame la Princesse de Gonzague sur L'Italie, La France,*

L'Allemagne et les Beaux-Arts. Nouvelle Édition corrigée et augmentée. 2 vols. Hamburg: Fauche, 1797.

Gray, Robert. *Letters during the Course of a Tour through Germany, Switzerland and Italy, in the Years 1791 and 1792 with Reflections on the Manners, Literature, and Religion of those Countries.* London: F. and C. Rivington, 1794.

GutsMuths, J. C. F. *Gymnastik für die Jugend: Enthaltend eine praktische Anweisung zu Leibesübungen.* Schnepfenthal: Verlag der Erziehungsanstalt, 1793; 2nd ed., reprint, Frankfurt: Wilhelm-Limbert Verlag, 1970. Translated into English and published by Joseph Johnson in 1800.

Howitt, William. *The Rural and Domestic Life of Germany: Characteristic Sketches of Its Cities and Scenery, Collected . . . in the Years 1840, 41, and 42.* London: Longman, Brown, Green and Longmans, 1842.

Humboldt, Wilhelm von. *Ideen zu einem Versuch, die Grenzen der Wirksamkeit des Staats zu bestimmen.* Breslau: Trewendt, 1851.

Jameson, Anna. *Commonplace Book of Thoughts, Memories, and Fancies.* London: Longman, 1854.

Jameson, Anna. *Diary of an Ennuyée* (1826). In *Visits and Sketches at Home and Abroad with Tales and Miscellanies.* London: Saunders and Otley, 1834.

Jameson, Anna. "Erinnerungen an Dresden." Translated by D. Vogel. *Zeitung für die Elegante Welt* 35, nos. 61–68 (1835).

Jameson, Anna. *Letters and Friendships. 1812–1860.* Edited by Mrs. Steuart Erskine. New York: E. P. Dutton & Company, 1915.

Jameson, Anna. *Sisters of Charity and the Communion of Labour: Two Lectures on the Social Employments of Women.* London: Longman, Brown, Green, Longmans, and Roberts, 1859.

Jameson, Anna. *Visits and Sketches at Home and Abroad with Tales and Miscellanies Now First Collected and a New Edition of the Diary of an Ennuyée.* 4 vols. London: Saunders and Otley, 1834.

Jameson, Anna. *Winter Studies and Summer Rambles in Canada.* 3 vols. London: Saunders and Otley, 1838. Translated by Amalie Winter as *Winterstudien und Sommerstreifereien in Canada. Ein Tagebuch von Mrs. Jameson. Aus dem Englischen uebersetzt von A. W.* 3 vols. Braunschweig: Vieweg und Sohn, 1839.

Jameson, Anna. "Women's Mission and Women's Position." *Athenaeum* (1843).

Jerusalem, Johann Friedrich Wilhelm. "Absicht und erste Einrichtung des Collegii Carolini." In *Nachgelassene Schriften.* 2 vols. Braunschweig: n.p., 1793.

Jerusalem, Johann Friedrich Wilhelm. *Ueber die Teutsche Sprache und Litteratur. An Ihro Koenigliche Hoheit die verwittwete Frau Herzogin von Braunschweig und Lueneburg.* Berlin: n.p., 1781.

Keyßler, Johann Georg. *Reisen durch Deutschland, Boehmen, Ungarn, die Schweiz, Italien, und Lothringen,* 2 vols. Der Königlichen Grossbrittanischen Societät der Wissenschaften Mitglied. Hannover: In der Helwingschen Hof-Buchhandlung, 1776.

Kühne, Ferdinand Gustav. "Anna Jameson." In *Zeitung für die elegante Welt* 35, no. 206 (19 October 1835): 824. Reprinted in *Portraits und Silhouetten.* Hannover: Kius, 1843.

Lalande, Joseph Jérôme le Français de. *Voyage d'un François en Italie, fait dans les Années 1765 & 1766.* 8 vols. (text), 1 vol. (maps and illustrations). Venice and Paris: Desaint, 1769.

Lichtenberg, Georg Christoph, ed. *Goettinger Taschen Calender vom Jahr 1781.* Facsimile edition with an afterword by Wolfgang Promies. Mainz: Dieterich, 1989.

Liebeskind, Johann Heinrich. *Rückerinnerungen von einer Reise durch einen Teil von Deutschland, Preußen, Kurland und Livland—während des Aufenthaltes der Franzosen in Mainz und der Unruhen in Polen.* Strasburg and Königsberg, 1795.

Loudon, John Claudius, et al. *An Encyclopaedia of Gardening.* London: Longman, Rees, Orme, Brown, Green and Longman, 1835 (first shorter edition, 1822).

Marryat, Frederick. *A Diary in America.* 6 vols. London: Longmans, 1839.

Martineau, Harriet. *Society in America.* New York: Saunders and Otley, 1837.

Meyer, Friedrich Johann Lorenz. *Darstellungen aus Italien.* Berlin: Vossische Buchhandlung, 1792.

Michaelis, Johann David. *Allerunterthänigste Bittschrifft an Seine Königliche Majestät in Preussen, um Anlegung einer Universität für das schöne Geschlecht.* Göttingen, 1747.

Michaelis, Johann David. "Vorrede: von dem Geschmack der Morgenlaendischen Dichtkunst." Preface to Johann Friedrich Loewens, *Poetische Nebenstunden in Hamburg.* Leipzig: Johann Wendler, 1752.

Miller, Lady Anne Riggs. *Letters from Italy, Describing the Manners, Customs, Antiquities, Paintings, &c. of that Country, In the Years 1770 and 1771 to a Friend residing in France. By an English Woman.* 2nd ed., rev. and corrected. 2 vols. London: Edward and Charles Dilly, 1777.

Misson, Maximilien. *Nouveau Voyage D'Italie.* 4th ed., 3 vols. La Haye: Henry van Bulderen, 1702.

Moore, John. *A View of Society and Manners in Italy: with Anecdotes relating to some Eminent Characters.* 2 vols., 3rd ed. London: W. Strahan and T. Cadell, 1783.

Morgan, Sydney Owenson, Lady. *Italy: A New Edition.* 3 vols. London: Henry Colburn, 1821.

Piozzi, Hester Lynch. *Observations and Reflections made in the Course of a Journey through France, Italy, and Germany.* 2 vols. London: Strahan and Cadell, 1789.

Report of the Royal Commission on the Employment of Women and Young People in Mines. 1842.

Richardson, Samuel. *Clarissa, die Geschichte eines vornehmen Frauenzimmers.* Translated by Johann David Michaelis. Göttingen: Verlegts Abram Vandenhoeck, 1748–53.

Rode, August von. *Beschreibung des Fürstlichen Anhalt-Dessauischen Landhauses und Englischen Gartens zu Wörlitz.* Dessau: Heinrich Tänzer, 1814; facsimile, Wörlitz: Kettmann Verlag, 1996.

Salzmann, Christian Gotthilf. *Livre Élémentaire de morale. Avec une introduction pour s'en servir utilement; ouvrage traduit de l'allemand de M. Salzmann, Professeur & Prédicateur à l'Institut de Dessau.* Leipzig: chez Siegried Lebrecht Crusius, 1785.

Salzmann, Christian Gotthilf. *Moralisches Elementarbuch, nebst einer Anleitung zum nützlichen Gebrauch desselben.* Neue verbesserte Auflage. Leipzig: Siegfried Lebrecht Crusius, 1785. Repr. with afterword by Hubert Göbels. Dortmund: Harenberg, 1980. Translated by Mary Wollstonecraft as *Elements of Morality for the Use of Children.* London: J. Johnson, 1790.

Salzmann, Christian Gotthilf. *Über die heimlichen Sünden der Jugend* [On the secret sins of youth]. Frankfurt, 1786.

Schlegel-Schelling, Caroline. *Die Kunst zu Leben,* edited and with a preface by Sigrid Damm. Frankfurt: Insel Verlag, 1997.

Schlözer, August Ludwig. *Entwurf zu einem Reise-Collegio.* Göttingen: Vandenhoeck, 1777.

Schlözer, August Ludwig. *Vorlesungen über Land- und Seereisen, nach dem Kollegheft des stud. Jur. E. F. Haupt.* Edited by Wilhelm Ebel. Göttingen: Musterschmidt-verlag, 1962.

Seume, Johann Gottfried. *Spaziergang nach Syrakus im Jahre 1802.* Edited by Jörg Drews. Frankfurt: Insel Verlag, 2001.

Sharp, Samuel. *Letters from Italy, Describing the Customs and Manners of that Country, in the Years 1765, and 1766.* London: J. Rivington et al., n.d.

Shelley, Mary. *The Journals of Mary Shelley 1814–1844.* Edited by Paula Feldman and Diana Scott-Kilvert. 2 vols. Oxford: Clarendon, 1987.

Shelley, Mary. *Letters of Mary Wollstonecraft Shelley.* Edited by Betty T. Bennett. 3 vols. Baltimore: Johns Hopkins University Press, 1980.

Shelley, Percy Bysshe. *Letters* in *Complete Works of Percy Bysshe Shelley,* edited by Roger Ingpen and Walter E. Peck. 10 vols. New York: Gordian Press; and London: Ernst Benn, 1965.

Somerville, William C. *Letters from Paris.* Baltimore: Edward Coale, 1822.

Staël, Madame de. *Corinne, or Italy* (1807). Translated by Sylvia Raphael, introduction by John Isbell. Oxford: Oxford University Press, 1998.

Starke, Mariana. *Letters from Italy, between the years 1792 and 1798, Containing a View of the Revolutions in that Country.* 2 vols. London: R. Phillips, 1800.

Tocqueville, Alexis de. *De la démocratie en Amerique.* 2 vols. Paris: Pagnerre [vol. 1], 1835, [vol. 2], 1840.

Traill, Catharine Parr. *The Backwoods of Canada.* London: Charles Knight, 1836.

Ueber die deutsche Litteratur: Koenig Friderich, Jerusalem, Tralles. Munich: Joh. Baptist Strobl, 1781.

Vandenhoeck, Abraham. *Bibliopolium Vandenhoeckianum: or, a catalogue of books in most faculties and languages. Collected in Italy, France, Germany, England and Holland, by Abram. Vandenh To be sold (the Price being mark'd [at the beginning] of each Book) Monday the 14th [of Decem]ber 1730, at his Shop, at the Sign of Virgil's Head opposite the New Church in the Strand.* London, 1730.

Vandenhoeck, Anna. *Vollständiges Verzeichniss der Bücher, welche um beygesezte Preise zu haben sind bey sel. Abraham Vandenhöcks Witwe, Universitätsbuchhändlerin zu Göttingen.* 2 vols. Göttingen: Vandenhoeck, 1785.

Vigée Lebrun, Elisabeth. *Memoirs of Elisabeth Louise Vigée Lebrun.* Translated by Lionel Strachey. New York: Doubleday, 1903.

Von der Recke, Elisa. *Tagebuch einer Reise durch einen Theil Deutschlands und durch Italien, in den Jahren 1804 bis 1806.* Edited by Hofrath Boettiger. 4 vols. Berlin: Nicolai, 1815.

Watkins, Thomas. *Travels through Swisserland, Italy, Sicily, the Greek Islands, to Constantinople in the Years 1787, 1788, 1789.* 2 vols. London: T. Cadell, 1792.

Weissenborn, Georg Friedrich Christian. "Über den Richterspruch in der Sache des weiblichen Geschlechts gegen das männliche" [On the verdict in the case of the female sex against the male]. In *Bibliothek der pädagogischen Literatur,* edited by J. C. F. GutsMuths. Gotha: Perdes, 1800.

Werner, Johann Adolph Ludwig. *Gymnastik für die weibliche Jugend, oder weibliche Körperbildung für Gesundheit, Kraft, und Anmuth* [Gymnastics for female Youth, or feminine physical development for Health, Strength, and Grace]. N.p.: Meissen, 1834.

Wilcox, John. *A catalogue of books, being The Libraries of A Right Reverend Prelate. Thomas Wickham, M. D. and J. Shaw, Attorney, deceas'd. Consisting Of many thousand Valuable Books in almost all Languages and Faculties.* London, 1735.

Williams, Helen Maria. *Letters Written in France, in the summer of 1790 to a friend in England.* London: T. Cadell, 1790.

Wilmot, Catherine. *An Irish Peer on the Continent (1801–1803).* Edited by Thomas U. Sadleir. London: Willimans and Norgate, 1920.

Winckelmann, Johann Joachim. *Critical Account of the Situation and Destruction by the First Eruptions of Mount Vesuvius, of Herculaneum, Pompeii, and Stabia.* London: T. Carnan and F. Newbery, 1771.

Wollstonecraft, Mary. *Letters Written During a Short Residence in Sweden, Norway, and Denmark.* Edited by Carol Poston. Lincoln: University of Nebraska Press, 1976.

Wollstonecraft, Mary. *Vindication of the Rights of Men.* London: J. Johnson, 1790.

Wollstonecraft, Mary. *Vindication of the Rights of Woman.* London: J. Johnson, 1792.

Secondary Sources

Agorni, Mirella. *Translating Italy for the Eighteenth Century: Women, Translation and Travel Writing: 1739–1797.* Manchester: St. Jerome, 2002.

Agorni, Mirella. "The Voice of the 'Translatress': From Aphra Behn to Elizabeth Carter." *Yearbook of English Studies* 28 (1998): 181–95.

Alexander, Meena. *Women in Romanticism: Mary Wollstonecraft, Dorothy Wordsworth, and Mary Shelley.* London: Macmillan, 1989.

Amadeus, Viktor, and Elise von Hessen-Rotenburg. *The Corvey Library and Anglo-German Cultural Exchanges, 1770–1837.* Munich: Wilhelm Fink, 2004.

Anderson, Benedict. *Imagined Communities: Reflections on the Origin and Spread of Nationalism.* Rev. ed. London: Verso, 1994.

Anderson, Perry. "Components of the National Culture." *New Left Review* 50 (1968): 3–20.

Appiah, Kwame Anthony. "Cosmopolitan Patriots." *Critical Inquiry* 23 (Spring 1997): 617–39. Reprinted in *Cosmopolitics: Thinking and Feeling Beyond the Nation,* edited by Pheng Cheah and Bruce Robbins, 91–114. Minneapolis: University of Minnesota Press, 1998.

Armstrong, Isobel. "Natural and National Monuments—Felicia Hemans's 'The Image in Lava': A Note." In *Felicia Hemans: Reimagining Poetry in the Nineteenth Century,* edited by Nanora Sweet and Julie Melnyk, 212–30. Basingstoke: Palgrave, 2001.

Arnold, Hans. "Die Aufnahme von Thomas Paines Schriften in Deutschland." *PMLA* 74.4 (1959): 365–86.

Ashton, Rosemary. *The German Idea: Four English Writers and the Reception of German Thought 1800–1860.* Cambridge: Cambridge University Press, 1980.

Baker, Keith, and Peter Hanns Reill. *What's Left of Enlightenment? A Postmodern Question.* Stanford: Stanford University Press, 2001.

Batchelor, Jennie, and Cora Kaplan, eds. *Women and Material Culture, 1660–1830.* Basingstoke: Palgrave Macmillan, 2007.

Beck, Doris, and Paul Beck, eds. *Flora Tristan: Utopian Feminist.* Bloomington: Indiana University Press, 1993.

Becker-Cantarino, Barbara, ed. *German Literature of the Eighteenth Century: The Enlightenment and Sensibility.* Vol. 5 of the Camden House History of German Literature. Rochester, NY: Camden House, 2005.

Becker-Cantarino, Barbara, ed. *Martin Opitz: Studien zu Werk und Person.* Amsterdam: Rodopi, 1982.

Beebee, Thomas O. *"Clarissa" on the Continent: Translation and Seduction.* University Park: Pennsylvania State University Press, 1990.

Behdad, Ali. "The Politics of Adventure: Theories of Travel, Discourses of Power." In *Travel Writing, Form, and Empire: The Poetics and Politics of Mobility,* edited by Julia Kuehn and Paul Smethurst, 80–94. New York: Routledge, 2009.

Bell, David A. *The First Total War: Napoleon's Europe and the Birth of Warfare as We Know It.* Boston: Houghton Mifflin, 2007.

Bender, John, and Michael Marrinan. *The Culture of Diagram.* Stanford: Stanford University Press, 2010.

Benhabib, Seyla. "On Hegel, Women and Irony." In *Situating the Self: Gender, Community and Postmodernism in Contemporary Ethics,* by Seyla Benhabib. Cambridge: Polity, 1992.

Bennett, Judith M. *History Matters: Patriarchy and the Challenge of Feminism.* Philadelphia: University of Pennsylvania Press, 2006.

Berger, Joachim. *Anna Amalia von Sachsen-Weimar-Eisenach (1739–1807): Denk- und Handlungsräume einer "aufgeklärten" Herzogin.* Heidelberg: Universitätsverlag Winter, 2003.

Besterman, Theodore. *Voltaire.* New York: Harcourt, Brace & World, 1969.

Biskup, Thomas. "The University of Göttingen and the Personal Union, 1737–1837." In *The Hanoverian Dimension in British History, 1714–1837,* edited by Brendan Simms and Torsten Riotte. Cambridge: Cambridge University Press, 2007.

Black, Jeremy. *The British Abroad: The Grand Tour in the Eighteenth Century.* London: St. Martin's, 1992.

Blackbourn, David. "'The Horologe of Time': Periodization in History." *PMLA* 127.2 (March 2012): 301–7.

Blix, Göran. *From Paris to Pompeii: French Romanticism and the Cultural Politics of Archaeology.* Philadelphia: University of Pennsylvania Press, 2009.

Blok, Anders, and Torben Elgaard Jensen, *Bruno Latour: Hybrid Thoughts in a Hybrid World.* London: Routledge, 2011.

Bohls, Elizabeth. *Women Travel Writers and the Language of Aesthetics, 1716–1818.* Cambridge: Cambridge University Press, 1995.

Bothe, Rolf, and Ulrich Haussmann. *Goethes "Bildergalerie": Die Anfänge der Kunstsammlungen zu Weimar.* Berlin: G + H Verlag, 2002.

Braeunig-Oktavio, Herrmann. "Die Bibliothek der grossen Landgräfin Caroline von Hessen." *Archiv für Geschichte des Buchwesens* 6 (1966): 682–875.

Braithwaite, Helen. *Romanticism, Publishing and Dissent: Joseph Johnson and the Cause of Liberty.* Basingstoke: Palgrave Macmillan, 2003.

Brown, Hilary. *Benedikte Naubert (1756–1819) and Her Relations to English Culture.* Leeds: Maney Publishing; and London: MHRA and Institute of Germanic Studies, 2005.

Brown, Hilary. "The Reception of the Bluestockings by Eighteenth-Century German Women Writers." *Women in German Yearbook* 18 (2002): 111–32.

Brown, Marshall. "Romanticism and Enlightenment." In *The Cambridge Companion to British Romanticism,* edited by Stuart Curran, 25–47. Cambridge: Cambridge University Press, 1993.

Brown, Sarah Annes. "Women Translators." In *The Oxford History of Literary Translation in English: Volume 3 1660–1790,* edited by Stuart Gillespie and David Hopkins, 111–20. Oxford: Oxford University Press, 2005.

Burke, Peter. *Cultural Hybridity*. London: Polity, 2009.

Burwick, Frederick. "Romantic Theories of Translation." *Wordsworth Circle* 39.3 (Summer 2008): 68–74.

Callon, Michel, and John Law. "After the Individual in Society: Lessons on Collectivity from Science, Technology and Society." *Canadian Journal of Sociology* 22.2 (Spring 1997): 165–82.

Campbell Orr, Clarissa. "Charlotte of Mecklenburg–Strelitz, Queen of Great Britain and Electress of Hanover: Northern Dynasties and the Northern Republic of Letters." In *Queenship in Europe 1660–1815: The Role of the Consort*, edited by Clarissa Campbell Orr. Cambridge: Cambridge University Press, 2004.

Canning, Joseph, and Hermann Wellenreuther, eds. *Britain and Germany Compared: Nationality, Society and Nobility in the Eighteenth Century*. Göttingen: Wallstein Verlag, 2001.

Chard, Chloe. *Pleasure and Guilt on the Grand Tour: Travel Writing and Imaginative Geography 1600–1830*. Manchester: Manchester University Press, 1999.

Cheah, Pheng, and Bruce Robbins eds. *Cosmopolitics: Thinking and Feeling beyond the Nation*. Minneapolis: University of Minnesota Press, 1998.

Clark, Steve. Introduction to *Travel Writing and Empire: Postcolonial Theory in Transit*, edited by Steve Clark. London: Zed Books, 1999.

Cohen, Roger. "Iran's Second Sex." *New York Times* (27 June 2009), A19.

Conger, Syndy. "Fellow Travelers: Eighteenth-Century Englishwomen and German Literature." In *Studies in Eighteenth-Century Culture*, edited by O. M. Brack, vol. 14, 109–28. Madison: University of Wisconsin Press, 1985.

Craciun, Adriana. *British Women Writers and the French Revolution: Citizens of the World*. Basingstoke: Palgrave Macmillan, 2005.

Curl, James Stevens. *The Art and Architecture of Freemasonry*. London: B. T. Batsford, 1991.

Davis, John A. *Naples and Napoleon: Southern Italy and the European Revolutions, 1780–1860*. Oxford: Oxford University Press, 2006.

Dawson, P. M. S. *The Unacknowledged Legislator: Shelley and Politics*. Oxford: Clarendon, 1980.

Dawson, Ruth P. *The Contested Quill: Literature by Women in Germany, 1770–1800*. Cranbury, N.J.: Associated University Presses, 2002.

Dawson, Ruth P. "Philippine Gatterer Engelhard." In *Bitter Healing: German Women Writers from 1700 to 1830*, edited by Jeannine Blackwell and Susanne Zantop, 189–200. Lincoln: University of Nebraska Press, 1990.

DeJean, Joan. "Transnationalism and the Origins of the French(?) Novel." In *The Literary Channel: The Inter-National Invention of the Novel*, edited by Margaret Cohen and Carolyn Dever, 37–49. Princeton: Princeton University Press, 2002.

Deložel, L. "Narratives of Counterfactual History." In *Essays on Fiction and Perspective*, edited by G. Rossholm, 109–28. Bern: Peter Lang, 2004.

D'Monte, Rebecca, and Nicole Pohl, eds. *Female Communities 1600–1800: Literary Visions and Cultural Realities*. London: St. Martin's, 2000.

Dolan, Brian. *Ladies of the Grand Tour*. London: Flamingo, 2001.

Dow, Gillian E., ed. *Translators, Interpreters, Mediators: Women Writers 1700–1900*. Oxford: Peter Lang, 2007.

Droysen, Hans, ed. *Aus den Briefen der Herzogin Philippine Charlotte von Braunschweig 1732–1801*. Vol. 1, 1732–1768. Wolfenbüttel: Zwissler, 1916.

Eger, Elizabeth. *Bluestockings: Women of Reason from Enlightenment to Romanticism*. Basingstoke: Palgrave Macmillan, 2010.

Eger, Elizabeth, and Lucy Peltz, eds. *Brilliant Women: Eighteenth-Century Bluestockings*. London: National Portrait Gallery, 2008.

Eisenberg, Christiane. *"English Sports" und deutsche Bürger: Eine Gesellschaftsgeschichte 1800–1939*. Paderborn: Schöningh, 1999.

Eisenberg, Christiane. "'German Gymnastics' in Britain, or the Failure of Cultural Transfer." In *Migration and Transfer from Germany to Britain 1660–1914*, edited by Stefan Manz, Margrit Schulte Beerbühl, and John R. Davis, 131–46. Munich: Saur, 2007.

El-Akramy, Ursula. "Caroline Schlegel-Schelling als Salonniere und Shakespeare Übersetzerin." In *Mittlerin zwischen den Kulturen: Mittlerin zwischen den Geschlechtern? Studie zur Theorie und Praxis feministischer Übersetzung*, edited by Sabine Messner and Michaela Wolf. Graz: Institut für Theoretische und Angewandte Translationswissenschaft, 2000.

Erdmannsdorf, Friedrich Wilhelm von. *Kunsthistorisches Journal einer fürstlichen Bildungsreise nach Italien 1765/66*. Translated from the French and edited by Ralf-Torsten Speler. Munich: Deutscher Kunstverlag, 2001.

Ernstrom, Adele M. "The Afterlife of Mary Wollstonecraft and Anna Jameson's *Winter Studies and Summer Rambles in Canada*." *Women's Writing* 4.2 (1997): 277–97.

Espagne, Michel. *Les transferts culturels franco-allemands*. Paris: Presses Universitaires de France, 1999.

Evelyn, John. *The Diary of John Evelyn*. Edited by E. S. de Beer. 6 vols. Oxford: Clarendon, 1955.

Fabian, Bernhard. "English Books and Their Eighteenth-Century German Readers." In *The Widening Circle: Essays on the Circulation of Literature in Eighteenth-Century Europe*, edited by Paul J. Korshin. Philadelphia: University of Pennsylvania Press, 1976.

Ferguson, Moira, and Janet Todd. *Mary Wollstonecraft*. Boston: Twayne, 1984.

Flotow, Luise von. *Translation and Gender*. Manchester: St Jerome, 1997.

Freeman, Barbara. *The Feminine Sublime: Gender and Excess in Women's Fiction*. Berkeley: University of California Press, 1995.

Gäbler, Burkhard. "Die kunsttheoretischen und erziehungstheoretischen Anschauungen Georg Forsters und seine Beziehungen zur Dessau-Wörlitzer Aufklärung." In *Georg Forster: Leben, Werk, Wirkung*, 39–52. Wissenschaftliches Kolloquium 30. Juni 1984 anlässlich der Eröffnung der Forster-Stätte in Wörlitz. Wörlitz: Staatliche Schlösser und Gärten, 1985.

Gardner Coates, Victoria C. "Making History: Pliny's Letters to Tacitus and Angelica Kauffmann's *Pliny the Younger and His Mother at Misenum*." In *Pompeii in the Public Imagination*, edited by Shelley Hales and Joanna Paul. Oxford: Oxford University Press, 2011.

Geertz, Clifford. *The Interpretation of Culture*. New York: Basic Books, 1973.

Geldbach, Erich. "The Beginning of German Gymnastics in America." *Journal of Sport History* 3.3 (1976): 236–72.

Georgii, Augustus. *A Biographical Sketch of the Swedish Poet and Gymnasiarch, Peter Henry Ling*. London: Bailliere, 1854.

Gerry, Thomas. "'I am translated': Anna Jameson's Sketches and *Winter Studies and Summer Rambles in Canada*." *Journal of Canadian Studies* 25.4 (1990–91): 34–49.

Gibbels, Elisabeth. *Mary Wollstonecraft zwischen Feminismus und Opportunismus: Die discursiven Strategien in deutschen Übersetzungen von "A Vindication of the Rights of Woman."* Tübingen: Gunter Narr Verlag, 2004.

Gilleir, Anke, and Alicia C. Montoya. Introduction to *Women Writing Back/Writing Women Back: Transnational Perspectives from the Late Middle Ages to the Dawn of the Modern Era*, edited by Anke Gilleir, Alicia Montoya, and Suzan van Dijk. Leiden: Brill, 2010.

Gillespie, Stuart. "Translation and Canon-Formation." In *The Oxford History of Literary Translation in English: Volume 3, 1660–1790*, edited by Stuart Gillespie and David Hopkins, 7–20. Oxford: Oxford University Press, 2005.

Gillespie, Stuart, and David Hopkins, eds. *The Oxford History of Literary Translation in English: Volume 3, 1660–1790*. Oxford: Oxford University Press, 2005.

Gillespie, Stuart, and Robin Sowerby. "Translation and Literary Innovation." In *The Oxford History of Literary Translation in English, Volume 3: 1660–1790*, edited by Stuart Gillespie and David Hopkins, 21–37. Oxford: Oxford University Press, 2005.

Gilli, Marita. "George Forsters Modernität: Ein Porträt." In *Weltbürger-Europäer-Deutscher-Franke: Georg Forster zum 200. Todestag*, edited by Rolf Reichardt and Geneviève Roche, 3–14. Mainz: Universitätsbibliothek, 1994.

Gioberti, Vincenzo. *Opere: Del Primato Morale e Civile degli Italiani*. Vol. 3. Losanna: Bonamici e Compagnia, 1846.

Gleixner, Ulrike, and Marion W. Gray, eds. *Gender in Transition: Discourse and Practice in German-Speaking Europe, 1750–1830*. Ann Arbor: University of Michigan Press, 2006.

Goodden, Angelica. *Madame de Staël: The Dangerous Exile*. Oxford: Oxford University Press, 2008.

Goodman, Dena. *The Republic of Letters: A Cultural History of the French Enlightenment*. Ithaca: Cornell University Press, 1996.

Gordon, Daniel. "On the Supposed Obsolescence of the French Enlightenment." In *Postmodernism and the Enlightenment*, edited by Daniel Gordon. New York: Routledge, 2001.

Graeber, Wilhelm, and Geneviève Roche, *Englische Literatur des 17. und 18. Jahrhunderts in französischer Übersetzung und deutscher Weiterübersetzung*. Tübingen: Max Niemeyer Verlag, 1988.

Guest, Harriet. *Small Change: Women, Learning, Patriotism, 1750–1810*. Chicago: University of Chicago Press, 2000.

Hamblyn, Richard. "Private Cabinets and Popular Geology: The British Audiences for Volcanoes in the Eighteenth Century." In *Transports: Travel, Pleasure, and Imaginative Geography, 1600–1830*, edited by Chloe Chard and Helen Langdon, 179–205. New Haven: Yale University Press, 1996.

Haraway, Donna. "A Game of Cat's Cradle: Science Studies, Feminist Theory, Cultural Studies." *Configurations* 2.1 (1994): 59–71.

Harding, Nick. *Hanover and the British Empire 1700–1837*. Woodbridge: Boydell Press, 2007.

Hatton, Ragnhild. *George I*. London: Thames and Hudson, 1978.

Haug, Christine. "'Diese Arbeit unterhält mich, ohne mich zu ermüden': Georg Forsters Übersetzungsmanufaktur in Mainz in den 1790er Jahren." *Georg-Forster-Studien* 13 (2008): 99–128.

Heißler, Sabine. "Christine Charlotte von Ostfriesland (1645–1699) und Ihre Bücher, oder, Lesen Frauen Anderes?" *Daphnis: Zeitschrift für Mittlere Deutsche Literatur* 27 (1998): 335–418.

Henderson, Jennifer. *Settler Feminism and Race Making in Canada*. Toronto: University of Toronto Press, 2003.

Henry, Thomas. *Memoirs of Albert de Haller*. London: Joseph Johnson, 1783.

Heringman, Noah. "The Style of Natural Catastrophes." *Huntington Library Quarterly* 66 (2003): 97–133.

Hermand, Jost. "Rousseau, Goethe, Humboldt: Their Influence on Later Advocates of the Nature Garden." In *Nature and Ideology: Natural Garden Design in the Twentieth Century*, edited by Joachim Wolschke-Bulmahn. Dumbarton Oaks Research Library and Collection, vol. 18, 35–58. Washington, D.C: Harvard University, 1997.

Hess, Jonathan M. "Johann David Michaelis and the Colonial Imaginary: Orientalism and the Emergence of Racial Antisemitism in Eighteenth-Century Germany." *Jewish Social Studies* 6.2 (2000): 56–101.

Hesse, Carla. *The Other Enlightenment: How French Women Became Modern*. Princeton: Princeton University Press, 2001.

Houben, H. H. Introduction to Ottilie von Goethe, *Erlebnisse und Geständnisse 1832–1857*. Leipzig: Klinkhardt & Biermann, 1923.

Huber, Werner, ed. *The Corvey Library and Anglo-German Cultural Exchanges, 1770–1837*. Munich: Wilhelm Fink Verlag, 2004.

Hufton, Olwen. *The Prospect before Her: A History of Women in Western Europe, Volume One, 1500–1800*. London: Fontana Press, 1997.

Johns, Alessa. "Anna Jameson in Germany: 'A.W.' and Women's Translation." *Translation and Literature* 19 (2010): 190–95.

Johns, Alessa. "Feminism and Utopianism." In *The Cambridge Companion to Utopian Literature*, edited by Gregory Claeys. Cambridge: Cambridge University Press, 2010.

Johns, Alessa. "Gender and Utopia in Eighteenth-Century England." PhD diss., University of California, Berkeley, 1994.

Johns, Alessa. *Women's Utopias of the Eighteenth Century*. Urbana: University of Illinois Press, 2003.

Johnston, Judith. *Anna Jameson: Victorian, Feminist, Woman of Letters*. Aldershot: Scolar Press, 1997.

Kammerer-Grothaus, Helke. "'Voyage d'Italie' (1755): Markgräfin Wilhelmine von Bayreuth im Königreich Neapel." In *Wilhelmine und Friedrich II. und die Antiken*, edited by Helke Kammerer-Grothaus and Detlev Kreikenbom, 7–41. Stendal: Winckelmann-Gesellschaft, 1998.

Kelleher, Margaret. "Woman as Famine Victim: The Figure of Woman in Irish Famine Narratives." In *Gender and Catastrophe*, edited by Ronit Lentin, 241–54. London: Zed Books, 1997.

Kelly, Gary. "Death and the Matron: Felicia Hemans, Romantic Death, and the Founding of the Modern Liberal State." In *Felicia Hemans: Reimagining Poetry in the Nineteenth Century*, edited by Nanora Sweet and Julie Melnyk, 196–211. Basingstoke: Palgrave, 2001.

Kelly, Gary. "General Introduction." *Bluestocking Feminism: Writings of the Bluestocking Circle, 1738–1785*. 6 vols. London: Pickering and Chatto, 1999.

Kelly, Gary. "Introduction: Felicia Hemans, the Reading Public, and the Political Nation." In *Felicia Hemans: Selected Poems, Prose, and Letters*, edited by Gary Kelly, 15–85. Peterborough, Ontario: Broadview Press, 2002.

Kelly, Gary. *Revolutionary Feminism: The Mind and Career of Mary Wollstonecraft.* London: Macmillan, 1992.

Kern, Bärbel, and Horst Kern. *Madame Doctorin Schlözer: Ein Frauenleben in den Widersprüchen der Aufklärung.* Munich: Verlag C. H. Beck, 1990.

Kleingeld, Pauline. "Six Varieties of Cosmopolitanism in Late Eighteenth-Century Germany." *Journal of the History of Ideas* 60.3 (1999): 505–24.

Klessmann, Eckart. *Universitätsmamsellen: Fünf aufgeklärte Frauen zwischen Rokoko, Revolution und Romantik.* Frankfurt: Eichborn Verlag, 2008.

Korte, Barbara. *English Travel Writing from Pilgrimages to Postcolonial Explorations.* Translated from the German by Catherine Matthias. London: Macmillan; and New York: St. Martin's, 2000.

Krake, Astrid. "'Translating to the moment'—Marketing and Anglomania: The First German Translation of Richardson's *Clarissa*." In *Cultural Transfer through Translation*, edited by Stefanie Stockhorst, 103–19. Amsterdam: Rodopi, 2010.

Krüger, Michael, ed. *Johann Christoph Friedrich GutsMuths (1759–1839) und die philanthropische Bewegung in Deutschland.* Hamburg: Feldhaus, 2010.

Lamarra, Annamaria, and Eleonora Federici, eds. *Nations, Traditions and Cross-Cultural Identities: Women's Writing in English in a European Context.* Bern: Peter Lang, 2010.

Laqueur, Thomas W. *Solitary Sex: A Cultural History of Masturbation.* New York: Zone Books, 2003.

Latour, Bruno. "An Attempt at a 'Compositionist' Manifesto." *New Literary History* 41.3 (Summer 2010): 471–90.

Latour, Bruno. *Reassembling the Social: An Introduction to Actor-Network-Theory.* Oxford: Oxford University Press, 2005.

Law, John. *After Method: Mess in Social Science Research.* London: Routledge, 2004.

Law, John. "Notes on the Theory of the Actor-Network: Ordering, Strategy, and Heterogeneity." *Systems Practice* 5 (August 1992): 379–93.

Lefevere, André, ed. *Translation / History / Culture.* London: Routledge, 1992.

Lehmann, Christine. *Das Modell Clarissa: Liebe, Verführung, Sexualität und Tod der Romanheldinnen des 18. und 19. Jahrhunderts.* Stuttgart: Metzler, 1991.

Lempa, Heikki. *Beyond the Gymnasium: Educating the Middle-Class Bodies in Classical Germany.* Lanham, Md.: Lexington, 2007.

Lentin, Ronit. "Introduction: (En)gendering Genocides." In *Gender and Catastrophe*, edited by Ronit Lentin, 2–17. London: Zed Books, 1997.

Leonard, Fred E. *Pioneers of Modern Physical Training.* New York: Physical Directors' Society of the Young Men's Christian Association of North America, 1915.

Lerner, Gerda. *The Creation of Feminist Consciousness.* Oxford: Oxford University Press, 1993.

Leuthy, Johann Jakob. *Geschichte des Cantons Zürich von 1831–1840.* Zürich: Leuthy's Verlags-Bureau, 1845.

Lifschitz, Avi. "Translation in Theory and Practice: The Case of Johann David Michaelis's Prize Essay on Language and Opinions (1759)." In *Cultural Transfer through Translation: The Circulation of Enlightened Thought in Europe by Means of Translation*, edited by Stefanie Stockhorst. Amsterdam: Rodopi, 2010.

Littlejohns, Richard. "Early Romanticism." In *The Literature of German Romanticism*, edited by Dennis F. Mahoney, vol. 8 of the Camden House History of German Literature. Rochester: Camden House, 2004.

Lokke, Kari. "Schiller's *Maria Stuart*: The Historical Sublime and the Aesthetics of Gender." *Germanisch-Romanische Monatshefte* 82 (1990): 123–41.

Lösel, Barbara. *Die Frau als Persönlichkeit im Buchwesen: Dargestellt am Beispiel der Göttinger Verlegerin Anna Vandenhoeck. 1709–1787.* Wiesbaden: Otto Harrassowitz, 1991.

Lowndes, Thomas. *The Bibliographer's Manual of English Literature.* London: Bell and Daldy, 1865.

Lüsebrink, Hans-Jürgen. *Interkulturelle Kommunikation: Interaktion, Fremdwahrnehmung, Kulturtransfer.* 2nd ed. Stuttgart: J. B. Metzler, 2008.

Lüsebrink, Hans-Jürgen, and Rolf Reichardt, eds. *Kulturtransfer im Epochenumbruch Frankreich-Deutschland 1770 bis 1815.* 2 vols. Leipzig: Leipziger Universitätsverlag, 1997.

MacDonogh, Giles. *Frederick the Great.* New York: St. Martin's, 1999.

Macedo, Ana Gabriela, and Margarida Esteves Pereira, eds. *Identity and Cultural Translation: Writing across the Borders of Englishness.* Bern: Peter Lang, 2006.

Macpherson, Gerardine. *Memoirs of the Life of Anna Jameson.* London: Longmans, Green, and Co., 1878.

Manz, Stefan, Margrit Schulte Beerbühl, and John R. Davis, eds. *Migration and Transfer from Germany to Britain 1660–1914.* Munich: Saur, 2007.

Marshall, David. "The Problem of the Picturesque." *Eighteenth-Century Studies* 35.3 (2002): 413–37.

Maurer, Michael. *Aufklärung und Anglophilie in Deutschland.* Göttingen: Vandenhoeck & Ruprecht, 1987.

McIntosh, Christopher. *Gardens of the Gods: Myth, Magic, and Meaning in Horticulture.* London: I. B. Tauris, 2005.

McMurran, Mary Helen. "National or Transnational? The Eighteenth-Century Novel." In *The Literary Channel: The Inter-National Invention of the Novel,* edited by Margaret Cohen and Carolyn Dever, 50–72. Princeton: Princeton University Press, 2002.

McMurran, Mary Helen. *The Spread of Novels: Translation and Prose Fiction in the Eighteenth Century.* Princeton: Princeton University Press, 2009.

Meli, D. Bertoloni. "Caroline, Leibniz, and Clarke." *Journal of the History of Ideas* 60 (1999): 469–86.

Mellor, Anne. *Romanticism and Gender.* New York and London: Routledge, 1993.

Minier, Márta. "'The Translatress in Her Own Person Speaks': A Few Marginal Notes on Feminist Translation in Practice, in Creative Writing and in Criticism." In *Identity and Cultural Translation: Writing across the Borders of Englishness,* edited by Ana Gabriela Macedo and Margarida Esteves Pereira, 39–54. Oxford: Peter Lang, 2006.

Moe, Nelson. *The View from Vesuvius: Italian Culture and the Southern Question.* Berkeley: University of California Press, 2002.

Möhle, Sylvia. *Ehekonflikte und sozialer Wandel: Göttingen 1740–1840.* Frankfurt: Campus Verlag, 1997.

Monk, Samuel. *The Sublime: A Study of Critical Theories in 18th-Century England.* New York: Modern Language Association of America, 1935.

Morgan, B. Q., and A. R. Hohlfeld. *German Literature in British Magazines 1750–1860.* Madison: University of Wisconsin Press, 1949.

Moses, Claire Goldberg. *French Feminism in the 19th Century.* Albany: SUNY Press, 1984.

Müller, F. Max. "Royalties." *Cosmopolis* 7 (July 1897): 16–38.

Münch, Ingrid. "Testament und Begräbnis der Herzogin Philippine Charlotte v. Braunschweig-Lüneburg (1716–1801)." *Braunschweigisches Jahrbuch* 68 (1987): 51–82.

Myers, Mitzi. "Impeccable Governesses, Rational Dames, and Moral Mothers: Mary Wollstonecraft and the Female Tradition in Georgian Children's Books." *Children's Literature* 14 (1986): 31–59.

Myers, Mitzi. "Pedagogy as Self-Expression in Mary Wollstonecraft." In *The Private Self*, edited by Shari Benstock, 192–210. Chapel Hill: University of North Carolina Press, 1988.

Myers, Mitzi. "Reform or Ruin: 'A Revolution in Female Manners'." *Studies in Eighteenth-Century Culture* 11 (1982): 199–216.

Myers, Sylvia Harcstark. *The Blustocking Circle: Women, Friendship, and the Life of the Mind in Eighteenth-Century England*. Oxford: Clarendon Press, 1990.

Naul, Roland. *Olympic Education*. Maidenhead: Meyer and Meyer, 2008.

Needler, G. H., ed. *Letters of Anna Jameson to Ottilie von Goethe*. London: Oxford University Press, 1939.

O'Brien, Karen. *Women and Enlightenment in Eighteenth-Century Britain*. Cambridge: Cambridge University Press, 2009.

Offen, Karen. *European Feminisms 1700–1950: A Political History*. Stanford: Stanford University Press, 2000.

O'Neill, Patrick. *Ireland and Germany: A Study in Literary Relations*. New York: Peter Lang, 1985.

Oppenheimer, Clive. "Climatic, Environmental and Human Consequences of the Largest Known Historic Eruption: Tambora Volcano, Indonesia, 1815." *Progress in Physical Geography* 27.2 (2003): 230–59.

Pangels, Charlotte. *Friedrich der Grosse: Bruder, Freund, und König*. Munich: Callwey, 1979.

Paulmann, Johannes. "Interkultureller Transfer zwischen Deutschland und Grossbritannien: Einführung in ein Forschungskonzept." In *Aneignung und Abwehr: Interkultureller Transfer zwischen Deutschland und Großbritannien im 19. Jahrhundert*, edited by Rudolf Muhs, Johannes Paulmann, and Willibald Steinmetz, 21–43. Bodenheim: Philo, 1998.

Pearson, Jacqueline. *Women's Reading in Britain 1750–1835: A Dangerous Recreation*. Cambridge: Cambridge University Press, 1999.

Perry, Ruth. *The Celebrated Mary Astell: An Early English Feminist*. Chicago: University of Chicago Press, 1986.

Phillips, Roderick. *Untying the Knot: A Short History of Divorce*. Cambridge: Cambridge University Press, 1991.

Plumb, J. H. *The First Four Georges*. London: Batsford, 1956.

Pohl, Nicole, and Betty Schellenberg, eds. *Reconsidering the Bluestockings*. San Marino, Calif.: Huntington Library, 2003.

Pratt, Mary Louise. *Imperial Eyes: Travel Writing and Transculturation*. London: Routledge, 1992.

Price, Mary Bell, and Lawrence Marsden Price. *The Publication in the Eighteenth Century of English Literature in Germany*. Berkeley: University of California Press, 1934.

Pufelska, Agnieszka, and Iwan Michelangelo D'Aprile, eds. *Aufklärung und Kulturtransfer in Mittel- und Osteuropa*. Saarbrücken: Wehrhahn Verlag, 2009.

Raabe, Mechthild. *Leser und Lektüre im 18. Jahrhundert: Die Ausleihbücher der Herzog August Bibliothek Wolfenbüttel 1714–1799*. Munich: K. G. Saur, 1989.

Raschke, Bärbel. "Die Bibliothek der Herzogin Anna Amalia." In *Herzogin Anna Amalia Bibliothek: Kulturgeschichte einer Sammlung*, edited by Michael Knoche and Ingrid Arnhold. Munich: Hanser Verlag, 1999.

Raven, James. "An Antidote to the French? English Novels in German Translation and German Novels in English Translation." *Eighteenth-Century Fiction*, 14.3–4 (2002): 715–34.

Raven, James, Peter Garside, and Rainer Schöwerling, *The English Novel 1770–1829: A Bibliographical Survey of Prose Fiction Published in the British Isles*. Oxford: Oxford University Press, 2000.

Reichardt, Rolf. "Die visualisierte Revolution: Die Geburt des Revolutionärs Georg Forster aus der politischen Bildlichkeit." *Forster-Studien* 5 (2000): 163–227.

Reinhart, Kai, and Michael Krüger. "Funktionen des Sports im modernen Staat und in der modernen Diktatur." *Historical Social Research* 32.1 (2007): 43–77.

Rivière, Marc Serge, and Annett Volmer, eds. *The Library of an Enlightened Prussian Princess: Catalogue of the Non-music Sections of the Amalien-Bibliothek*. Berlin: Verlag Arno Spitz, 2002.

Ross, Hartmut, et al. *Belehren und nützlich seyn: Franz von Anhalt-Dessau, Fürst der Aufklärung 1740–1817*. Exhibition catalog. Wörlitz: Staatliche Schlösser und Gärten, 1990.

Ross, Marlon B. "Romantic Quest and Conquest: Troping Masculine Power in the Crisis of Poetic Identity." In *Romanticism and Feminism*, edited by Anne Mellor, 26–51. Bloomington: Indiana University Press, 1988.

Roworth, Wendy Wassyng. "Kauffman and the Art of Painting in England." In *Angelica Kauffman: A Continental Artist in Georgian England*, edited by Wendy Wassyng Roworth, 11–95. London: Reaktion Books, 1992.

Roy, Wendy. *Maps of Difference: Canada, Women, and Travel*. Montreal: McGill-Queen's University Press, 2005.

Ruprecht, Wilhelm. *Väter und Söhne: Zwei Jahrhunderte Buchhändler in einer deutschen Universitätsstadt*. Göttingen: Vandenhoeck & Ruprecht, 1935.

Saine, Thomas P. *Georg Forster*. New York: Twayne Publishers, 1972.

Sanislo, Teresa. "Protecting Manliness in the Age of Enlightenment: The New Physical Education and Gymnastics in Germany, 1770–1800." In *Gender in Transition: Discourse and Practice in German-Speaking Europe, 1750–1830*, edited by Ulrike Gleixner and Marion W. Gray, 265–81. Ann Arbor: University of Michigan Press, 2006.

Schellenberg, Betty. *The Professionalization of Women Writers in Eighteenth-Century Britain*. Cambridge: Cambridge University Press, 2005.

Schmidt-Haberkamp, Barbara, Uwe Steiner, and Brunhilde Wehinger, eds. *Europäischer Kulturtransfer im 18. Jahrhundert: Literaturen in Europa—Europäische Literatur?* Berlin: Berliner Wissenschaftsverlag, 2003.

Schröder, Willi. *Johann Christoph Friedrich GutsMuths: Leben und Wirken des Schnepfenthaler Pädagogen*. Sankt Augustin: Academia, 1996.

Scott, Grant F. "The Fragile Image: Felicia Hemans and Romantic Ekphrasis." In *Felicia Hemans: Reimagining Poetry in the Nineteenth Century*, edited by Nanora Sweet and Julie Melnyk, 36–54. Basingstoke: Palgrave, 2001.

Selle, Götz von, ed. *Die Matrikel der Georg-August-Universität zu Göttingen 1734–1837*. Hildesheim: August Lax, 1937.

Sheehan, James J. *German History 1770–1866*. Oxford: Clarendon, 1989.

Shoemaker, Robert B. *Gender in English Society 1650–1850: The Emergence of Separate Spheres?* London: Longman, 1998.

Siegel, Monika. "'Ich hatte einen Hang zur Schwärmerey': Das Leben der Schriftstellerin und Übersetzerin Meta Forkel-Liebeskind im Spiegel ihrer Zeit." PhD diss., Technische Universität Darmstadt, 2001.

Simms, Brendan, and Torsten Riotte, eds. *The Hanoverian Dimension in British History, 1714–1837.* Cambridge: Cambridge University Press, 2007.

Simon, Sherry. *Gender in Translation: Cultural Identity and the Politics of Transmission.* London: Routledge, 1996.

Singleton, Vicky. "Feminism, Sociology of Scientific Knowledge and Postmodernism." *Social Studies of Science* 26 (1996): 445–68.

Smith, Bonnie G. *The Gender of History: Men, Women, and Historical Practice.* Cambridge, Mass.: Harvard University Press, 1998.

Sosulski, Michael. *Theater and Nation in Eighteenth-Century Germany.* Aldershot: Ashgate, 2007.

Spieckermann, Marie-Luise. "Dorothea Margareta Liebeskind (1765–1853): Übersetzerin zwischen wissenschaftlicher Literatur und Unterhaltungsromanen englischer Autorinnen." In *Übersetzungskultur im 18. Jahrhundert: Übersetzerinnen in Deutschland, Frankreich und der Schweiz,* edited by Brunhilde Wehinger and Hilary Brown, 141–64. Saarbrücken: Wehrhahn Verlag, 2008.

Stafford, Barbara Maria. *Voyage into Substance: Art, Science, Nature, and the Illustrated Travel Account, 1760–1840.* Cambridge, Mass.: MIT Press, 1984.

Stagl, Justin. *A History of Curiosity: The Theory of Travel 1550–1800.* Chur, Switzerland: Harwood Academic Publishers, 1995.

Star, Susan Leigh. "Power, Technologies and the Phenomenology of Conventions: On Being Allergic to Onions." In *A Sociology of Monsters? Essays on Power, Technology and Domination,* edited by J. Law. London: Routlege, 1991.

Stark, Susanne. *"Behind Inverted Commas": Translation and Anglo–German Cultural Relations in the Nineteenth Century.* Clevedon: Multilingual Matters, 1999.

Stark, Susanne. "Women." In *The Oxford History of Literary Translation in English: Volume 4 1790–1900,* edited by Peter France and Kenneth Haynes.Oxford: Oxford University Press, 2006.

Staves, Susan. *A Literary History of Women's Writing in Britain, 1660–1800.* Cambridge: Cambridge University Press, 2006.

Steiner, T. R. *English Translation Theory 1650–1800.* Amsterdam: Van Gorcum, 1975.

Steinmetz, Horst, ed. *Friedrich II, König von Preussen, und die deutsche Literatur des 18. Jahrhunderts: Texte und Dokumente.* Stuttgart: Reclam, 1985.

Stemmler, Theo. "Einleitung." In *Die Rechte des Menschen,* by Thomas Paine. Frankfurt: Suhrkamp Verlag, 1973.

Stockhorst, Stefanie, ed. *Cultural Transfer through Translation: The Circulation of Enlightened Thought in Europe by Means of Translation.* Amsterdam: Rodopi, 2010.

Stockley, V. *German Literature as Known in England 1750–1830.* Port Washington, N.Y.: Kennikat Press, 1929; facsimile, 1969.

Stone, Lawrence. *The Road to Divorce.* Oxford: Oxford University Press, 1990.

Struminger, Laura. "The Vésuviennes: Images of Women Warriors in 1848 and Their Significance for French History." *History of European Ideas* 8 (1987): 451–88.

Stummann-Bowert, Ruth. "Philippine Engelhard." In *Des Kennenlernens Werth: Bedeutende Frauen Göttingens,* edited by Traudel Weber-Reich, 27–52. Göttingen: Wallstein Verlag, 2002.

Taylor, Barbara. *Mary Wollstonecraft and the Feminist Imagination.* Cambridge: Cambridge University Press, 2003.

Terrall, Mary. *The Man Who Flattened the Earth: Maupertuis and the Sciences in the Enlightenment.* Chicago: University of Chicago Press, 2002.

Thomas, Christa Zeller. "'I shall take to translating': Transformation, Translation and Transgression in Anna Jameson's *Winter Studies and Summer Rambles in Canada.*" In *Translators, Interpreters, Mediators: Women Writers 1700–1900*, edited by Gillian E. Dow, 175–90. Bern: Peter Lang, 2007.

Thomas, Clara. *Love and Work Enough: The Life of Anna Jameson.* Toronto: University of Toronto Press, 1967.

Thompson, E. P. *The Making of the English Working Class.* New York: Vintage Books, 1966.

Thomson, Ann, Simon Burrows, and Edmond Dziembowski. Introduction to *Cultural Transfers: France and Britain in the Long Eighteenth Century*, edited by Ann Thomson, Simon Burrows, and Edmond Dziembowski. Oxford: Voltaire Foundation, 2010.

Todd, Jan. *Physical Culture and the Body Beautiful.* Macon, Ga.: Mercer University Press, 1998.

Todd, Janet, ed. *The Collected Letters of Mary Wollstonecraft.* London: Allen Lane/Penguin, 2003.

Todd, Janet, ed. *Mary Wollstonecraft: A Revolutionary Life.* London: Weidenfeld & Nicolson, 2000.

Tyson, Gerald P. *Joseph Johnson: A Liberal Publisher.* Iowa City: University of Iowa Press, 1979.

Uhlig, Ludwig. *Georg Forster: Lebensabenteuer eines gelehrten Weltbürgers.* Göttingen: Vandenhoeck & Ruprecht, 2004.

Ulfkotte, Josef. "'Dem Wakkern fügte sich die glückliche Stunde': Zur wechselseitigen Wahrnehmung von Johann Christoph Friedrich GutsMuths und Friedrich Ludwig Jahn." In *Johann Christoph Friedrich GutsMuths (1759—1839) und die philantropische Bewegung in Deutschland*, edited by Michael Krüger. Hamburg: Czwalina, 2010.

Umbach, Maiken. *Federalism and Enlightenment in Germany, 1740–1806.* London: Hambledon Press, 2000.

Umbach, Maiken. "Visual Culture, Scientific Images and German Small-State Politics in the Late Enlightenment." *Past & Present* 158 (February 1998): 110–45.

Van der Kiste, John. *The Georgian Princesses.* Stroud: Sutton Publishing, 2000.

Venuti, Lawrence, ed. *The Translation Studies Reader.* London: Routledge, 2000.

Vertovec, Steven, and Robin Cohen eds. *Conceiving Cosmopolitanism: Theory, Context, and Practice.* Oxford: Oxford University Press, 2002.

Von der Osten, Jenny. *Luise Dorothee Herzogin von Sachsen-Gotha 1732–1767.* Leipzig: Breitkopf und Härtel, 1893.

von Sachsen-Weimar-Eisenach, Anna Amalia. *Briefe über Italien.* St. Ingbert: Röhrig Universitätsverlag, 1999.

Wardle, Ralph M. *Collected Letters of Mary Wollstonecraft.* Ithaca: Cornell University Press, 1979.

Wardle, Ralph M. *Mary Wollstonecraft.* Lawrence: University of Kansas Press, 1951.

Warneke, Sara. *Images of the Educational Traveller in Early Modern England.* Leiden: E. J. Brill, 1995.

Weber-Reich, Traudel, ed. *"Des Kennenlernens Werth": Bedeutende Frauen Göttingens.* Göttingen: Wallstein Verlag, 1993.

Weisbrod, Bernd. "Der englische 'Sonderweg' in der neueren Geschichte." *Geschichte und Gesellschaft* 16 (1990): 233–52.

Wellenreuther, Hermann. "England und Europa: Überlegungen zum Problem des englischen Sonderwegs in der europäischen Geschichte." In *Liberalitas*, edited by Norbert Finzsch and Hermann Wellenreuther, 89–123. Stuttgart: Steiner, 1992.

Wellenreuther, Hermann. "Göttingen und England im 18. Jahrhundert." In *250 Jahre Vorlesungen an der Georgia Augusta 1734–1984*, edited by Norbert Kamp, Hermann Wellenreuther, and Friedrich Hund. Göttingen: Vandenhoeck & Ruprecht, 1985.

Wellenreuther, Hermann. "Von der Interessenharmonie zur Dissoziation: Kurhannover und England zur Zeit der Personalunion." *Niedersächsisches Jahrbuch für Landesgeschichte* 67 (1995).

Werner, Michael, and Bénédicte Zimmermann. "Vergleich, Transfer, Verflechtung: Der Ansatz der 'histoire croisée' und die Herausforderung des Transnationalen." *Geschichte und Gesellschaft* 28.4 (2002): 607–36.

Werrett, Simon. *Fireworks: Pyrotechnic Arts and Sciences in European History*. Chicago: University of Chicago Press, 2010.

Wesling, Donald. "Michel Serres, Bruno Latour, and the Edges of Historical Periods." *Clio* 26.2 (Winter 1997): 189–204.

Wiggin, Bethany. "Dating the Eighteenth Century in German Literary History." *Eighteenth-Century Studies* 40.1 (2006): 126–32.

Wilkeson, Samuel. "Historical Writing of Judge Samuel Wilkeson." *Publications of the Buffalo Historical Society* 5 (1902): 176.

Wolfson, Susan J. Introduction to *Felicia Hemans: Selected Poems, Letters, Reception Materials*, edited by Susan J. Wolfson, xiii–xxix. Princeton: Princeton University Press, 2000.

Wolpers, Theoder. "Literaturvermittlung zwischen Göttingen und England im 18. Jahrhundert." In *"Eine Welt Allein ist Nicht Genug": Grossbritannien, Hannover und Göttingen 1714–1837*, edited by Elmar Mittler, 401–35. Göttingen: Niedersächsische Staats- und Universitätsbibliothek, 2005.

Wolter, Ingrid-Charlotte. *Mary Wollstonecraft und Erziehung: Eine Erziehungskonzeption zur Entkulturation*. Trier: Wissenschaftlicher Verlag, 2008.

Zinsser, Judith P. *History and Feminism: A Glass Half Full*. New York: Twayne, 1993.

Index

Printed and bound by CPI Group (UK) Ltd, Croydon, CR0 4YY

09/06/2025

14685646-0002